PLINY

Correspondence with Trajan from Bithynia
(*Epistles X 15–121*)

with an Introduction, Translation and Commentary by

Wynne Williams

Aris & Phillips is an imprint of
Oxbow Books

First published 1990. Reprinted with addenda 2007.

ISBN 0-85668-408-2
ISBN 978-0-85668-408-1

A CIP record for this book is available from the British Library

Printed in Great Britain
by CPI Antony Rowe, Eastbourne

Contents

PREFACE AND ACKNOWLEDGEMENTS

This edition of Pliny's correspondence with Trajan from the province of Bithynia-Pontus has been prepared with the needs of undergraduates and sixth-formers in mind. The notes therefore include much more in the way of elementary information, and much less by way of scholarly analysis, than does the great Commentary on all of Pliny's Letters by A. N. Sherwin-White. This commentary is repeatedly referred to in the notes, and the debt I owe to my old tutor's work is even greater than might appear from these references, many of which register dissent from his interpretations: this in some measure obscures the extent of my agreement with, and dependence upon, Mr Sherwin-White's Commentary. The reader should of course consult it for fuller discussion on most points.

To assist readers, and to save space, they have, where possible, been directed for further information to one or two books only, and books which are likely to be accessible and available to them (on most questions of Roman law, for example, to Professor Crook's superb account for the general reader, *Law and Life of Rome*, rather than to textbooks written for students of law).

The translation makes no claim to literary merit: it is intended to be as literal a version as is compatible with the rules of English syntax. This is in order that the notes, which are keyed to the translation (as is the usual practice in this series), can discuss Pliny's meaning very much as notes on the Latin text would do.

I am indebted to the University of Keele, and to the cooperation of my colleagues in its Classics Department, for a period of study leave, during which the first version of the translation and the notes was composed. Professor A. L. F. Rivet has been so kind as to allow an adapted version of part of a map drawn by him to be reproduced here. Dr Byron Harries subjected the translation to a vigilant scrutiny. I am especially indebted to Mrs B. Morris for transcribing my manuscript on to disc: without her devoted efforts this book would have taken much longer to produce.

I dedicate this book to the memory of my parents, and, in gratitude, to my second mother.

Wynne Williams

Department of Classics
University of Keele

v

Addenda & Corrigenda

Introduction

p.8, Gii, 1.8	Additional reference: F. Millar, *Rome, The Greek World and the East*, vol.1, chs.11 and 13.

Correspondence with Trajan

p.33, ep.34, 1.7	For "make use of them" read "prevent them from spreading".
p.35, ep.39 (2), 1.5	For "soft and crumbling" read "light and crumbling".
p.36, ep.XXXIX (6), 1.2	For "collecetur" read "collocetur".
p.48, ep.LVIII (8), 1.1	For "tamem" read "tamen"
p.51, ep.62, 1.6	For "those province of yours are not lacking" read "those provinces are not lacking".
p.55, ep.70 (1), 1.1	For "When I was investigating" read "Sir, when I was investigating".
p.55, ep.70 (1), 1.6	For "are enlarged and improved" read "are cleared away as an improvement".
p.60, ep.LXXIX (5), 1.3	For "effetctum" read "effectum".
p.69, ep.93, 1.6	For "is forbidden" read "is to be forbidden".
p.72, ep.XCIX, 1.2	For "Amastrianourm" read "Amastrianorum".
p.75, ep.105, 1.1	For "prudent" read "prompt".
p.79, ep.113, 1.5	For "oututstrip" read "outstrip".
p.79, ep.114 (1), 1.1	For "Bythinian" read "Bithynian".
p.79, ep.114 (1), 1.3	For "Bythinia" read "Bithynia".
p.81, ep.117, 1.5	For "might exercise" read "might yourself exercise".
p.82, ep.CXIX, 1.2	For "εἰσήλασεν" read "εἰσήλασεν".

Commentary

p.88, ep.17A, 1.19	For "*Hellenique*" read "*Hellénique*".
p.90, ep.19, 1.10	For "remanding custody" read "remanding in custody".
p.96, ep.31, 2, 1.4	For the ref. to Millar, *Papers* ... etc., see now Millar, *Rome, the Greek World and the East*, vol.2, ch.7.
p.96, ep.31, 2, 1.7	For the ref. to Millar, 127, see now Millar, 124.
p.96, ep.31, 2, 1.26	For "The spread of the bloodthirsty" read "The bloodthirsty".

ADDENDA & CORRIGENDA

p.102, ep.41, l.7	For "Sophon" read "lacus Sunonensis" and ignore the incorrect ref. to "ancient Melas".
p.104, l.3	For "(, title of Part 2)" refer to Jones, G.C., title of Part 2.
p.109, ep.52, ll.14/15	For "Antony" read "Antonius".
p.112, ep.58, 1, l.33	For the ref. to Millar, *JRS* ... etc., see now Millar, *Rome, the Greek World and the East*, vol.2, ch.16, p.340.
p.114, l.6	On imperial edicts see Introd. IIGiii(a).
p.115, ep.61, 4, l.2	For "catarractae" read "cataractae".
p.116, ep.62, l.3	For "**and those provinces of yours are not lacking**" read "**and those provinces are not lacking**".
p.117, ep.65, 1, l.18	For the ref. to Strabo 17,824, see now Strabo 17,2,5.
p.118, ep.65, 3, l.36	For the ref. to 67, 1n. see now 66, 1n.
p.119, ep.66, l.22	Above line 22, "**the right of free status ...**" left sub-heading: **66, 2**.
p.119, ep.66, 2, l.22	For "T.'s ruling" read "Domitian's ruling".
p.121, ep.70, 1, l.1	For "When I was ..." read "Sir, when I was ...".
p.123, ep.74, 1, l.16–17	For the ref. to Millar, *Papers* ... etc., see now Millar, *Rome, the Greek World and the East*, vol.2, p.145.
p.124, ep.74, 2, l.18	For "**things which was wearing**" read "**things which he was wearing**".
p.124, ep.74, 3, l.1	See note on section 2 (not 1).
p.126, ep.78	Prior to **78, 1**, centre heading: **Epistle 78**.
p.128, ep.79, 3, l.9	For "found at Prusias" read "found at Prusias ad Hypium".
p.131, ep.84, l.6	For "and only if were no such heirs" read "and only if there were no such heirs".
p.134, ep.88, l.2	For the ref. to 17A, n., see 17A, 2n.
p.136, ep.93, l.5	For "as evidence hat" read "as evidence that".
p.138, ep.95, l.24	For "on the Banasa ablet" read "on the Banasa tablet".
p.140, ep.96, 3, l.18	For "apostacies" read "apostasies".
p.141, ep.96, 5, l.8–9	For the ref. to Millar see now *Rome, the Greek World and the East*, vol.2, ch.14, and on this passage, pp.152–3.
p.143, ep.96, 10, l.8	For the ref. to forthcoming in *JRS Monographs*, see now *Journal of Roman Studies Monographs* no.7.
p.146, ep.104, l.11	For "Paulino" read "*Paulino*".
p.156, l.16	For "Suetononius" read "Suetonius".
p.158, Ap: ep.113, l.3	For "Mynor's *OCT*" read "Mynors' *OCT*".

ABBREVIATIONS AND SHORT TITLES USED IN THE INTRODUCTION AND NOTES

(1) The main subjects
P. = the younger Pliny (Gaius Plinius Caecilius Secundus)
T. = the emperor Trajan (Imperator Caesar Nerva Traianus Augustus)
BP = the Roman province of Bithynia-Pontus.

(2) Texts, translations and commentaries on Pliny's epistles

Hardy	E. G. Hardy, *Pliny's Correspondence with Trajan* (Macmillan, 1889)
Merrill	E. T. Merrill, *Selected Letters of the Younger Pliny* (Macmillan, 1903).
OCT	R. A. B. Mynors (ed), *C. Plini Caecili Secundi Epistularum Libri Decem* (Clarendon Press, 1963)
Radice	B. Radice (trans), *The Letters of the Younger Pliny* (Penguin,1963); the translation is also printed in Pliny, *Letters and Panegyricus* (Loeb Classical Library, 1969)
SW	A. N. Sherwin-White, *The Letters of Pliny: A Historical and Social Commentary* (Clarendon Press, 1966)
Veyne	P. Veyne, *"Autour d'un commentaire de Pline le Jeune"*, Latomus, 26, 1967, 723-51

(3) Periodicals

JRS	Journal of Roman Studies
ZPE	Zeitschrift für Papyrologie und Epigraphik
ANRW	H. Temporini (ed), *Aufstieg und Niedergang des römischen Reichs* (de Gruyter, 1972-)

(4) Books

Armies and Frontiers	S. Mitchell (ed), *Armies and Frontiers in Roman and Byzantine Anatolia* (British Archaeological Reports, International Series 156, 1983)
Campbell	J. B. Campbell, *The Emperor and the Roman Army* (Clarendon Press, 1984)
Cod.Iust.	*Codex Iustiniani* (Corpus Iuris Civilis, Vol.2, Weidmann, 1895)
Crook	J. A. Crook, *Law and Life of Rome* (Thames and Hudson, 1967)
D	*Digesta* (Corpus Iuris Civilis, Vol.1, Weidmann, 1895)
Eck	W. Eck, "Jahres - und Provinzialfasten der senatorischen Staathalter von 69/70 bis 138/139", in *Chiron*, Vol.12, 1982, 281-362 (a revised version of chap.7 of *Senatoren von Vespasian bis Hadrian*, 1970).
ILS	H. Dessau, *Inscriptiones Latinae Selectae* (Weidmann, 1892-1916)
Jolowicz-Nicholas	H. F. Jolowicz and B. Nicholas, *Historical Introduction to the Study of Roman Law* (third edition, Cambridge, 1972)
Jones, *Dio*	C. P. Jones, *The Roman World of Dio Chrysostom* (Harvard, 1978)

Jones, *GC*   A. H. M. Jones, *The Greek City from Alexander to Justinian* (Clarendon Press, 1940)

Lewis and Reinhold   N. Lewis and M. Reinhold: *Roman Civilisation, A Sourcebook,* Vols.1-2 (Harper Torchbooks, 1966)

Millar   Fergus Millar, *The Emperor in the Roman World, 31BC-AD337* (Duckworth, 1977)

OLD   *The Oxford Latin Dictionary* (ed P. G. W. Glare and others)

PIR   *Prosopographia Imperii Romani saec.I, II , III* (Ed.2, E. Groag, A. Stein, L Petersen; Berlin, de Gruyter, 1933-)

Rom.Arch. in Greek World   Sarah Macready and F. H. Thompson (eds), *Roman Architecture in the Greek World* (Society of Antiquaries of London, 1987)

Smallwood   E. Mary Smallwood, *Documents illustrating the principates of Nerva, Trajan and Hadrian* (Cambridge, 1966)

Syme, *RP*   R. Syme, *Roman Papers*, Vols.1-5 (Clarendon Press, 1979-1988)

Talbert   R. J. A. Talbert, *The Senate of Imperial Rome* (Princeton, 1984)

Ward-Perkins   J. B. Ward-Perkins, *Roman Imperial Architecture* (Pelican History of Art, 1981)

Watson   G. R. Watson, *The Roman Soldier* (Thames and Hudson, 1969)

(5)Cross-references

(i) Letters in Books I-IX of the Epistles: a Roman numeral is used for the book, an Arabic numeral for the number of the letter within each book.

(ii) Letters in Book X: the Arabic numeral of the letter is given, without the number of the book.

(iii) Sections into which the text of each letter is divided in the *OCT*: the Arabic numeral is used, after sect. in the case of the particular letter being discussed, or after the number of the letter, in the case of other letters.

THE PROVINCE OF BITHYNIA-PONTUS

Map labels:

0 — 200 miles / 320 kilometres

SEATS OF PROVINCIAL COUNCILS
ROMAN COLONIES
CITIES

Amisus
Amasia
Zela
Neoclaudiopolis
Sinope
Pompeiopolis
Tavium
Abonuteichos Ionopolis
Gangra Germanicopolis
Amastris
PONTUS ET PHLAGONIA
Tium
Ancyra
Crateia Flaviopolis
Heraclea Pontica
Bithynium Claudiopolis
Germa
Pessinus
Cierus Prusias
Juliopolis
Nicomedia
GALATIA
BITHYNIA
Byzantium
Chalcedon
Cius Nicaea
Apamea Prusa
Caesarea Germanica
ASIA
Appia

INTRODUCTION

Table of contents

I

Pliny's Correspondence with Trajan: uniqueness and survival

(A)   The uniqueness of Book X
The tenth book of the *Epistulae* of the Younger Pliny includes a unique documentary source for the government of the Roman Empire, a series of letters addressed by the governor of a Roman province to the reigning emperor, together with the latter's replies. There is no exact parallel to this collection in Latin literature: Cicero, when proconsul of Cilicia in the last years of the Republic, addressed some official reports to the Senate and People, but most of his surviving letters from that period were written to personal friends; Fronto, half a century after Pliny, corresponded with the emperors Antoninus Pius, Marcus Aurelius and Lucius Verus (the latter pair being his former pupils), but Fronto never took up the proconsulship which he had been allotted; texts of imperial epistles addressed to governors are preserved on inscriptions, in papyri and in the writings of Roman jurists, but these are hardly ever accompanied by the epistles from the governors, to which most of the imperial epistles were replies.

(B)   The contents of Book X
The letters written by Pliny from (or en route to) the province of Bithynia-Pontus, together with Trajan's replies, comprise nos.15-121 of Book X; nos.1-14 comprise the letters addressed by Pliny to Trajan between the latter's accession in 98 (no.1 is Pliny's message of congratulation on Trajan's accession) and his departure for his province in 110 (see IV(A) below), with only 3 of Trajan's replies. This miscellaneous group of what SW calls "private letters" to Trajan are not included in this volume.

(C)   The differences between Book X and Books I-IX
Book X as a whole differs in four significant ways from Books I-IX.
(i) Books I-IX were prepared for publication by Pliny himself in his lifetime (between c.104 and 110: see SW, 54-6), and in most cases exhibit a more polished style than the purely official letters of Book X. It is usually assumed that Pliny died suddenly in BP soon after writing X.120, and that Book X must have been collected and published by someone else (an 'editor') in an unrevised form (see (D) below).
(ii) The letters in Books I-IX are presented as personal messages to a wide range of friends and acquaintances; those in Book X are addressed to a single, 'official', correspondent, the emperor.
(iii) All the letters in Books I-IX are written by Pliny himself, whereas Book X includes Trajan's replies to Pliny (and all of Trajan's letters are replies).
(iv) In Books I-IX Pliny presumably made a selection from his own letters to suit his literary aims; whether Book X is a complete file of letters exchanged between Pliny and Trajan is a problem which needs to be discussed next.

(D) The completeness of Book X

At first sight it would be a natural thing to assume that nos.15-121 comprise the complete file of the letters exchanged between Pliny and Trajan in the years 110-112. The subject-matter of these letters is highly various; messages of congratulation on formal occasions, together with Trajan's notes of acknowledgement, are faithfully reproduced five times (35-6; 52-3; 78-9; 100-1; 102-3); personal messages which have no direct bearing on Pliny's presence in the province are included (26, 87, 94). So it does not seem likely that any particular category of letters has been deliberately omitted by an editor, nor is there any good reason to suppose that any letters were mislaid.

There are, however, some arguments which could be used to support the hypothesis that there were some omissions. (a) The most obvious omission is that of those documents which were neither in Pliny's nor in Trajan's own words. No.58 is the only letter which is followed by four such documents (2 epistles of Domitian, 1 edict and 1 epistle of Nerva), although Pliny in several other letters informs Trajan (as he does in 58,4) that he has 'appended' or 'sent' copies of documents (56,5; 65,3; 70,4; 79,5; 106; 114,3) and Trajan also refers to a copy appended to one of his replies (22,1). Since such copies were written on the same sheet of papyrus as the actual letters (see 22,1n.), the editor of Book X must have taken a deliberate decision to omit them in every case except that of 58, where he retained a selection of the texts copied at the end of the letter. The same would have applied to the texts of the original documents which had been 'attached' to some letters (22,1n.), if these were still available to the editor. (b) Trajan instructs Pliny to inform him of the result of his enquiries about who was responsible for waste at Nicomedia and about the decision Pliny reached about the theatre at Nicaea (38;40), but no later letters of Pliny deal with either matter: in the former case Pliny may well have failed to fasten responsibility on anyone, and in the latter he may have forgotten an 'instruction' which was not issued in very strong terms ("it will be enough for me to be informed"). In 57,1 Trajan tells Pliny he will write later after consulting an ex-proconsul, yet there is no such letter: it may be that this man could throw no light on the matter, but it would not be surprising if a busy emperor just forgot to follow the matter up. In 73 Trajan tells Pliny he will answer Pliny's question if Pliny sends him a text of the resolution of the Senate which has caused Pliny's anxiety, but there is no later letter from Pliny appending such a text, nor one from Trajan giving his decision. It may be that Pliny was referring to the resolution from memory and had no text to send but, if so, it would be surprising that he did not write to tell Trajan this. (c) Eleven of Pliny's letters evoked no reply from Trajan (25, 26, 51, 63, 64, 67, 74, 85, 86A, 86B, 87). Most were routine reports which called for no comment from T., and one was an effusive letter of thanks (51). However, SW (533-4) believes that two requests for favours for Pliny's protégés (26;87) would have received answers, and hence that these must be missing. Emperors may not always have informed applicants on behalf of others that their requests had been granted; it is true that Trajan did inform Pliny that he had granted the privilege Pliny had sought for Suetonius (94,95), but this may have been done to stress that he was doing so as an exceptional favour (see 95n.).

To sum up, only 73 presents any real difficulty, and it would not be surprising if Pliny on one occasion failed to respond to Trajan's instructions. There is no good reason to believe that any of the letters written by Pliny or Trajan were mislaid before they came into the hands of the editor of Book X, or that they were omitted by that editor: the only excision he made was of documents appended to the letters, but all Pliny's and Trajan's own words were kept.

(E)   The publication of Book X
There is no external evidence of the conditions under which this took place, but there are some assumptions which can reasonably be made.
(i) The inspiration for the unique publication of such a file (after all, such a collection could have been assembled of the correspondence of numerous governors) was provided by the fact that Pliny had already published nine books of his own letters.
(ii) Publication can only have taken place with the permission of the reigning emperor, either Trajan himself, or, possibly, his successor Hadrian.
(iii) An editor was needed to prepare the correspondence for publication. He excised the texts of documents which had been appended to some of the letters (see (D) above). The texts were also shorn of any formulaic elements such as greetings at the beginning or end, or a statement of the date and place of writing. In the headings the names and titles of the governor and the emperor have been abbreviated to *C.Plinius* and *Traiano Imperatori* (in Trajan's replies to *Traianus* and *Plinio*).
(iv) The identity of the editor can only be a subject for speculation, but there is one obvious candidate. As a voluminous author himself, Suetonius (see 94,1n.) would be equipped to do the job; he had been Pliny's protégé and had probably accompanied him to BP; subsequently, down to 121, he held posts in the imperial secretariat, culminating in that of *ab epistulis* (responsible for the emperor's correspondence: Smallwood, no.281); and his biographies of the Caesars reveal an interest in the texts of imperial letters.
(v) The originals of Pliny's letters would, at the time of his death, have been in the imperial archives at Rome, and those of Trajan among Pliny's own papers. The imperial archives also kept copies of imperial epistles to governors (66,1n.), so the collection could have been prepared at Rome from the archives. On the other hand, if Pliny had kept file copies of his own letters, it could have been prepared from Pliny's own papers (SW,535). There is no way of deciding between the alternatives.

(F)   The survival of Book X
Although there are a number of surviving medieval MSS which contain the first 9 books of Pliny's Epistles, knowledge of the text of Book X depends mainly on two early printed editions: those published at Venice by Hieronymus Avantius in 1502, which included only the letters numbered 41-121 in modern texts, and by Aldus Manutius at Venice in 1508, which included all the letters (1-121) in Book X. Avantius had used a copy made from a single manuscript which preserved the complete text of all ten books and which survived until 1508 at the Abbey of St Victor in Paris, but Aldus was probably able to have this ancient codex sent to him in Venice (where it was subsequently lost, apart from some sheets, now in New York, with the text of II,20,13–III,5,4; these indicate that the MS dated from the 6th century). One further source of information about what the lost MS contained was identified by E.G. Hardy in 1888 in the Bodleian Library: it was a volume prepared for the great French scholar Budé, in which Avantius' printed text of X,41-121 was supplemented by a manuscript text of X,1-40 derived from the St Victor MS, and with marginal corrections to Avantius' text

from the same source in Budé's own hand. (See SW, 83-4; *OCT*, pp.v-vi, xviii-xx; L.D. Reynolds (ed), *Texts and Transmission*, 316-20).

The Latin text printed below reproduces Sir Roger Mynors' Oxford Classical Text (1963), except that at 58.5 *Prusam* has been printed instead of *Prusiadam,* at 65,3 *Achaiam* instead of *Andaniam,* and at 81,6 *Prusae* instead of *Prusiade,* and at 118,2 the five words *scribo iselastici nomine itaque eorum* have been omitted (see nn. on these passages). Since the notes are annotations to the translation, textual difficulties are only discussed when they raise serious problems of historical interpretation (113 is the most difficult of these cases).

II

Roman provincial government under the early emperors

(A) Provinces

The whole territory under Roman rule outside Italy was divided into 'provinces' with clearly defined boundaries; each of these provinces was under the control of a single 'governor'. The Latin term *provincia* was originally used to refer to any kind of 'job' or 'sphere of responsibility' assigned to Roman magistrates.   The most coveted of *provinciae* under the Republic were the 'war-zones' allotted to consuls and praetors, and such 'war-zones' often developed into permanent territorial provinces. Hence a particular province of this kind did not necessarily have any geographical, historical or cultural unity (on BP see III below).

(B) Status and appointment of governors

The Roman officials in charge of individual provinces might have one of four different titles, which reflected the way they were appointed or their status.

(i) Proconsul. This was the title of the governors of the 'public' provinces, i.e. those which continued to have their governors appointed under the system which had developed under the Republic. Proconsuls held office for one year only, and were replaced by other senators chosen by lot from those with appropriate rank and seniority. All but two (the proconsuls of Asia and Africa, chosen from ex-consuls with as much as 16-18 years seniority) were chosen from among those ex-praetors who had five years' seniority and who were not otherwise engaged in jobs given to them by the emperor. Until Pliny's appointment BP's governors had been proconsuls of praetorian rank: Pliny was the first governor with the title of *legatus Augusti* (see IVC).

(ii) Legatus Augusti pro praetore. From 27 B.C. onwards the governors of the majority of provinces were appointed by the emperor and held their posts at the emperor's pleasure: in Pliny's day the average term was about three years. Senators, some of them ex-consuls (as Pliny was in 110) and some ex-praetors, who were appointed to govern such provinces, were given this title, which means 'deputy of the Emperor (with the rank of) pro-praetor'. In constitutional theory the emperor was the proconsul of all these provinces, and the actual governor only his deputy, with the inferior rank of propraetor (see Trajan's remark in 18,2). This was Pliny's own title in BP, but an inscription which records Pliny's official career (Smallwood, no.230, line 3) reveals that it was qualified by the additional words 'with consular power' (*consulari potestate*): this probably only entitled him to the same outward dignity as his proconsular predecessors, namely to be attended by 6 lictors and not just the 5 to which ordinary *legati* were entitled (see SW,82; and Dio Cassius 53,13,3-6 on numbers of lictors).

(iii) Procurator and **(iv) Praefectus.** The emperors appointed as governors of some of 'their' provinces men who were not senators, but belonged to the next highest rank in Roman society, the Equestrian Order. Governors of this rank bore one or other of these two titles.

(C)   The powers and functions of governors

(i) Military. Governors were the commanders-in-chief of all army units stationed in their provinces, and would be expected to take the field in person for major campaigns. The few units stationed in BP would only have 'police functions', and Pliny in the letters refers only to the disposition of soldiers 'on secondment' (19, 21, 27, 77).

(ii) Judicial. The governor was the only judge (with the exception of his deputy: (D) below) for all serious criminal and civil cases in his province. In provinces without serious military problems, such as BP, most of a governor's time must have been spent going on circuit from one assize-centre (see below) to another, clearing up the backlog of cases which had accumulated since his last visit or that of his predecessor.

Several cities in each province were designated as 'assize-centres' (Latin *conventus*, Greek *dioikesis*), to which litigants from neighbouring cities had to come to have access to the governor's tribunal (see G.P. Burton and C. Habicht in *JRS.* 1975,92f and 64f; J. Reynolds, *JRS.* 1978, 119-20, with Williams, *ZPE.* 48, 265; Jones, *Dio*, 67-8). Pliny refers in 58 to holding assizes, and in 81,2 to hearing a case on his tribunal, and several other enquiries put to Trajan clearly arose from cases brought before Pliny as judge (31, 56, 65, 72, 96, 110).

(iii) Administrative. Pliny had special instructions from Trajan to investigate the finances of the self-governing communities (*civitates*) of BP, but the general supervision and inspection of the administration of these 'cities' was supposed to be part of the duty of every governor (see G.P. Burton, *JRS.*1975,102-6).

One function of provincial administration in which governors did not have a part was the collection of the taxes due to the imperial government (see (D)(ii) below).

(D)   Other Roman officials in the provinces
(i) Subordinates of the governor

On the military side, these would be commanders of individual legions (usually senators, and called *legati legionis*) or of units of 'auxiliary' infantry and cavalry (usually *equites* in rank, and called *praefecti*): there should have been at least two of the latter serving under P., but they are not alluded to in his letters. On the civilian side, each proconsul of praetorian rank had a single deputy (a *legatus*), chosen by himself, who exercised jurisdiction delegated by the proconsul: these *legati proconsulis* were senators, often ex-praetors, but not always that senior in rank. The *legati* of the imperial provinces were in theory themselves only the 'deputies' of the emperor and did not usually have *legati* of their own. Pliny did have a *legatus* of his own, Servilius Pudens (25): presumably, like his 'consular power' (see B(ii) above), this appointment was intended to put Pliny on the same footing as his proconsular predecessors.

(ii) Officials of lower rank but with independent appointments

The most important of these was the emperor's senior procurator in the province, who would be of equestrian status. In the 'public' provinces such procurators were in charge of the administration of the extensive imperial properties to be found in every province, but in the emperor's own provinces they were also in charge of the collection of the taxes due to the imperial government. When BP became an 'imperial' province in 110 (see IVC), the 'patrimonial' procurator, who had been in charge of imperial properties, must have taken over the latter task in place of the quaestor (a junior senator) who would have carried it out while BP was still a 'public' province. Pliny and Trajan refer to Virdius Gemellinus who must have been holding the post of procurator when Pliny arrived (27-28), and he was still holding it some time later (84). He had subordinates, also called procurators, who were freed slaves of the emperor, and hence part of the *familia Caesaris*, 'Caesar's household', which supplied lower level administrators in the provinces as well as at Rome: among these freedmen were Maximus (27-28, 85) and Epimachus (84), both stationed in BP and associated with Virdius. The imperial freedman Lycormas was only travelling through BP on a diplomatic mission for Trajan (63, 67).

Pliny also refers to two military men operating in BP who were not his own subordinates. One was conducting a levy of recruits for the army (29-30 nn.). The other, Gavius Bassus, is decribed as "the prefect of the Pontic shore", but what his exact functions were is quite uncertain (21-22n; 86A).

(E) Cities in the provinces

Most provinces were divided up between the territories of self-governing communities known in Latin as *civitates* ('states' or 'cities'). Since the Roman government did not employ a large staff of civil servants in the provinces, most of the routine work of government was carried out by the local authorities in the cities. The functions they had to perform on behalf of the imperial government included the actual collection of the direct taxes imposed by Rome, the provision of lodging and transport for travellers on official business (see 45-46 nn.), as well as of supplies for the army, which were obtained by compulsory purchase. The importance of these tasks explains Trajan's concern about the financial solvency of the cities of BP (see IV(C) below).

'Cities' in the Greek world (Greek *poleis*) had traditionally had three main organs of government: (i) an Assembly (Greek *ekklesia*), open to all adult male citizens, which in working democracies had been the sovereign body; (ii) a Council (Greek *boule*) much smaller than the Assembly, which had prepared the agenda for the Assembly; (iii) executive officials, usually holding office for one year only, under a great variety of titles; the generic Latin term for such officials was *magistratus*, 'magistrates', in the older English sense of the term. Under Roman overlordship the actual working of the government of Greek cities became steadily less democratic, with Assemblies becoming little more than rubber-stamps for decisions taken by the Councils (see Jones, *GC*, chap.11; G. de Ste Croix, *The Class Struggle in the Ancient Greek World*, Appendix 4, pp.518-37).

(F) 'Provincial councils'

In most, but not all, provinces, there existed, by Pliny's day, bodies made up of delegates from the 'cities', which met once every year to celebrate a religious festival for the cult of the emperor, linked with that of the goddess 'Rome'. In the West such a body was known as a 'council' (*consilium*), but in the East as the 'common body' (Latin *commune*, Greek *koinon*). In BP there were two separate 'councils' for the two parts of the province: there is no direct reference to either body in Book X, but it was probably the members of one or other of the councils which took the New Year vows (see 36 n.) and the oath of loyalty on Trajan's birthday (see 52 n.); see also 79 n. and 100 n.. Pliny's silence helps to underline the fact that these bodies were by no means 'provincial parliaments': they had no power to issue regulations which would be binding on their constituent cities. Their only political importance was that they might be the place where provincials decided on a concerted effort to prosecute at Rome a former governor (see VII,6,1 for the role of the Bithynian council in the prosecution of Varenus Rufus). See J.A.O. Larsen, *Representative Government in the Greek and Roman World*, chaps 6-7; J. Deininger, *Die provinziallandtage in der römischen Kaiserzeit.*

(G) Roman regulations for the provinces

There was no complete code of administrative law in existence to regulate the way governors should act, and they enjoyed very wide discretion. Pliny, however, did regard himself as bound by existing regulations of various kinds.

(i)The 'provincial charter', a body of rules drawn up by the Roman authority responsible for the original organisation of the province: in BP's case this was Pompeius, and on the content of the *lex Pompeia* see III(A) iii, below.

(ii)'Resolutions of the Senate' (*senatus consulta*). Under the Republic only the voting Assemblies of the Roman People could pass statutes, but under the emperors the Senate's resolutions came to be treated as if they were statutes. The majority of those of which we have any record dealt with changes in the rules of Roman private law, and resolutions which were of any political significance would only have been passed at the emperor's initiative. Apart from letter 72, there is no evidence that the Senate passed resolutions binding on the 'public' provinces governed by proconsuls alone (see 72 n.). See Talbert, chap 15; Jolowicz-Nicholas, 363-5.

(iii)'Constitutions' of the emperors (*constitutiones principum*). A 'constitution' was any decision of an emperor, made public in any one of a variety of forms, which was treated subsequently as a binding precedent. The jurist Gaius wrote that it had never been doubted that what the emperor 'constituted,' whether by a *decretum* or by an edict or by an epistle, had the force of law (Gaius 1,5), and the jurist Ulpian that "it is agreed that whatever the emperor has laid down by epistle and subscript or 'decreed' when acting as judge or pronounced extra-judicially or ordered by edict is law" (D.1,4,1,1). These two passages list the forms which 'constitutions' might take:-

(a) Edicts. An imperial edict was a pronouncement introduced by the emperor's titles and the one word 'says' (*dicit*), addressed not to any specific person or group, but 'to whomsoever it may concern'. Edicts might apply either to the whole empire or to particular areas (see 65,2-3 nn.).

(b) Epistles. These were letters addressed by the emperors to persons of high status (such as Pliny) or to corporate bodies such as cities or provincial councils. The addressees received greetings from the emperor at the beginning and the end of the epistle. Most imperial epistles were replies to epistles addressed to the emperor, and hence they could be described as *rescripta* ('things written in reply').

(c) Subscripts. These were imperial replies to petitions from persons or groups of low status; as the word suggests they were actually written at the foot of the original petition, and the addressees, unlike those of epistles, did not receive any greetings. All subscripts were by reason of their formal character *rescripta*.

(d) Decreta. These were the texts of the judgments delivered by the emperors at the end of cases heard before their court.

(e) Extra-judicial pronouncements. There is some evidence that oral pronouncements made by emperors, in response to a deputation, for instance, were recorded and could be treated as 'constitutions': see Williams, *ZPE*. 22,240-45.

On constitutions in general, see Jolowicz-Nicholas, 365-73; Millar, chap 5.

(f) The emperor's instructions (*mandata*) to a governor. Although not included by the jurists among the types of imperial constitution, the *mandata* of the emperor are often cited by them as sources of law. There is evidence that they were being issued to proconsuls, as well as to *legati*, and to other officials directly appointed by the emperor (e.g 30,1), as early as the reign of Claudius (see G.P. Burton, *ZPE*.21,63). There seems to have been a standard core included in the *mandata* of every governor: when Trajan wished to follow the example of his predecessors and make the wills of soldiers on active service valid even if they did not meet the stringent formal requirements of the jurists, he began to have a chapter (*caput*) inserted in the *mandata* (D.29,1,1, praef.); for another example of a standard clause, see 17A,1 n. The letters in Book X provide examples of specific instructions intended to deal with conditions in one particular province: the numbers of soldiers to be assigned to an official (22,1); a ban on the recall of anyone banished by earlier governors or by Pliny himself (56,3); a ban on clubs (96,7); a ban on ex-gratia payments by city councils (110-111). See SW,547-8, 589-91; Jolowicz-Nicholas, 370-1; Millar, 314-17.

(iv) The governor's edict. In the Republican period it had become standard practice for Roman magistrates whose functions were mainly judicial (in the first instance, the *praetor urbanus* and the *praetor peregrinus* at Rome, but also provincial governors) to issue upon entering office a long edict listing the legal principles they would enforce in their tribunals throughout their term of office (hence it was a 'perpetual' edict, *edictum perpetuum*). The greater part of the content of such edicts was 'tralatician', i.e. carried over from the edict of the previous governor (or praetor). One of Pliny's letters shows that a governor's edict might also include novel rules: in 96,7 he reveals that in his edict he had announced that clubs would be forbidden, to give effect to one of Trajan's instructions. See Jolowicz-Nicholas, 97-101, 358-9.

III

The province of Bithynia-Pontus and its cities

(A)   Origins of the province
Its double name reflected the history of the area before its annexation by Rome.
(i) Bithynia. Its name derives from that of a people which originally lived in the interior of the Roman province, the *Bithynoi*. In 297 B.C. a chieftain of this people, Zipoetes, asserted his independence of the warring Successors of Alexander by taking the Greek title *Basileus* (king); the kings of this dynasty brought under their rule the territory which formed the western part of the Roman province, including some of the old-established Greek cities on the Sea of Marmara. Later members of the dynasty became 'clients' of Rome, and the last of them, Nicomedes IV, who died in 74 B.C., left a will bequeathing his kingdom to the Roman People. It was then annexed as a province, but it was at once invaded by Mithridates VI of Pontus, and the new province was not properly organised until after his final defeat.
(ii) Pontus. The word is originally a Greek word for 'sea', and it was applied to the Black Sea, and thence to the coastal strip along the south coast of that sea. In this area, in the 3rd century B.C., a family of Iranian ancestry carved out an independent kingdom. Mithridates VI, a member of this dynasty, fought three wars against Rome, the last of which, in 74-65 B.C., ended in his flight to the Crimea and, eventually, his suicide. His territories in Pontus were annexed by Rome to Bithynia to form a single province.
(iii) The organisation of the province by Pompeius. The Roman general responsible for Mithridates' final defeat, Gnaeus Pompeius, had been granted wide powers by a law of the Roman People in 66 B.C., and it was he who decided to form the province of Bithynia-Pontus, and who drew up a body of regulations for its administration: this is referred to in the correspondence as 'the Pompeian law' (*lex Pompeia*: 79,112,114). Pompeius followed the usual Roman practice of imposing much of the 'donkey-work' of administration on the gentry who held elective offices in the self-governing cities (see II (E) above). Along the northern coasts of the area there were cities with traditions of self-government, both ancient Greek 'colonies' and more recent royal foundations, but there were areas in the interior which had been administered directly by royal officials: such areas were either added to the territories of existing cities, or became the territories of new cities founded by Pompeius. It was anxiety on his part to ensure that wealthy families did not migrate from these new foundations to older, more comfortable ones which, so it is argued by A.J. Marshall (*JRS.* 1968, 107 ff.), provides the explanation for two rules in the Pompeian law: first, that no city might confer honorary citizenship on anyone who was by birth the citizen of another city within the new province (114,1): second, that 'the child of a Pontic mother should be Pontic' (D. 50,1,1,2). Marshall holds that Pompeius made it possible for his new cities in Pontus to impose financial obligations on persons whose mothers alone, and not their fathers, were citizens of one of these cities. Pompeius also imposed standardised constitutions on all the cities which brought them more into line with the institutions of Rome itself (see 79,1 n.).

(B) The province's history between Pompeius and Pliny
The size of the Pontic half of the province was greatly reduced by Marcus Antonius, who controlled the eastern provinces in 42-31 B.C. Cities were allocated to client rulers of Paphlagonia and of a revived kingdom of Pontus, and, even after these areas were later annexed by Rome (in 4 B.C. and A.D 64), these cities became part of the neighbouring province of Galatia. Two new Greek cities were founded in Bithynia (Caesarea and Iuliopolis), and two Roman citizen colonies were planted at the site of long-established Greek cities (Apamea and Sinope): see (C) below. When Augustus took direct control of about half the provinces in 27 B.C, BP remained one of the 'public' provinces, and was ruled by proconsuls of praetorian rank, until Pliny's appointment. These proconsuls showed a propensity to misgovern: BP comes top of the list in a survey of the number of prosecutions of governors for maladministration recorded from the period between Augustus and Trajan (see P.A. Brunt, *Historia* 10, 1961, 224-7). Two of these cases, those against Iulius Bassus and Varenus Rufus, were heard by the Senate in the first decade of Trajan's reign and are reported in the earlier books of Pliny's letters (IV,9; V,20; VI,5 and 13; VII,6 and 10).

(C) The cities of the province in Pliny's day
(i) BITHYNIA
Of the twelve cities of Bithynia referred to by the Elder Pliny (*Natural History* V, 143), only seven are mentioned in Book X. The other five were Caesarea-Germanice; Prusias ad Mare; Chalcedon; Prusias ad Hypium; Flaviopolis-Creteia. The seven cities which do appear in Book X were the following.
Apamea (47-8) had been a Greek city, probably founded by Nicomedes II and named after his mother, on the site of the old Greek colony of Myrlea (destroyed in 200 B.C): a *colonia* of Roman citizens had been planted at the site by either Julius Caesar or Marcus Antonius under the name Colonia Iulia Concordia Apamea. It enjoyed the additional privilege known as *ius Italicum*, under which the territory of a provincial community was treated as if it were part of Italy, i.e., it was exempt from direct taxation (D.50,15,1,10). It may have been an assize-centre (see Jones, *Dio*, 108-9).
Prusa ad Olympum (17A-B; 23-4; 58; 70-71; 81). A city founded on the northern slopes of Mt Olympus in SW Bithynia by King Prusias I and named after himself. In Pliny's day it was the home of one of the great Greek literary figures of the age, Dio Chrysostom (the "Golden-mouthed"). His influence with Trajan secured for the city promotion to the status of an assize-centre, and the right to enlarge the city council (see Jones, *Dio*, 52,107-8; and Dio, *Or.* 40,33; 44,11).
Nicaea (31; 39-40; 83-4). Founded in 301 B.C. by King Lysimachus and named after his first wife. With its extensive territory, Nicaea was, with the possible exception of its immediate neighbour Nicomedia, the wealthiest city in Bithynia: the two were bitter rivals in a contest for recognition as the most important city in Bithynia. It was an assize-centre.
Nicomedia (31; 33-4; 37-8; 41; 49; 74). Founded in 264 B.C. as a new royal capital by King Nicomedes I on the site of an old Greek colony, Olbia, and named after himself. Under Roman rule, Nicomedia was an assize-centre, used the titles 'mother-city' and 'first-city', and was the meeting place where the Bithynian council celebrated the annual

festival of the imperial cult (II (E) above). It is only in this sense that it could be described as the 'capital' , but the capital of Bithynia alone; however, it can hardly be described as "the seat of Roman governor" (as it is by SW,604), because Roman governors did not have any permanent headquarters in one city in their provinces (as Pliny's own travels show).

Iuliopolis (77-8). A comparatively poor city in the SE corner of Bithynia, founded at the site of his birthplace, Gordiucome, by a minor ruler (and ex-brigand) named Cleon, in the time of Antonius and Augustus. It was presumably incorporated in the province after his death.

Claudiopolis (39-40). This city, in the east of Bithynia, had originally been called Bithynium, a name which should indicate that it had been founded by one of the Bithynian kings, possibly Nicomedes I. It had been renamed in honour of the emperor Claudius.

Byzantium (43-4; 77-8). This Greek colony, on the site of modern Istanbul, did not strictly form part of Bithynia proper, since it lies on the other, European, shore of the Bosporus, in Thrace. It was probably when Vespasian deprived it of the status of a free city, earlier conferred on it by Nero, that it was made the responsibility of the proconsul of BP rather than of the equestrian procurator of Thrace.

(ii) PONTUS

Of the six cities in that part of Pontus which remained in the province in Pliny's day, only one, Abonuteichos, is not mentioned in Book X. The other five were the following.

Heraclea (75). A Greek colony, dating from the 6th century B.C., which maintained its independence until 74 B.C. It then admitted a garrison of Mithridates VI and was subsequently besieged and sacked by the Romans; its prosperity was diminished and it became a tribute-paying provincial city.

Tium (75). A small Greek city, under the overlordship of Heraclea, its neighbour, until annexed by King Prusias I of Bithynia; hence it became part of the new province.

Amastris (98-9). Founded by the divorced wife of King Lysimachus, early in the third century B.C., by the merger of several small Greek cities, and named after herself. It was later incorporated in the kingdom of Pontus, and thus became part of Pompeius' new province. It appears to have been the meeting-place of the Pontic council in the 2nd century. It may also have been an assize-centre (see SW,693).

Sinope (90-1). An ancient Greek colony, forcibly incorporated in the kingdom of Pontus in 183 B.C. A *colonia* of Roman citizens was planted there by Julius Caesar in 46/5 B.C. under the name of Colonia Iulia Felix Sinopensis. Like Apamea it had the privilege of *ius Italicum* (D.50,15,1,10: see on Apamea).

Amisus (92-3; 110). The most easterly city on the coast and another old Greek colony conquered by the Pontic kings, and included in the new province by Pompeius. It was awarded the status of a 'free city' by Julius Caesar as compensation for what it had suffered at the hands of Pharnaces, son of Mithridates. After an interval under royal rule in the time of Antonius, it had this status restored by Augustus and was still a 'free and allied city' in Pliny's day. The term 'and allied (or federate)' would normally mean that the city was 'free' because it had made a treaty of alliance with Rome when it was an independent state, but in some cases (including that of Amisus) the status was just an additional honour conferred unilaterally by Rome (see Jones, *GC* 131).

On the history of these cities, see A.H.M. Jones, *Cities of the Eastern Roman Provinces* (2nd edition, 1971), chap 6, and also Jones, *Dio*, chaps 1, 8, 10

IV

Pliny's mission in Bithynia-Pontus

(A) Chronology

The letters themselves do not indicate the year when Pliny was sent to the province. They do show that he was there for a period of less than two years: he arrived on September 17th of one calendar year, on the day before Trajan's birthday (17A and B); he was there for New Year's Day and the anniversary of Trajan's accession in January of the next year (35,52), and celebrated Trajan's birthday in that year, twelve months after his arrival (88); he was still there for the New Year and the Accession Day of the following year (100, 102), but there is no reference to Trajan's birthday in the September after that. The usual assumption is that Pliny died suddenly in the province, soon after his wife's departure for Italy (120), at some time between January 28th and September 18th of the third calendar year in which he was there: (i) there is no later reference to P.; (ii) he died before Trajan himself died in 117, because the inscription which records some of Pliny's bequests (Smallwood, no.230) refers to Trajan as the living emperor; (iii) his sudden death is the simplest way to explain the sudden interruption in the correspondence.

It is generally accepted that the years involved can only be 109-111 (favoured by SW,81), 110-112 (favoured by Eck, 349f. and Syme, *RP* IV, 477f.) or 111-113 (favoured by Mommsen: see Syme, *loc.cit.*). An earlier year for Pliny's arrival than 109 is held to be excluded by the probable dates of letters written from Rome in Books VII-IX, and a later year for the end of the correspondence than 113 by the silence of Book X about Trajan's journey to the eastern provinces (in the later part of that year), to conduct a war with Parthia. SW, 81, held that, if Pliny had been alive and in BP in January 112, there should have been a reference in letter 100 to Trajan's assumption of his sixth consulship on January 1st of that year, and so preferred 109-111. Eck held that P. Calpurnius Macer, mentioned as governor of Lower Moesia in a letter dating from January of P's first year (42, which comes between nos.35 (New Year vows) and 52 (Accession Day)), could hardly have taken up this post before the middle of 110, so that the earliest possible date for Pliny's arrival was September 110; and Syme argued that several letters in Book IX date from 109, and deduced from a remark in IX,28,4 that Pliny was aware of his appointment by the autumn of 109 (Syme's interpretation of IX,28,4 is rejected by SW,80), and left for BP in summer 110. In the commentary below, to avoid recurrent use of circa or a question mark, the letters have been firmly dated to 110, 111 or 112. However, it must be stressed that these dates are provisional, and it is possible that new discoveries (e.g., about the dates of Calpurnius Macer's term in Lower Moesia) may make it necessary to change the dates.

(B)   Pliny's earlier career

Pliny's full name was Gaius Plinius Caecilius Secundus. Gaius was his personal name, Caecilius and Secundus the family names of his own father (who died when Pliny was still a boy), and Plinius the name of his mother's brother, the Elder Pliny, who adopted Pliny as his son and heir (Syme, *RP* IV,160; V,644). The Elder Pliny was not only a voluminous author (only his vast encyclopaedia, the *Natural History*, survives) but also a senior imperial official of equestrian rank under Vespasian (69-79): at the time of his death during the eruption of Vesuvius in 79 (described in VI,16) he was commander of the fleet based at Misenum on the bay of Naples. His status as a trusted servant of the ruling dynasty probably helped his adopted son to pursue a successful career as a senator, despite being a 'new man' (i.e. the first member of his family to enter the Senate). Before entering the Senate by becoming quaestor (probably after being 'recommended' to the Senate by the emperor Domitian, since he became one of the two quaestors attached to the emperor himself), Pliny saw his only experience of service in the army as a junior officer (*tribunus militum laticlavius*) in the Third Gallic Legion in Syria: he was detached from his service with this legion by the governor of Syria and sent to examine the accounts of the 'auxiliary' army units in the province; in most cases he found evidence of greed and negligence (VII,31,2). After the quaestorship he proceeded to the next rungs in the senatorial ladder, the tribunate and the praetorship. The emperors had at their disposal a considerable number of provincial appointments (legionary commands as well as governorships) open to ex-praetors, but Pliny's praetorian appointments were both held at Rome, and both were concerned with financial administration: he served for three years as one of the two Prefects of the Military Treasury (*praefectus aerarii militaris*), and then for another three years as one of the two Prefects of the Treasury of Saturn (*praefectus aerarii Saturni*; the original treasury of the Republican period). These two terms must have filled most of the interval between his praetorship (probably in 93) and his consulship (September and, probably, October 100). Pliny had acquired a reputation as an orator, with a successful practice as an advocate in the civil courts, but the only sample of his oratory to have survived is his *Panegyric* on Trajan, delivered as consul before the Senate, in Trajan's presence (the published version is probably revised and expanded).

As an ex-consul (*vir consularis*) Pliny had attained to the highest rank in the Roman state, but it was to be ten years before he was appointed to a provincial governorship by Trajan. Syme suggested that this was because Pliny had no close ties with the men who were themselves influential with Trajan and indeed was not highly thought of by Trajan (Syme, *Tacitus*, Vol.1,83; *RP* II, nos.36 and 54). Yet Trajan did nominate Pliny for membership of the second most senior college of priests, the augurs, and Pliny also served as the consular in charge of the maintenance of flood defences and drainage in the city of Rome (*curator alvei Tiberis et cloacarum urbis*). As for provincial appointments, there were only ten imperial legateships for consulars, and, with the usual term for a legate being three years, there must have been intense pressure for appointments from a large body of consulars: in the decade 101-110, in the years for which the record is complete, there were between 5 (103, 105, 107) and 8 (110) new consulars a year (6 in 109: see Smallwood, pp.4-5). All but two of these consular provinces (Hispania Tarraconensis, Dalmatia) involved a serious prospect of commanding in the field, and Pliny had no real experience of military command (which surely mattered for an emperor such as Trajan who prided himself on his military achievements). On the other hand, it is surely evidence of Trajan's esteem for Pliny's competence as a civilian administrator that he did eventually choose him to carry out a provincial mission where Pliny's rather specialised experience in financial management (both in Syria and in Rome) would be an asset .

(C)   The circumstances of Pliny's appointment

A resolution of the Senate changed the status of BP from public province to an imperial one: on an inscription from Como Pliny is described as *"legatus pro praetore* of the province of Pontus and Bithynia with consular power (see II (B)ii), having been sent to that province under a resolution of the Senate by the Emperor Caesar Nerva Trajan etc." (Smallwood, no.230, ll.2-4). The initiative for this resolution must have come from Trajan, but one can only speculate about what prompted him in around 109 to make what was a very rare decision to intervene in what had been a public province since 27 B.C. Two ex-proconsuls of BP had been tried for misgovernment before the Senate in recent years, Iulius Bassus in 101 or 102 (IV,9) and Varenus Rufus (V, 20). These hearings may have brought to Trajan's attention the existence of problems which worried him, but Trajan would also have had confidential sources of information: his own procurators (II(D)ii), and eminent Bithynians such as the orator Dio of Prusa (see Jones, *Dio*, chap.13). At any rate, what he was especially concerned with, to judge from the letters, was extravagance and corruption in the running of the finances of cities (especially in the case of new buildings: e.g. 18,3; 38), and disorder fomented by quarrels between political cliques in the cities (e.g.34). He came to the conclusion that to clean up the mess a senior ex-consul, known to have been chosen especially for the job by the emperor (18,2), was needed; furthermore, the term of office of an imperial legate, unlike a proconsul's, could last for as long as Trajan thought fit.

(D)   Pliny's qualities as an administrator.

A conventional picture of Pliny as an administrator is that of a nervous and fussy man unwilling to take responsibility and forever pestering the emperor about trivial questions which he should have settled on his own initiative. SW attacked this conventional picture and sought to show that a considerable number of Pliny's queries (15 out of 39) arise from the interpretation of Trajan's own *mandata* to Pliny (II(G)iv above); others arose from proposals to modify the effects of existing rules, or challenges to the existing privileges of individuals or groups (in two cases granted by Trajan himself); yet others applied for technical help or guidance not available in BP (see SW,546-51). A more fundamental criticism of the conventional picture of Pliny is that it takes it for granted that Trajan had far more serious grand issues of policy with which to concern himself and should not have been, indeed would not have wished to be, bothered by minor local problems. But Professor Millar has shown that the emperors did not engage in the active formulation of general policies to be imposed on the whole empire, but spent their time dealing with highly specific problems presented to them by cities, private individuals or their own subordinates acting as channels for the requests or protests of cities and individuals, just in the way Pliny did. "What passes for 'administration' was in fact largely either jurisdiction and the settlement of disputes or diplomacy --- the Imperial power was largely static or inert, and its activity stimulated by pressures and initiatives from below" (Millar, Rome, etc., vol.1, p.290). Of course, it is impossible to assess whether Pliny pestered Trajan with queries (even given his special mission) to a greater extent than other governors, because we do not have the files of other governors with which to make a comparison. One ought not therefore to assume, on the basis of a misleading present-day view of how government should work, that any other senator in Pliny's position would have written fewer letters to Trajan

V

The authorship of Trajan's replies

A corollary of the conventional picture of what a Roman emperor did with his time is the assumption that Trajan would have been far too busy with grand issues of policy to compose in person the replies sent out in his name to Pliny (or to any other governor or to cities or private individuals): that job would have been entrusted to a senior *eques* who was 'in charge of' imperial correspondence (the *ab epistulis*). The modern parallel, which has perhaps influenced unduly the conventional picture of the relationship between an emperor and his 'secretary' (*ab epistulis*), is that of a British civil servant drafting a reply for his minister to deliver to a parliamentary question. Syme assumes that epistles issued in the names of Domitian, Nerva and Trajan would all have been composed by the same man: "Titinius Capito was the secretary *ab epistulis* under Domitian, Nerva and Trajan: it will not be fancied that this man was compelled to transform his prose style twice in two years" (*RP* I, 86).

SW, 536-46, pointed out that in Trajan's replies there were passages of sarcasm and bad temper which revealed the emperor's own hand (or, rather, tongue, given that the texts were probably dictated), but he still adhered to the 'model' of the senior civil servant preparing a draft for his master's approval: he refers to "the reasonable opinion" of H.Peter "that Trajan did not draft the rescripts himself or manage the details of law and administration which they involve, that being the work of the secretary" (SW, 536). He therefore accepted that the presence of a "verbose chancellery style" indicated "the hand of the secretary". He also tried to use evidence of content as well as style to detect Trajan's personal interventions. However, he does concede that "nowhere in the drafting of the rescripts is it ever clearly admitted that 'a senior civil servant' was involved. Pains were taken to give the opposite impression" (p.546).

Professor Millar (ch.5; and Rome, etc., vol.2, ch.1.) and the present author (*JRS*. 1976, 67f.; and *Latomus* 1979, 67f.) have argued that this "impression" corresponded to the reality, and that there was no involvement of 'a senior civil servant' to be concealed. All the ancient references to "emperors at work", collected by Millar, take it for granted that emperors read (or had read to them) all incoming letters and dictated their replies to amanuenses. The actual texts of imperial pronouncements (in the century from Hadrian to Caracalla) reveal the individual stylistic quirks of each emperor, even in the most routine replies (Williams, *articles cited*). Only the *a priori* assumption that emperors would have been too busy, or felt themselves too unqualified, to handle their own correspondence, stands in the way of accepting the clear implication of the ancient sources. Trajan did compose all his replies in person, and used the clerks (freedmen or slaves), who were supervised by the *ab epistulis* (himself a glorified chief clerk, or 'office manager'), only as amanuenses and for the kinds of task which are mentioned in the replies: appending a copy of a letter to another official (22,1); searching for documents in the imperial archives (66,1); and making entries in the registers of imperial grants (95; 105).

Further illustrations of Trajan's direct involvement will be pointed out in the notes to individual letters, as well as cases where the alleged effort "to give the opposite impression" (SW, 546) would have led to extremes of hypocrisy. One aspect of Trajan's replies which fits much better with the 'model' of a very busy man listening to Pliny's letters and dictating his replies immediately is the occasional tendency to "go off at a tangent", to pick up some marginal element in Pliny's original letter and belabour it: in his letter on the aqueduct at Nicomedia, after two lines telling Pliny to carry on with his plan, five are devoted to instructing him to investigate possible corruption (38); in his letter on the Christians, Trajan ends by ticking Pliny off for paying attention to an anonymous accusation (97). On the other hand, the cases in which Trajan's reply closely follows the wording of Pliny's original letter (see SW, 537-8) also suit the "model" of a busy man responding immediately rather than that of a civil servant preparing a draft (despite SW's claim that "this habit may well be held to be that of a secretary set to draft his principal's replies", p.538): anyone with experience of having to answer a number of letters quickly will know the temptation to fall back on extensive repetition of the wording of the originals. Millar pointed out (*JRS*. 1968, 223) that Pliny himself once repeated (in X,10) the wording of a letter of Trajan's (X,7); "and no one has yet suggested that Pliny did not write his (own) letters".

VI

Dates and Modes of Address in the Epistles

(A) Dates

The evidence of epigraphic and papyrus texts of imperial epistles indicates that all Trajan's epistles (and Pliny's as well) ended with a formula which recorded the date and place of writing. These formulae were omitted by the editor. It can be assumed that Trajan's epistles were written at Rome or at one of the imperial villas nearby, and that each was written within a few weeks (at the most) of the date of the epistle of Pliny to which it was a response. As for Pliny's epistles, it is clear in some cases from internal evidence where a particular epistle was written, and in other cases this can be deduced from the preceding and following epistles: see the head-note in each case. Seven of P's epistles can be assigned precise dates (17A, 25, 35, 52, 88, 100, 105), and, since it is quite clear that they are all arranged in chronological order (the first in the sequence (15) was written while Pliny was still on his journey, the second and third (17A, 17B) immediately after his arrival, and 17A, 25, 35, and 52 are in correct chronological order (see IV (A) above), the other epistles can be dated by reference to these seven, thus:–

17B–23 : between 18 Sept. 110, and 24 Nov., 110.
26–33   : between 24 Nov. 110, and 3 Jan., 111.
37–51   : between 3 Jan. and 28 Jan., 111.
54–87   : between 28 Jan. and 18 Sept., 111.
90–98   : between 18 Sept. 111, and 3 Jan., 112.
104–120: between 28 Jan. and 18 Sept., 112.

(B) Modes of Address
Pliny regularly addresses Trajan as "sir" (this word is used in the translation as a more natural English equivalent for *domine* than the literal rendering, "O Lord", would be) and Trajan frequently addresses Pliny as "my dearest Secundus". Trajan follows standard practice in using Pliny's *cognomen* (see IV (B) above), and there is a parallel for the use by an emperor of the epithet "dearest" in addressing an official: Marcus Aurelius' codicils of appointment for a procurator ended "farewell, my Marsianus, most dear to me" (*Année Epigraphique* 1962, no. 183, line 18). Pliny's use of the term *dominus* ("lord", "master") is more suprising, in view of some of his own remarks in his *Panegyric* on Trajan: e.g., that Trajan "holds the place of a *princeps*, in order that there shall be no place for a *dominus*" (*Pan.* 55,7; see also 2,3; 7,6; 45,3). His protégé Suetonius also recorded that Augustus and Tiberius had repudiated this appellation (*Div. Aug.* 53,1; *Tib.* 27), whereas the hated Domitian had welcomed it (*Dom.* 13). Only an excerpt from one epistle from a senator (in fact a proconsul) to an emperor survives from this period: in it Hadrian is addressed as 'most excellent emperor' (*optime Imperator*: see *Coll. Leg. Mos. et Rom.*1,11,2), so it is impossible to tell whether Pliny was just using what had become a conventional form in such epistles. (See also SW, 557–8).

CORRESPONDENCE WITH TRAJAN FROM BITHYNIA

EPISTULAE

XV. C. Plinivs Traiano Imperatori

Quia confido, domine, ad curam tuam pertinere, nuntio tibi me Ephesum cum omnibus meis ὑπὲρ Μαλέαν nauigasse quamuis contrariis uentis retentum. Nunc destino partim orariis nauibus, partim uehiculis prouinciam petere. Nam sicut itineri graues aestus, ita continuae nauigationi etesiae reluctantur.

XVI. Traianvs Plinio

Recte renuntiasti, mi Secunde carissime. Pertinet enim ad animum meum, quali itinere prouinciam peruenias. Prudenter autem constituis interim nauibus, interim uehiculis uti, prout loca suaserint.

XVIIA. C. Plinivs Traiano Imperatori

(1) Sicut saluberrimam nauigationem, domine, usque Ephesum expertus ita inde, postquam uehiculis iter facere coepi, grauissimis aestibus atque etiam febriculis uexatus Pergami substiti. (2) Rursus, cum transissem in orarias nauculas, contrariis uentis retentus aliquanto tardius quam speraueram, id est xv kal. Octobres, Bithyniam intraui. Non possum tamen de mora queri, cum mihi contigerit, quod erat auspicatissimum, natalem tuum in prouincia celebrare. (3) Nunc rei publicae Prusensium impendia, reditus, debitores excutio; quod ex ipso tractatu magis ac magis necessarium intellego. Multae enim pecuniae uariis ex causis a priuatis detinentur; praeterea quaedam minime legitimis sumptibus erogantur. (4) Haec tibi, domine, in ipso ingressu meo scripsi.

XVIIB. C. Plinivs Traiano Imperatori

(1) Quinto decimo kal. Octob., domine, prouinciam intraui, quam in eo obsequio, in ea erga te fide, quam de genere humano mereris, inueni. (2) Dispice, domine, an necessarium putes mittere huc mensorem. Videntur enim non mediocres pecuniae posse

EPISTLES X

15. C. Plinius to Traianus Imperator

Because I feel sure, sir, that you are interested, I am reporting to you that, together with all my people, I have reached Ephesus by sea, after "rounding Malea", despite being held up by opposing winds. Now I intend to set out for the province, by coastal vessels for part of the way, by carriages for the rest. For, just as oppressive heat is an obstacle to travel by land, so are the Etesian winds to an unbroken voyage by sea.

16. Traianus to Plinius

You were right to report to me, my dearest Secundus. For I do feel concern about what kind of journey you are having on the way to the province. It is a wise decision of yours to use ships for part of the time, and carriages for part of the time, according to what local conditions require.

17A. C. Plinius to Traianus Imperator

(1) Although I had a very healthy voyage, as far as Ephesus, sir, yet thereafter, when I had begun to pursue my journey by carriage, I was troubled by the most oppressive heat and also by slight attacks of fever, and I halted at Pergamum. (2) Subsequently, when I had shifted to coastal vessels, I was held back by opposing winds, and I entered Bithynia rather later than I had hoped, that is on September 17th. I cannot, however, complain about this delay, since it was my good fortune to celebrate your birthday in the province, which was a very good omen. (3) At the moment I am examining the expenditures, revenues and debtors of the state of Prusa; from the very process of investigation I am learning more and more that this is necessary. For many sums of money are being kept in their possession by private persons under different pretexts; moreover some sums are being paid out on wholly unlawful outlays. (4) I have written to you about this, sir, at the very moment of my arrival.

17B. C. Plinius to Traianus Imperator

(1) On September 17th, sir, I entered the province, which I found in that state of reverence and of loyalty to yourself which you deserve from the human race. (2) Consider, sir, whether you think it necessary to send a surveyor here. For it appears that considerable sums of money could be recovered from the administrators of public

reuocari a curatoribus operum, si mensurae fideliter agantur. Ita certe prospicio ex ratione Prusensium, quam cum maxime tracto.

XVIII. Traianvs Plinio

(1) Cuperem sine querela corpusculi tui et tuorum peruenire in Bithyniam potuisses, ac simile tibi iter ab Epheso ei nauigationi fuisset, quam expertus usque illo eras. (2) Quo autem die peruenisses in Bithyniam, cognoui, Secunde carissime, litteris tuis. Prouinciales, credo, prospectum sibi a me intellegent. Nam et tu dabis operam, ut manifestum sit illis electum te esse, qui ad eosdem mei loco mittereris. (3) Rationes autem in primis tibi rerum publicarum excutiendae sunt; nam et esse eas uexatas satis constat. Mensores uix etiam iis operibus, quae aut Romae aut in proximo fiunt, sufficientes habeo; sed in omni prouincia inueniuntur, quibus credi possit, et ideo non deerunt tibi, modo uelis diligenter excutere.

XIX. C. Plinivs Traiano Imperatori

(1) Rogo, domine, consilio me regas haesitantem, utrum per publicos ciuitatium seruos, quod usque adhuc factum, an per milites adseruare custodias debeam. Vereor enim, ne et per publicos parum fideliter custodiantur, et non exiguum militum numerum haec cura distringat. (2) Interim publicis seruis paucos milites addidi. Video tamen periculum esse, ne id ipsum utrisque neglegentiae causa sit, dum communem culpam hi in illos, illi in hos regerere posse confidunt.

XX. Traianvs Plinio

(1) Nihil opus sit, mi Secunde carissime, ad continendas custodias plures commilitones conuerti. Perseueremus in ea consuetudine, quae isti prouinciae est, ut per publicos seruos custodiantur. (2) Etenim, ut fideliter hoc faciant, in tua seueritate ac diligentia positum est. In primis enim, sicut scribis, uerendum est, ne, si permisceantur seruis publicis milites, mutua inter se fiducia neglegentiores sint; sed et illud haereat nobis, quam paucissimos a signis auocandos esse.

works if measurements were carried out honestly. Such at any rate is my estimate on the basis of the balance-sheet of Prusa with which I am dealing at this very moment.

18. Traianus to Plinius

(1) I could wish that you had been able to reach Bithynia without any complaint about your own physical condition or that of your people, and that your journey from Ephesus had been similar to your experience of the voyage as far as there. (2) The date of your arrival in Bithynia I learnt from your letter, my dearest Secundus. The provincials, I believe, will understand that I have taken thought for their interests. For you in your turn will see to it that it is evident to them that you have been picked out to be sent to them in my place. (3) Moreover, you must above all examine the accounts of the communities: for it is an established fact that they have been in confusion. I have scarcely enough surveyors for those works which are in progress at Rome or nearby; but men who can be trusted are to be found in every province, and therefore you will have no lack of them, if only you are willing to search for them diligently.

19. C. Plinius to Traianus Imperator

(1) I ask you, sir, to guide me with your advice in my doubts about whether I ought to have prisoners guarded by public slaves owned by the cities, which has hitherto been the practice, or by soldiers. For I fear both that an insufficiently reliable watch will be kept by the public slaves and also that this responsibility will call a considerable number of soldiers away from their duties. (2) For the time being I have included a few soldiers among the public slaves. However, I see that there is a risk that this may itself be a reason for neglect of duty by both groups, as the former feel certain that they can throw the burden of their shared guilt upon the latter, and the latter upon the former.

20. Traianus to Plinius

(1) There should be no necessity, my dearest Secundus, for more of my fellow-soldiers to be transferred to guarding prisoners. Let us persist with what is the custom in that province, to have prisoners guarded by public slaves. (2) And in fact it is up to you by your strictness and thoroughness to see that they do it conscientiously. For, as you say in your letter, what is to be feared above all is that, if soldiers were to be mixed in with public slaves, they would become more negligent as a result of either group relying upon the other; but let us also stick to this rule, that as few of them as possible should be called away from their units.

XXI. C. Plinivs Traiano Imperatori

(1) Gauius Bassus praefectus orae Ponticae et reuerentissime et officiosissime, domine, uenit ad me et compluribus diebus fuit mecum, quantum perspicere potui, uir egregius et indulgentia tua dignus. Cui ego notum feci praecepisse te ut ex cohortibus, quibus me praeesse uoluisti, contentus esset beneficiariis decem, equitibus duobus, centurione uno. (2) Respondit non sufficere sibi hunc numerum, idque se scripturum tibi. Hoc in causa fuit, quominus statim reuocandos putarem, quos habet supra numerum.

XXII. Traianvs Plinio

(1) Et mihi scripsit Gauius Bassus non sufficere sibi eum militum numerum, qui ut daretur illi, mandatis meis complexus sum. Cui quae rescripsissem, ut notum haberes, his litteris subici iussi. Multum interest, res poscat an hoc nomine eis uti latius uelit. (2) Nobis autem utilitas demum spectanda est, et, quantum fieri potest, curandum ne milites a signis absint.

XXIII. C. Plinivs Traiano Imperatori

(1) Prusenses, domine, balineum habent; est sordidum et uetus. Itaque magni aestimant nouum fieri; quod uideris mihi desiderio eorum indulgere posse. (2) Erit enim pecunia, ex qua fiat, primum ea quam reuocare a priuatis et exigere iam coepi; deinde quam ipsi erogare in oleum soliti parati sunt in opus balinei conferre; quod alioqui et dignitas ciuitatis et saeculi tui nitor postulat.

XXIV. Traianvs Plinio

Si instructio noui balinei oneratura uires Prusensium non est, possumus desiderio eorum indulgere, modo ne quid ideo aut intribuatur aut minus illis in posterum fiat ad necessarias erogationes.

XXV. C. Plinivs Traiano Imperatori

Seruilius Pudens legatus, domine, viii kal. Decembres Nicomediam uenit meque longae exspectationis sollicitudine liberauit.

21. C. Plinius to Traianus Imperator

Gavius Bassus, the Prefect of the Pontic shore, has come to me, sir, showing me the greatest respect and attention, and has been with me for several days, a worthy man, so far as I have been able to judge, and one deserving of your generosity. I informed him that you had given instructions that he should be satisfied with 10 privileged men, two cavalrymen and one centurion, drawn from the cohorts which you wanted me to have under my command. (2) He replied that this number was not enough for him, and that he would write to you to this effect. It was for this reason that I decided that the soldiers he has in excess of the total should not be recalled at once.

22. Traianus to Plinius

Gavius Bassus has also written to me that the number of soldiers which I laid down in my instructions should be given to him was not large enough for him. I have ordered a copy of what I wrote back to him to be appended to this letter, for your information. It makes a great difference whether the situation requires it or whether he wants to make wider use of them on this pretext. (2) But we should consider only what is useful, and, as far as possible, ensure that soldiers are not absent from their units.

23. C. Plinius to Traianus Imperator

(1) The people of Prusa, sir, have a bath-house: it is squalid and old. They therefore regard it as of great importance to have a new one built; it seems to me that you can grant their request in this matter. (2) For there will be the money for it to be built: in the first place that which I have already begun to recover and to exact from private persons; in the second place they are ready to transfer to the building of the bath-house the money which they have themselves been in the practice of spending on olive-oil; besides it is something which both the standing of the city and the splendour of your age requires.

24. Traianus to Plinius

If the building of a bath-house is not going to put a burden on the resources of the people of Prusa, we can grant their request, provided that no special tax is imposed for that purpose and that they do not have less available for necessary expenditures in the future.

25. C. Plinius to Traianus Imperator

Servilius Pudens, my deputy, came to me at Nicomedia on November 24th, sir, and freed me from the anxiety caused by a long period of waiting.

XXVI. C. Plinivs Traiano Imperatori

(1) Rosianum Geminum, domine, artissimo uinculo mecum tua in me beneficia iunxerunt; habui enim illum quaestorem in consulatu. Mei sum obseruantissimum expertus; tantam mihi post consulatum reuerentiam praestat, et publicae necessitudinis pignera priuatis cumulat officiis. (2) Rogo ergo, ut ipse apud te pro dignitate eius precibus meis faueas. Cui et, si quid mihi credis, indulgentiam tuam dabis; dabit ipse operam ut in iis, quae ei mandaueris, maiora mereatur. Parciorem me in laudando facit, quod spero tibi et integritatem eius et probitatem et industriam non solum ex eius honoribus, quos in urbe sub oculis tuis gessit, uerum etiam ex commilitio esse notissimam. (3) Illud unum, quod propter caritatem eius nondum mihi uideor satis plene fecisse, etiam atque etiam facio teque, domine, rogo, gaudere me exornata quaestoris mei dignitate, id est per illum mea, quam maturissime uelis.

XXVII. C. Plinivs Traiano Imperatori

Maximus libertus et procurator tuus, domine, praeter decem beneficiarios, quos adsignari a me Gemellino optimo uiro iussisti, sibi quoque confirmat necessarios esse milites sex. Hos interim, sicut inueneram, in ministerio eius relinquendos existimaui, praesertim cum ad frumentum comparandum iret in Paphlagoniam. Quin etiam tutelae causa, quia ita desiderabat, addidi duos equites. In futurum, quid seruari uelis, rogo rescribas.

XXVIII. Traianvs Plinio

Nunc quidem proficiscentem ad comparationem frumentorum Maximum libertum meum recte militibus instruxisti. Fungebatur enim et ipse extraordinario munere. Cum ad pristinum actum reuersus fuerit, sufficient illi duo a te dati milites et totidem a Virdio Gemellino procuratore meo, quem adiuuat.

XXIX. C. Plinivs Traiano Imperatori

(1) Sempronius Caelianus, egregius iuuenis, repertos inter tirones duos seruos misit ad me; quorum ego supplicium distuli, ut te conditorem disciplinae militaris firmatoremque consulerem de modo poenae. (2) Ipse enim dubito ob hoc maxime quod, ut iam dixerant sacramento, ita nondum distributi in numeros erant. Quid ergo

26. C. Plinius to Traianus Imperator

(1) Your kindnesses to me have bound Rosianus Geminus to me by the closest of links, sir: for I had him as quaestor in my consulship. I have found him to be most attentive to me: so great is the respect he shows me since my consulship, and he heaps personal services on top of the tokens of our official relationship. (2) So I ask that you yourself in response to my prayers show him on your side the favour appropriate to his rank. You will also, if you have any trust in my judgment, show him your generosity; he himself will devote his efforts in those tasks which you will have entrusted to him to show he deserves greater honours. What makes me more sparing in my praise is the fact that I hope his integrity and honesty and diligence are very well known to you, as a result not only of the offices which he has filled in the city under your own eyes, but also from his military service with you. (3) This one request I keep making again and again, something which, because of my affection for him, I cannot convince myself that I have yet done in full measure, and I beg you, sir, to allow me as soon as possible to rejoice in the enhanced standing of my quaestor, and so, through him, in my own.

27. C. Plinius to Traianus Imperator

Your freedman and procurator Maximus, sir, asserts that he too needs six soldiers apart from the ten privileged soldiers whom you ordered to be allocated by me to that excellent man Gemellinus. For the time being I have decided that these men should be left in attendance upon him, just as I had found them, especially since he was setting off for Paphlagonia to collect grain. In fact I even added two cavalrymen to guard him, since he requested it. I ask you to write back about the rule you wish to have followed in future.

28. Traianus to Plinius

Since he was in fact at that moment setting off to collect grain you were right to supply my freedman Maximus with soldiers. For he too was undertaking a special duty. When he has returned to his old post, two soldiers supplied by you and the same number by my procurator Virdius Gemellinus, whose assistant he is, will be enough for him.

29. C. Plinius to Traianus Imperator

(1) Sempronius Caelianus, an excellent young man, has sent two slaves who had been discovered among the recruits to me. I postponed their sentence until I could ask your advice as the founder and upholder of military discipline about the manner of their punishment. (2) For I am myself in doubt principally because of the fact that, while they had already sworn the oath, they had not yet been enrolled in the ranks. So I ask

debeam sequi rogo, domine, scribas, praesertim cum pertineat ad exemplum.

XXX. Traianvs Plinio

(1) Secundum mandata mea fecit Sempronius Caelianus mittendo ad te eos, de quibus cognosci oportebit, an capitale supplicium meruisse uideantur. Refert autem, uoluntarii se obtulerint an lecti sint uel etiam uicarii dati. (2) Lecti ⟨si⟩ sunt, inquisitio peccauit; si uicarii dati, penes eos culpa est qui dederunt; si ipsi, cum haberent condicionis suae conscientiam, uenerunt, animaduertendum in illos erit. Neque enim multum interest, quod nondum per numeros distributi sunt. Ille enim dies, quo primum probati sunt, ueritatem ab iis originis suae exegit.

XXXI. C. Plinivs Traiano Imperatori

(1) Salua magnitudine tua, domine, descendas oportet ad meas curas, cum ius mihi dederis referendi ad te, de quibus dubito. (2) In plerisque ciuitatibus, maxime Nicomediae et Nicaeae, quidam uel in opus damnati uel in ludum similiaque his genera poenarum publicorum seruorum officio ministerioque funguntur, atque etiam ut publici serui annua accipiunt. Quod ego cum audissem, diu multumque haesitaui, quid facere deberem. (3) Nam et reddere poenae post longum tempus plerosque iam senes et, quantum adfirmatur, frugaliter modesteque uiuentes nimis seuerum arbitrabar, et in publicis officiis retinere damnatos non satis honestum putabam; eosdem rursus a re publica pasci otiosos inutile, non pasci etiam periculosum existimabam. (4) Necessario ergo rem totam, dum te consulerem, in suspenso reliqui. Quaeres fortasse, quem ad modum euenerit, ut poenis in quas damnati erant exsoluerentur: et ego quaesii, sed nihil comperi, quod adfirmare tibi possim. Vt decreta quibus damnati erant proferebantur, ita nulla monumenta quibus liberati probarentur. (5) Erant tamen, qui dicerent deprecantes iussu proconsulum legatorumue dimissos. Addebat fidem, quod credibile erat neminem hoc ausum sine auctore.

XXXII. Traianvs Plinio

(1) Meminerimus idcirco te in istam prouinciam missum, quoniam multa in ea

you, sir, to write to me about what course I should follow, especially since this would set a precedent.

30. Traianus to Plinius

(1) Sempronius Caelianus acted in obedience to my instructions in sending to you those persons who will need to be the subject of a hearing to decide whether they should be held to have deserved the capital penalty. Now it makes a difference whether they put themselves forward as volunteers or were conscripted or even offered as substitutes. (2) If they are conscripts, it is the examination which was at fault; if they were offered as substitutes, blame lies at the door of those who offered them; if they came forward on their own initiative, when they had full knowledge of their status, they will deserve execution. For the fact that they have not yet been enrolled in the ranks is of no great importance. For that day on which they were first approved demanded that they tell the truth about their origin.

31. C. Plinius to Traianus Imperator

(1) You can condescend to attend to my worries, sir, without injury to your dignity, since you have given me the privilege of placing before you matters about which I am in doubt. (2) In very many of the cities, and at Nicomedia and Nicaea in particular, individuals who were sentenced to forced labour or to appearing at the games and similar kinds of penalties to these are carrying out the functions and duties of public slaves, and even receiving a yearly allowance as public slaves. When I had learned of this, I was for a long time in great uncertainty about what I ought to do. (3) For I both considered it excessively harsh to send back to finish their sentences after a long interval a considerable number of men who are now old and who, so it is claimed, lead a simple and respectable life, and I also thought it quite improper to continue to use convicts in official posts; again I reflected that it was inexpedient to have these same men supported in idleness at public expense, but also dangerous not to have them supported at all. (4) Of necessity, therefore, I left the whole matter undecided, until I could take your advice. You will perhaps enquire how it came about that they were released from the penalties to which they had been sentenced; I too enquired, but I found out nothing which I could tell you for certain. Although the judgments in which they had been sentenced were produced, yet there were no documents in which they could be shown to have been set free. (5) There were, however, some who claimed that, upon appealing for mercy, they had been released at the orders of proconsuls or legates. What made this more convincing was the fact that it was unbelievable that anyone should have ventured to do this without authority.

32. Traianus to Plinius

(1) Let us remember that it was for this reason that you were sent to that province, because many things in it evidently stood in need of correction. Now this will

emendanda adparuerint. Erit autem uel hoc maxime corrigendum, quod qui damnati ad poenam erant, non modo ea sine auctore, ut scribis, liberati sunt, sed etiam in condicionem proborum ministrorum retrahuntur. (2) Qui igitur intra hos proximos decem annos damnati nec ullo idoneo auctore liberati sunt, hos oportebit poenae suae reddi; si qui uetustiores inuenientur et senes ante annos decem damnati, distribuamus illos in ea ministeria, quae non longe a poena sint. Solent et ad balineum, ad purgationes cloacarum, item munitiones uiarum et uicorum dari.

XXXIII. C. Plinivs Traiano Imperatori

(1) Cum diuersam partem prouinciae circumirem, Nicomediae uastissimum incendium multas priuatorum domos et duo publica opera, quamquam uia interiacente, Gerusian et Iseon absumpsit. (2) Est autem latius sparsum, primum uiolentia uenti, deinde inertia hominum quos satis constat otiosos et immobiles tanti mali spectatores perstitisse; et alioqui nullus usquam in publico sipo, nulla hama, nullum denique instrumentum ad incendia compescenda. Et haec quidem, ut iam praecepi, parabuntur; (3) tu, domine, dispice an instituendum putes collegium fabrorum dumtaxat hominum cl. Ego attendam, ne quis nisi faber recipiatur neue iure concesso in aliud utantur; nec erit difficile custodire tam paucos.

XXXIV. Traianvs Plinio

(1) Tibi quidem secundum exempla complurium in mentem uenit posse collegium fabrorum apud Nicomedenses constitui. Sed meminerimus prouinciam istam et praecipue eas ciuitates eius modi factionibus esse uexatas. Quodcumque nomen ex quacumque causa dederimus iis, qui in idem contracti fuerint, hetaeriae eaeque breui fient. (2) Satius itaque est comparari ea, quae ad coercendos ignes auxilio esse possint, admonerique dominos praediorum, ut et ipsi inhibeant ac, si res poposcerit, adcursu populi ad hoc uti.

XXXV. C. Plinivs Traiano Imperatori

Sollemnia uota pro incolumitate tua, qua publica salus continetur, et suscepimus, domine, pariter et soluimus precati deos, ut uelint ea semper solui semperque signari.

especially need to be put right, that men sentenced to punishment have not only been released from it without authority, as you say in your letter, but are also restored to the position of respectable officials. (2) So it will be necessary for those who were sentenced within these last ten years, and were released without any proper authorisation, to be sent back to their punishment; if any shall be found to be convicts of longer standing and old men sentenced more than ten years ago, we should assign them to those functions which would not be very different from a punishment. They are usually allocated to the public baths, to cleaning sewers, likewise to the repair of roads and streets.

33. C. Plinius to Traianus Imperator

(1) While I was travelling through a distant part of the province, a very extensive fire in Nicomedia destroyed many houses belonging to private persons and two public buildings, the Gerusia and the temple of Isis, even though there was a road separating them. (2) It spread quite widely, in the first place because there was a strong wind, in the second place because of the inactivity of the people: it is generally agreed that they stood around, idle and motionless spectators of so great a disaster; besides, nowhere was there publicly available any pump, any bucket, indeed any apparatus at all for fighting fires. These things too will in fact be supplied in accordance with instructions I have already given; (3) pray consider, sir, whether you think an association of firemen should be set up, provided that it has only 150 members. I shall myself see to it that no one except a fireman is admitted and that they do not use the permission they have been granted for any other purpose; and it will not be hard to keep watch over so few.

34. Traianus to Plinius

You are in fact following the example set by very many people in conceiving a plan that an assocation of firemen could be established at Nicomedia. But let us recall that that province and especially those cities have been troubled by cliques of that kind. Whatever name we may give, for whatever reason, to those who gather together for a common purpose, they will turn into political clubs, and that in a short time. (2) It is therefore more appropriate to have those things which can be of use in checking fires made available, and to urge the owners of properties both themselves to make use of them, and, if the situation requires it, to use for this purpose the crowd which gathers.

35. C. Plinius to Traianus Imperator

The customary vows for your preservation, upon which the safety of the state depends, we have both undertaken, sir, and at the same time fulfilled, praying to the gods that they be willing for these vows to be perpetually fulfilled and perpetually sealed.

XXXVI. Traianvs Plinio

Et soluisse uos cum prouincialibus dis immortalibus uota pro mea salute et incolumitate et nuncupasse libenter, mi Secunde carissime, cognoui ex litteris tuis.

XXXVII. C. Plinivs Traiano Imperatori

(1) In aquae ductum, domine, Nicomedenses impenderunt HS l̅x̅x̅x̅l c̅c̅c̅x̅v̅i̅i̅i̅, qui imperfectus adhuc omissus, destructus etiam est; rursus in alium ductum erogata sunt c̅c̅ Hoc quoque relicto nouo impendio est opus, ut aquam habeant, qui tantam pecuniam male perdiderunt. (2) Ipse perueni ad fontem purissimum, ex quo uidetur aqua debere perduci, sicut initio temptatum erat, arcuato opere, ne tantum ad plana ciuitatis et humilia perueniat. Manent adhuc paucissimi arcus: possunt et erigi quidam lapide quadrato, qui ex superiore opere detractus est; aliqua pars, ut mihi uidetur, testaceo opere agenda erit, id enim et facilius et uilius. (3) Sed in primis necessarium est mitti a te uel aquilegem uel architectum, ne rursus eueniat quod accidit. Ego illud unum adfirmo, et utilitatem operis et pulchritudinem saeculo tuo esse dignissimam.

XXXVIII. Traianvs Plinio

Curandum est, ut aqua in Nicomedensem ciuitatem perducatur. Vere credo te ea, qua debebis, diligentia hoc opus adgressurum. Sed medius fidius ad eandem diligentiam tuam pertinet inquirere, quorum uitio ad hoc tempus tantam pecuniam Nicomedenses perdiderint, ne, dum inter se gratificantur, et incohauerint aquae ductus et reliquerint. Quid itaque compereris, perfer in notitiam meam.

XXXIX. C. Plinivs Traiano Imperatori

(1) Theatrum, domine, Nicaeae maxima iam parte constructum, imperfectum tamen, sestertium (ut audio; neque enim ratio operis excussa est) amplius centies hausit: uereor ne frustra. (2) Ingentibus enim rimis desedit et hiat, siue in causa solum umidum et molle, siue lapis ipse gracilis et putris: dignum est certe deliberatione, sitne faciendum an sit relinquendum an etiam destruendum. Nam fulturae ac substructiones, quibus subinde suscipitur, non tam firmae mihi quam sumptuosae uidentur. (3) Huic theatro ex priuatorum pollicitationibus multa debentur, ut basilicae circa, ut porticus supra caueam. Quae nunc omnia differuntur cessante eo, quod ante peragendum est. (4) Iidem Nicaeenses gymnasium incendio amissum ante aduentum meum restituere

36. Traianus to Plinius
I learnt with pleasure from your letter, my dearest Secundus, that you along with the provincials had both fulfilled and pronounced vows to the immortal gods for my safety and preservation.

37. C. Plinius to Traianus Imperator

(1) The people of Nicomedia, sir, have spent 3,318,000 sesterces on an aqueduct, which was abandoned while still unfinished, and was also demolished; subsequently 200,000 were laid out on another aqueduct. Since this too was abandoned, fresh expenditure is required in order that those who have wasted so much money may get their water. (2) I have myself visited a very pure spring, from which it appears that the water must be brought, as was attempted on the first occasion, on an arched structure, so that it may not reach just the flat and low-lying parts of the city. A very few arches are still standing: some can also be built up from the dressed stone which was pulled down from the earlier structure; some part of it, in my judgment, should be made of brickwork, for this would be both easier and cheaper. (3) But what is needed above all is for you to send out a water engineer or an architect, in order that what has happened may not occur again. This one thing I assert, that both the usefulness and the beauty of the work are fully worthy of your age.

38. Traianus to Plinius

The effort must be made to bring water to the city of Nicomedia. I am truly confident that you will approach this task with the diligence which you ought to show. But, by heaven, it is also your duty diligently to investigate whose fault it is that the people of Nicomedia have until now wasted so much money, in case it was in the course of doing each other favours that they began and abandoned aqueducts. What you thus discover, bring to my attention.

39. C. Plinius to Traianus Imperator

A theatre at Nicaea, sir, most of which has already been built, though it is still incomplete, has swallowed up more than ten million sesterces (so I am informed; for the balance-sheet for the project has not been examined); I fear it may have been in vain. (2) For it is sinking and it gapes with huge cracks, either because the soil is wet and spongy, or because the stone itself is soft and crumbling; at all events it is worth considering whether it should be finished or abandoned or even demolished. For the supports and substructures, on which it is held up from below, appear to me not to be as strong as they are expensive. (3) Many embellishments for this theatre were promised by private persons and are still owed, for example halls around it, and a colonnade above the auditorium. All these are postponed now that the building which needs to be finished first is at a stop. (4) These same people of Nicaea began, before my arrival, to restore a gymnasium which had been destroyed in a fire, on a much more

coeperunt, longe numerosius laxiusque quam fuerat, et iam aliquantum erogauerunt; periculum est, ne parum utiliter; incompositum enim et sparsum est. Praeterea architectus, sane aemulus eius a quo opus incohatum est, adfirmat parietes quamquam uiginti et duos pedes latos imposita onera sustinere non posse, quia sint caemento medii farti nec testaceo opere praecincti.

(5) Claudiopolitani quoque in depresso loco, imminente etiam monte ingens balineum defodiunt magis quam aedificant, et quidem ex ea pecunia, quam buleutae additi beneficio tuo aut iam obtulerunt ob introitum aut nobis exigentibus conferent. (6) Ergo cum timeam ne illic publica pecunia, hic, quod est omni pecunia pretiosius, munus tuum male collecetur, cogor petere a te non solum ob theatrum, uerum etiam ob haec balinea mittas architectum, dispecturum utrum sit utilius post sumptum qui factus est quoquo modo consummare opera, ut incohata sunt, an quae uidentur emendanda corrigere, quae transferenda transferre, ne dum seruare uolumus quod impensum est, male impendamus quod addendum est.

XL. Traianvs Plinio

(1) Quid oporteat fieri circa theatrum, quod incohatum apud Nicaeenses est, in re praesenti optime deliberabis et constitues. Mihi sufficiet indicari, cui sententiae accesseris. Tunc autem a priuatis exige opera, cum theatrum, propter quod illa promissa sunt, factum erit. (2) Gymnasiis indulgent Graeculi; ideo forsitan Nicaeenses maiore animo constructionem eius adgressi sunt: sed oportet illos eo contentos esse, quod possit illis sufficere. (3) Quid Claudiopolitanis circa balineum quod parum, ut scribis, idoneo loco incohauerunt suadendum sit, tu constitues. Architecti tibi deesse non possunt. Nulla prouincia non et peritos et ingeniosos homines habet; modo ne existimes breuius esse ab urbe mitti, cum ex Graecia etiam ad nos uenire soliti sint.

XLI. C. Plinivs Traiano Imperatori

(1) Intuenti mihi et fortunae tuae et animi magnitudinem conuenientissimum uidetur demonstrari opera non minus aeternitate tua quam gloria digna, quantumque pulchritudinis tantum utilitatis habitura. (2) Est in Nicomedensium finibus amplissimus lacus. Per hunc marmora fructus ligna materiae et sumptu modico et labore usque ad uiam nauibus, inde magno labore maiore impendio uehiculis ad mare deuehuntur ... hoc opus multas manus poscit. At eae porro non desunt. Nam et in agris magna copia est hominum et maxima in ciuitate, certaque spes omnes

lavish and extensive scale than before, and they have already spent a considerable sum; the danger is that it will have been to little practical purpose; for it is ill-planned and rambling. Moreover, an architect, admittedly a rival of the one by whom the building was started, claims that the walls, despite being twenty-two feet thick, cannot support the load put upon them, because they are made up of a core of rubble and are not encased in brickwork.

(5) The people of Claudiopolis too are excavating rather than building a huge bath-house on a low-lying site which also has a mountain hanging over it, and indeed they are using that money which those members who were added to their council through your act of favour either have already paid upon their admission, or will contribute when we extract it from them. (6) Therefore, since I fear that in the former case the city's money, in the latter your gift, which is more valuable than any money, is being ill-spent, I am forced to ask you to send out an architect, not only on account of the theatre, but also of this bath-house, to consider whether it will be more expedient, after the expenditure which has already been made, to finish by some means or other the buildings in the form in which they have been started, or to put right what it appears can be corrected, and to change the sites where it appears they can be changed, in case we waste additional expenditure in our anxiety to save what has been spent.

40. Traianus to Plinius

(1) As the man on the spot you will be the best person to consider and decide what ought to be done with the theatre which has been begun at Nicaea. It will be enough for me to be informed of the decision you arrive at. After that make the private individuals add the embellishments, when the theatre in connection with which those embellishments were promised has been finished. (2) The Greeklings do enjoy their gymnasia; perhaps it was for that reason that the people of Nicaea set about building one in an over-ambitious spirit; but they must be content with the kind which can meet their needs. (3) You shall decide what advice should be given to the people of Claudiopolis about the bath-house they have begun to build on a site which, as you say in your letter, is quite unsuitable. You cannot be short of architects. There is no province which does not have men who are both expert and skilful; only do not suppose that it is quicker to have them sent from the capital, when they are actually accustomed to come from Greece to us.

41. C. Plinius to Traianus Imperator

When I reflect on the greatness of both your station and your character, it seems to me most appropriate that projects should be brought to your notice which are as worthy of your eternal fame as of your glory and will have as much utility as beauty. (2) There is a very large lake in the territory of the people of Nicomedia. Across it marble, grain, firewood and timber are carried by boat as far as the road with little expense and effort, but by cart from there to the sea with great effort and at even greater cost . . . [Probable lacuna in the text]. This project calls for many hands. But those are readily available. For there is both a plentiful supply of men in the countryside and a very

libentissime adgressuros opus omnibus fructuosum. (3) Superest ut tu libratorem uel architectum si tibi uidebitur mittas, qui diligenter exploret, sitne lacus altior mari, quem artifices regionis huius quadraginta cubitis altiorem esse contendunt. (4) Ego per eadem loca inuenio fossam a rege percussam, sed incertum utrum ad colligendum umorem circumiacentium agrorum an ad committendum flumini lacum; est enim imperfecta. Hoc quoque dubium, intercepto rege mortalitate an desperato operis effectu. (5) Sed hoc ipso (feres enim me ambitiosum pro tua gloria) incitor et accendor, ut cupiam peragi a te quae tantum coeperant reges.

XLII. Traianvs Plinio

Potest nos sollicitare lacus iste, ut committere illum mari uelimus; sed plane explorandum est diligenter, ne si emissus in mare fuerit totus effluat certe, quantum aquarum et unde accipiat. Poteris a Calpurnio Macro petere libratorem, et ego hinc aliquem tibi peritum eius modi operum mittam.

XLIII. C. Plinivs Traiano Imperatori

(1) Requirenti mihi Byzantiorum rei publicae impendia, quae maxima fecit, indicatum est, domine, legatum ad te salutandum annis omnibus cum psephismate mitti, eique dari nummorum duodena milia. (2) Memor ergo propositi tui legatum quidem retinendum, psephisma autem mittendum putaui, ut simul et sumptus leuaretur et impleretur publicum officium. (3) Eidem ciuitati imputata sunt terna milia, quae uiatici nomine annua dabantur legato eunti ad eum qui Moesiae praeest publice salutandum. Haec ego in posterum circumcidenda existimaui. (4) Te, domine, rogo ut quid sentias rescribendo aut consilium meum confirmare aut errorem emendare digneris.

XLIV. Traianvs Plinio

Optime fecisti, Secunde carissime, duodena ista Byzantiis quae ad salutandum me in legatum impendebantur remittendo. Fungentur his partibus, etsi solum psephisma per te missum fuerit. Ignoscet illis et Moesiae praeses, si minus illum sumptuose coluerint.

plentiful one in the town, and the sure prospect that they will all most gladly take part in a project which is of advantage to all. (3) It remains for you, if you see fit, to send a surveyor or an architect, to make a thorough investigation to see whether the lake is at a higher level than the sea; the experts in this district claim that it is forty cubits higher. (4) I myself learn that a ditch was cut through the same area by one of the kings, but it is uncertain whether it was done to drain off water from the surrounding fields or to link the lake to the river; for it is incomplete. It is also a matter of doubt whether the king was cut off by sudden death or whether the success of the enterprise was despaired of. (5) But what spurs me on and inspires me (you will bear with my aspirations to advance your glory) is my desire to see what the kings had merely begun completed by your agency.

42. Traianus to Plinius

That lake of yours can incite us to wish to link it to the sea; but clearly there must be a thorough investigation to find out how much water it collects and from what sources, in case, if let out into the sea, it would drain away entirely. You will be able to apply to Calpurnius Macer for a surveyor, and I shall send from here someone skilled in projects of this kind.

43. C. Plinius to Traianus Imperator

(1) When I was examining the very heavy expenditures which the state of the Byzantines has been making, it was pointed out to me, sir, that an envoy is sent every year with a resolution to bring you greetings, and that he is given twelve thousand sesterces. (2) Mindful, therefore, of your policy, I have decided that the envoy should be kept at home, but that the resolution should be sent on, in order that the expense may be lightened and the city's act of loyalty may at the same time be carried out. (3) Sums of three thousand sesterces have been charged to the account of the same city, which were being paid every year under the heading of travelling expenses to an envoy who went to bring the city's greetings to the person who is governor of Moesia. I thought this should be cut back for the future. (4) I ask you, sir, to write back what you think and to deign either to confirm my decision or to correct my mistake.

44. Traianus to Plinius

You acted quite correctly, dearest Secundus, in remitting to the Byzantines those twelve thousand sesterces which were being spent on an envoy to bring me greetings. They will be carrying out this duty even if the resolution on its own is sent on through you. The governor of Moesia also will excuse them if they pay their respects to him in a less expensive way.

XLV. C. Plinivs Traiano Imperatori

Diplomata, domine, quorum dies praeteriit, an omnino obseruari et quam diu uelis, rogo scribas meque haesitatione liberes. Vereor enim, ne in alterutram partem ignorantia lapsus aut inlicita confirmem aut necessaria impediam.

XLVI. Traianvs Plinio

Diplomata, quorum praeteritus est dies, non debent esse in usu. Ideo inter prima iniungo mihi, ut per omnes prouincias ante mittam noua diplomata, quam desiderari possint.

XLVII. C. Plinivs Traiano Imperatori

(1) Cum uellem, domine, Apameae cognoscere publicos debitores et reditum et impendia, responsum est mihi cupere quidem uniuersos, ut a me rationes coloniae legerentur, numquam tamen esse lectas ab ullo proconsulum; habuisse priuilegium et uetustissimum morem arbitrio suo rem publicam administrare. (2) Exegi ut quae dicebant quaeque recitabant libello complecterentur; quem tibi qualem acceperam misi, quamuis intellegerem pleraque ex illo ad id, de quo quaeritur, non pertinere. (3). Te rogo ut mihi praeire digneris, quid me putes obseruare debere. Vereor enim ne aut excessisse aut non implesse officii mei partes uidear.

XLVIII. Traianvs Plinio

(1) Libellus Apamenorum, quem epistulae tuae iunxeras, remisit mihi necessitatem perpendendi qualia essent, propter quae uideri uolunt eos, qui pro consulibus hanc prouinciam obtinuerunt, abstinuisse inspectatione rationum suarum, cum ipse ut eas inspiceres non recusauerint. (2) Remuneranda est igitur probitas eorum, ut iam nunc sciant hoc, quod inspecturus es, ex mea uoluntate saluis, quae habent, priuilegiis esse facturum.

XLIX. C. Plinivs Traiano Imperatori

(1) Ante aduentum meum, domine, Nicomedenses priori foro nouum adicere coeperunt, cuius in angulo est aedes uetustissima Matris Magnae aut reficienda aut transferenda, ob hoc praecipue quod est multo depressior opere eo quod cum maxime

45. C. Plinius to Traianus Imperator

I ask you to write, sir, and free me from my uncertainty about whether you would want passes which have reached their expiry date to be respected at all, and for how long. For I am concerned not to err in either direction through ignorance or to sanction what is unlawful or to stand in the way of essential business.

46. Traianus to Plinius

Passes which have reached their expiry date ought not to be in use. It is for that reason that I lay it upon myself as one of my first duties to send new passes out through all the provinces before they can be required.

47. C. Plinius to Traianus Imperator

(1) When I wanted, sir, to investigate the public debtors and revenue and expenditures at Apamea, the answer given to me was that the whole citizen-body was in fact anxious to have the colony's accounts examined by me, but that they had never been examined by any of the proconsuls; that they had had the privilege and long-established custom of running their community according to their own judgment. (2) I required them to include the statements they were making and the precedents they were quoting in a memorandum; this I have sent to you in the form in which I had received it, although I was aware that a great deal in it was not relevant to the issue which is in dispute. (3) I ask you to deign to guide me about the principle which you think I ought to follow. For I am concerned not to be thought either to have exceeded the bounds of my duty or not to have fulfilled it.

48. Traianus to Plinius

(1) The memorandum of the people of Apamea, which you had attached to your letter, has relieved me of the need to weigh the kind of reasons they had for wishing it to be seen that the proconsuls who ruled this province had refrained from an examination of their accounts, since they have not refused to let you examine them. (2) Their honesty should therefore be rewarded, so that they should now know that by my wish you will be carrying out this inspection which you are going to make without prejudice to the privileges which they now possess.

49. C. Plinius to Traianus Imperator

Before my arrival, sir, the people of Nicomedia began to add a new forum to their old one; in a corner of it there is a very ancient temple of the Great Mother which needs either to be rebuilt or moved to another site, principally for the reason that it is at a considerably lower level than the buildings which are going up at this very moment.

42

surgit. (2) Ego cum quaererem, num esset aliqua lex dicta templo, cognoui alium hic, alium apud nos esse morem dedicationis. Dispice ergo, domine, an putes aedem, cui nulla lex dicta est, salua religione posse transferri; alioqui commodissimum est, si religio non impedit.

L. Traianvs Plinio

Potes, mi Secunde carissime, sine sollicitudine religionis, si loci positio uidetur hoc desiderare, aedem Matris Deum transferre in eam quae est accommodatior; nec te moueat, quod lex dedicationis nulla reperitur, cum solum peregrinae ciuitatis capax non sit dedicationis, quae fit nostro iure.

LI. C. Plinivs Traiano Imperatori

(1) Difficile est, domine, exprimere uerbis, quantam perceperim laetitiam, quod et mihi et socrui meae praestitisti, ut adfinem eius Caelium Clementem in hanc prouinciam transferres. (2) Ex illo enim et mensuram beneficii tui penitus intellego, cum tam plenam indulgentiam cum tota domo mea experiar, cui referre gratiam parem ne audeo quidem, quamuis maxime possim. Itaque ad uota confugio deosque precor, ut iis, quae in me adsidue confers, non indignus existimer.

LII. C. Plinivs Traiano Imperatori

Diem, domine, quo seruasti imperium, dum suscipis, quanta mereris laetitia celebrauimus, precati deos ut te generi humano, cuius tutela et securitas saluti tuae innisa est, incolumem florentemque praestarent. Praeiuimus et commilitonibus ius iurandum more sollemni, eadem prouincialibus certatim pietate iurantibus.

LIII. Traianvs Plinio

Quanta religione et laetitia commilitones cum prouincialibus te praeeunte diem imperii mei celebrauerint, libenter, mi Secunde carissime, agnoui litteris tuis.

(2) When I enquired whether the temple had any foundation charter, I discovered that the practice of consecration here is different from ours. Consider therefore, sir, whether you think that a temple without any foundation charter can be moved to another site without any breach of religious law: apart from that, if religious law is not an obstacle, this is the most suitable course.

50. Traianus to Plinius

You can, my dearest Secundus, without anxiety about religious law, move the temple of the Mother of the Gods, if the situation of its site seems to require it, to that site which is more convenient; and do not let the fact that no foundation charter is to be found trouble you, since land in a foreign state is incapable of undergoing the consecration which takes place under our law.

51. C. Plinius to Traianus Imperator

(1) It is hard, sir, to put into words how much joy I felt because you granted both myself and my mother-in-law the favour of transferring her kinsman Caelius Clemens to this province. (2) For, from this, I also comprehend profoundly the scope of your kindness, when, along with my whole family, I experience generosity so full that I do not even venture to respond with equal gratitude, however much it may be in my power to do so. Accordingly I resort to prayers and I beg the gods that I may not be considered unworthy of those favours which you are constantly bestowing upon me.

52. C. Plinius to Traianus Imperator

The day, sir, upon which you saved the empire by taking it over, we have celebrated with as great a joy as you deserve, praying to the gods to bestow upon the human race, whose protection and safety have depended upon your well-being, the favour of keeping you unharmed and prosperous. We have also administered the oath to our fellow-soldiers in the customary manner, while the provincials vied with them in swearing the oath with the same loyalty.

53. Traianus to Plinius

With how much devotion and joy my fellow-soldiers, along with the provincials, celebrated the day of my accession under your guidance, I learnt with pleasure from your letter, my dearest Secundus.

LIV. C. Plinivs Traiano Imperatori

(1) Pecuniae publicae, domine, prouidentia tua et ministerio nostro et iam exactae sunt et exiguntur; quae uereor ne otiosae iaceant. Nam et praediorum comparandorum aut nulla aut rarissima occasio est, nec inueniuntur qui uelint debere rei publicae, praesertim duodenis assibus, quanti a priuatis mutuantur. (2) Dispice ergo, domine, numquid minuendam usuram ac per hoc idoneos debitores inuitandos putes, et, si nec sic reperiuntur, distribuendam inter decuriones pecuniam, ita ut recte rei publicae caueant; quod quamquam inuitis et recusantibus minus acerbum erit leuiore usura constituta.

LV. Traianvs Plinio

Et ipse non aliud remedium dispicio, mi Secunde carissime, quam ut quantitas usurarum minuatur, quo facilius pecuniae publicae collocentur. Modum eius, ex copia eorum qui mutuabuntur, tu constitues. Inuitos ad accipiendum compellere, quod fortassis ipsis otiosum futurum sit, non est ex iustitia nostrorum temporum.

LVI. C. Plinivs Traiano Imperatori

(1) Summas, domine, gratias ago, quod inter maximas occupationes ⟨ in⟩ iis, de quibus te consului, me quoque regere dignatus es; quod nunc quoque facias rogo. (2) Adiit enim me quidam indicauitque aduersarios suos a Seruilio Caluo, clarissimo uiro, in triennium relegatos in prouincia morari: illi contra ab eodem se restitutos adfirmauerunt edictumque recitauerunt. Qua causa necessarium credidi rem integram ad te referre. (3) Nam, sicut mandatis tuis cautum est, ne restituam ab alio aut a me relegatos, ita de iis, quos alius et relegauerit et restituerit, nihil comprehensum est. Ideo tu, domine, consulendus fuisti, quid obseruare me uelles, tam hercule quam de iis qui in perpetuum relegati nec restituti in prouincia deprehenduntur. (4) Nam haec quoque species incidit in cognitionem meam. Est enim adductus ad me in perpetuum relegatus ⟨ a⟩ Iulio Basso proconsule. Ego, quia sciebam acta Bassi rescissa datumque a senatu ius omnibus, de quibus ille aliquid constituisset, ex integro agendi, dumtaxat per biennium, interrogaui hunc, quem relegauerat, an adisset docuissetque proconsulem. ⟨Negauit.⟩ (5) Per quod effectum est, ut te consulerem, reddendum eum poenae suae an grauius aliquid et quid potissimum constituendum putares et in hunc et in eos, si qui

54. C. Plinius to Traianus Imperator

(1) The moneys of the cities, sir, by your foresight and my efforts have already been and are still being recovered; I am concerned that they do not lie idle. For there is no opportunity, or only a very rare one, of buying estates, and men who would be willing to become debtors to the community are not to be found, especially at a rate of twelve asses, the rate at which they borrow from private persons. (2) Consider, therefore, sir, whether you think the rate of interest should be lowered and suitable borrowers should be attracted by this means, and whether, if they are not forthcoming even on these terms, the money should be allocated among the decurions, on condition that they provide their community with adequate security; although they may be unwilling and refuse, this step will be less harsh if a lighter rate of interest is fixed.

55. Traianus to Plinius

I myself also see no other remedy, my dearest Secundus, than to reduce the amount of interest in order that the moneys of the cities may the more easily be put out on loan. Its level you shall determine in accordance with the numbers of those who will take up loans. To force men to accept against their will that which may perhaps lie idle on their hands is not in accordance with the justice of our age.

56. C. Plinius to Traianus Imperator

(1) I offer you my most profound thanks, sir, because in the midst of your most pressing duties you have deigned to guide me also on those points on which I have consulted you: which is what I ask you to do on this occasion as well. (2) For a man has come to me and informed me that his opponents, who had been banished for three years by that most distinguished man Servilius Calvus, were still residing in the province; they asserted in rebuttal that they had their status restored by the same governor and they read out his edict. For this reason I believed it necessary to refer the case to you as it stands. (3) For, while it is laid down in your instructions that I should not restore the status of men banished by another person or by myself, yet no provision is made for those whom another person has both banished and restored to their former status. So you had to be consulted, sir, about what rule you wish me to follow, as well, of course, as about those who, having been banished in perpetuity and not having had their status restored, are apprehended in the province. (4) For this category also has come before me for judgment. For a man who had been banished in perpetuity by the proconsul Iulius Bassus was brought before me. Because I was aware that Bassus' decisions had been revoked and that the right had been granted by the Senate to all those who had been involved in cases decided by him to plead their cases afresh, provided that they applied within two years, I asked this man whom he (Bassus) had banished whether he had approached a proconsul and informed him. He said he had not. (5) It was this which led me to consult you about whether you think he should be sent back to serve out his sentence or whether a heavier sentence should be imposed, and which sentence in particular, both on this man and on any others who may by chance

forte in simili condicione inuenirentur. Decretum Calui et edictum, item decretum Bassi his litteris subieci.

LVII. Traianvs Plinio

(1) Quid in persona eorum statuendum sit, qui a P. Seruilio Caluo proconsule in triennium relegati et mox eiusdem edicto restituti in prouincia remanserunt, proxime tibi rescribam, cum causas eius facti a Caluo requisiero. (2) Qui a Iulio Basso in perpetuum relegatus est, cum per biennium agendi facultatem habuerit, si existimat se iniuria relegatum, neque id fecerit atque in prouincia morari perseuerarit, uinctus mitti ad praefectos praetorii mei debet. Neque enim sufficit eum poenae suae restitui, quam contumacia elusit.

LVIII. C. Plinivs Traiano Imperatori

(1) Cum citarem iudices, domine, conuentum incohaturus, Flauius Archippus uacationem petere coepit ut philosophus. (2) Fuerunt qui dicerent non liberandum eum iudicandi necessitate, sed omnino tollendum de iudicum numero reddendumque poenae, quam fractis uinculis euasisset. (3) Recitata est sententia Veli Pauli proconsulis, qua probabatur Archippus crimine falsi damnatus in metallum: ille nihil proferebat, quo restitutum se doceret; adlegabat tamen pro restitutione et libellum a se Domitiano datum et epistulas eius ad honorem suum pertinentes et decretum Prusensium. Addebat his et tuas litteras scriptas sibi, addebat et patris tui edictum et epistulam, quibus confirmasset beneficia a Domitiano data. (4) Itaque, quamuis eidem talia crimina adplicarentur, nihil decernendum putaui, donec te consulerem de eo, quod mihi constitutione tua dignum uidebatur. Ea quae sunt utrimque recitata his litteris subieci.

Epistvla Domitiani Ad Terentivm Maximvm
(5) Flauius Archippus philosophus impetrauit a me, ut agrum ei ad c̄ circa Prusam, patriam suam, emi iuberem, cuius reditu suos alere posset. Quod ei praestari uolo. Summam expensam liberalitati meae feres.

Eivsdem Ad Lappivm Maximvm
(6) Archippum philosophum, bonum uirum et professioni suae etiam moribus respondentem, commendatum habeas uelim, mi Maxime, et plenam ei humanitatem tuam praestes in iis, quae uerecunde a te desiderauerit.

be found to be in a similar position. I have appended to this letter Calvus' judgment and edict, and likewise Bassus' judgment.

57. Traianus to Plinius

I shall write back to you presently about what decision should be taken about the status of those who had been banished for three years by the proconsul Publius Servilius Calvus and afterwards had their status restored by an edict of the same person, and have stayed on in the province, after I have ascertained from Calvus the reasons for this action. (2) The man who was banished in perpetuity by Iulius Bassus, since he had for two years the opportunity of going to law if he thought he had been banished wrongfully, and since he did not do this and persisted in staying on in the province, ought to be sent in chains to the Prefects of my Praetorian Guard. For it is not enough for him to be sent back to serve out his sentence which he insolently evaded.

58. C. Plinius to Traianus Imperator

(1) While I was calling out the names of jurymen, sir, as I was about to begin the assizes, Flavius Archippus started to apply for exemption as a philosopher. (2) Some people said he should not be freed from the obligation of jury service, but removed entirely from the ranks of jurymen, and sent back to suffer the punishment from which he had escaped by breaking out of his fetters. (3) A judgment of the proconsul Velius Paulus was read out, from which it was demonstrated that Archippus had been condemned to the mines on a charge of forgery: he was unable to produce anything by which he could show that his status had been restored; however, he advanced as evidence of his restoration both a petition submitted by himself to Domitian and epistles of the latter which had a bearing upon his reputation, as well as a resolution of the people of Prusa. To these he also added letters which you had written to him, he added both an edict and an epistle of your father's, in which he had confirmed the favours bestowed by Domitian. (4) Accordingly, although such serious charges were laid against this man, I thought no judgment should be reached until I consulted you about this matter, which seemed to me to be worthy of your decision. I have appended to this letter the documents which were read out on either side.

(5) Epistle of Domitian to Terentius Maximus
Flavius Archippus the philosopher has prevailed upon me to give instructions for the purchase of an estate worth up to 100,000 sesterces for him in the area of Prusa, his native city, on the income from which he can support his dependents. I wish this to be bestowed upon him. You will charge the full cost to my generosity.

(6) Of the same person to Lappius Maximus
I should wish you, Maximus my friend, to treat the philosopher Archippus, a good man whose character lives up to his profession, as a man recommended by me, and to show him your full kindness in those requests he may respectfully make of you.

Edictvm Divi Nervae

(7) Quaedam sine dubio, Quirites, ipsa felicitas temporum edicit, nec exspectandus est in iis bonus princeps, quibus illum intellegi satis est, cum hoc sibi ciuium meorum spondere possit uel non admonita persuasio, me securitatem omnium quieti meae praetulisse, ut et noua beneficia conferrem et ante me concessa seruarem. (8) Ne tamem aliquam gaudiis publicis adferat haesitationem uel eorum qui impetrauerunt diffidentia uel eius memoria qui praestitit, necessarium pariter credidi ac laetum obuiam dubitantibus indulgentiam meam mittere. (9) Nolo existimet quisquam, quod alio principe uel priuatim uel publice consecutus ⟨ sit⟩ ideo saltem a me rescindi, ut potius mihi debeat. Sint rata et certa, nec gratulatio ullius instauratis egeat precibus, quem fortuna imperii uultu meliore respexit. Me nouis beneficiis uacare patiantur, et ea demum sciant roganda esse quae non habent.

Epistvla Eivsdem ad Tvllivm Ivstvm

(10) Cum rerum omnium ordinatio, quae prioribus temporibus incohatae consummatae sunt, obseruanda sit, tum epistulis etiam Domitiani standum est.

LIX. C. Plinivs Traiano Imperatori

Flauius Archippus per salutem tuam aeternitatemque petit a me, ut libellum quem mihi dedit mitterem tibi. Quod ego sic roganti praestandum putaui, ita tamen ut missurum me notum accusatrici eius facerem, a qua et ipsa acceptum libellum his epistulis iunxi, quo facilius uelut audita utraque parte dispiceres, quid statuendum putares.

LX. Traianvs Plinio

(1) Potuit quidem ignorasse Domitianus, in quo statu esset Archippus, cum tam multa ad honorem eius pertinentia scriberet; sed meae naturae accommodatius est credere etiam statui eius subuentum interuentu principis, praesertim cum etiam statuarum ei honor totiens decretus sit ab iis, qui ⟨ non⟩ ignorabant, quid de illo Paulus proconsul pronuntiasset. (2) Quae tamen, mi Secunde carissime, non eo pertinent, ut si quid illi noui criminis obicitur, minus de eo audiendum putes. Libellos Furiae Primae accusatricis, item ipsius Archippi, quos alteri epistulae tuae iunxeras, legi.

(7)   Edict of the deified Nerva

Some things, citizens, the very happiness of our age proclaims for certain by edict, nor does a good emperor need to be waited for in matters where it is enough for him to be understood, since the confidence of my fellow-citizens can be assured, even without being explicitly told, of this fact, that I have placed the safety of all before my own tranquillity, in order that I might both grant new favours and confirm those conceded before my reign. (8) In order, however, that neither the uncertainty of those who obtained favours nor the reputation of him who conferred them should introduce any element of hesitation into the public rejoicing, I have judged it alike necessary and delightful to anticipate their doubts by my generosity. (9) I wish no man to suppose that what he has obtained in the reign of another emperor, whether as an individual or as a member of a community, would be revoked by me, for this reason at any rate, that he should be indebted for it to me instead. Let these favours be confirmed and secure, nor should the joy of anyone on whom the good fortune of the empire has looked with a kind face require renewed prayers. Let them permit me to keep my time free for new favours, and let them know that only those things which they do not possess need to be asked for.

(10) Epistle of the same person to Tullius Iustus

Since the arrangement of all matters which have been begun and completed in earlier times is to be respected, then one must also abide by the epistles of Domitian.

59. C. Plinius to Traianus Imperator

Flavius Archippus begs me in the name of your well-being and eternal fame to send you the memorandum which he has given to me. I decided that, since he has asked in this way, this request must be granted, on condition, however, that I made it known to the woman who is his accuser that I was going to send it. A memorandum which I have received from her in her turn I have attached to these epistles, that you may the more easily, having as it were listened to both parties, consider what you think should be decided.

60. Traianus to Plinius

(1) Domitian could, it is true, have been unaware of what the status of Archippus was at the time when he wrote so much that had a bearing upon his reputation; but it is more in accordance with my character to believe that support was given to his status by the emperor's intervention, especially since the honour of having his statue put up was voted to him on so many occasions by those who were not unaware of the judgment which the proconsul Paulus had delivered against him. (2) This, however, my dearest Secundus, does not imply that, if anything in the way of a fresh accusation is laid against him, you should suppose that less notice is to be taken of it. I have read the memoranda from his accuser Furia Prima, and also from Archippus himself, which you had attached to your second letter.

50

LXI.   C. Plinivs Traiano Imperatori

(1) Tu quidem, domine, prouidentissime uereris, ne commissus flumini atque ita mari lacus effluat; sed ego in re praesenti inuenisse uideor, quem ad modum huic periculo occurrerem. (2) Potest enim lacus fossa usque ad flumen adduci nec tamen in flumen emitti, sed relicto quasi margine contineri pariter et dirimi. Sic consequemur, ut neque aqua uiduetur flumini mixtus, et sit perinde ac si misceatur. Erit enim facile per illam breuissimam terram, quae interiacebit, aduecta fossa onera transponere in flumen. (3) Quod ita fiet si necessitas coget, et (spero) non coget. Est enim et lacus ipse satis altus et nunc in contrariam partem flumen emittit, quod interclusum inde et quo uolumus auersum, sine ullo detrimento lacus tantum aquae quantum nunc portat effundet. Praeterea per id spatium, per quod fossa fodienda est, incidunt riui; qui si diligenter colligantur, augebunt illud quod lacus dederit. (4) Enimuero, si placeat fossam longius ducere et altius pressam mari aequare nec in flumen, sed in ipsum mare emittere, repercussus maris seruabit et reprimet, quidquid e lacu ueniet. Quorum si nihil nobis loci natura praestaret, expeditum tamen erat cataractis aquae cursum temperare. (5) Verum et haec et alia multo sagacius conquiret explorabitque librator, quem plane, domine, debes mittere, ut polliceris. Est enim res digna et magnitudine tua et cura. Ego interim Calpurnio Macro clarissimo uiro auctore te scripsi, ut libratorem quam maxime idoneum mitteret.

LXII. Traianvs Plinio

Manifestum, mi Secunde carissime, nec prudentiam nec diligentiam tibi defuisse circa istum lacum, cum tam multa prouisa habeas, per quae nec periclitetur exhauriri et magis in usu nobis futurus sit. Elige igitur id quod praecipue res ipsa suaserit. Calpurnium Macrum credo facturum, ut te libratore instruat, neque prouinciae istae his artificibus carent.

LXIII. C. Plinivs Traiano Imperatori

Scripsit mihi, domine, Lycormas libertus tuus ut, si qua legatio a Bosporo uenisset urbem petitura, usque in aduentum suum retineretur. Et legatio quidem, dumtaxat in eam ciuitatem, in qua ipse sum, nulla adhuc uenit, sed uenit tabellarius Sauromatae ⟨ regis⟩, quem ego usus opportunitate, quam mihi casus obtulerat, cum

61. C. Plinius to Traianus Imperator

(1) You are indeed most far-sighted, sir, in your anxiety in case the lake, if linked to the river and so to the sea, drains away; I, however, believe that, being on the spot, I have found a means of forestalling this danger. (2) For the lake can be brought as far as the river by means of a canal, yet not be let out into the river, but, by leaving a bank as it were, it can be at the same time both brought together and kept separate. In this way we shall ensure that it is not deprived of its water by being mingled with the river, yet that it should be in the same position as if it were mingled. For it will be easy to transport to the river loads brought down on the canal across the very narrow strip of land which will lie in between. (3) It will be carried out in this way, if necessity forces us, and (I hope) it will not force us. For the lake is both deep enough in itself and at present pours a river out in the opposite direction. If the outlet is closed off on that side and turned aside in the direction we wish, it will only discharge the amount of water it carries at present, without any loss to the lake. Moreover streams run across the tract through which the canal will have to be dug; if these are carefully collected together, they will increase the supply of water which the lake will have provided. (4) Again, if it is decided to extend the canal further and, by cutting it deeper, to bring it to the level of the sea, and to let it out, not into the river, but into the sea itself, the counter-pressure of the sea will protect and push back whatever comes out of the lake. If the nature of the ground did not permit us any of these schemes, yet it would be practicable to restrain the flow of the water by means of sluice-gates. (5) However, a surveyor, whom you certainly should send out, sir, as you promise, will investigate and assess these and other schemes with far more skill. For the project is one worthy both of your greatness and your concern. I in the meantime have written, on your authority, to that most distinguished man Calpurnius Macer, to send as capable a surveyor as possible.

62. Traianus to Plinius

It is evident, my dearest Secundus, that you have spared neither forethought nor effort in the matter of that lake of yours, seeing that you have worked out so many devices to ensure that it would not be in danger of being drained and would be of greater use to us for the future. Choose therefore the scheme which the actual situation especially recommends. I believe that Calpurnius Macer will see to it that he supplies you with a surveyor, and those provinces of yours are not lacking in these experts.

63. C. Plinius to Traianus Imperator

Your freedman Lycormas has written to me, sir, to detain until his arrival any embassy which might have come from the Bosporus in order to make its way to the city. And in fact no embassy has yet come, at any rate to the city where I am myself staying, but a letter-carrier from king Sauromates has come. I decided to take advantage of the opportunity which chance had offered me and to send him along with the letter-carrier who arrived in advance of Lycormas on his journey, in order that you should be

tabellario qui Lycormam ex itinere praecessit mittendum putaui, ut posses ex Lycormae et regis epistulis pariter cognoscere, quae fortasse pariter scire deberes.

LXIV. C. Plinivs Traiano Imperatori

Rex Sauromates scripsit mihi esse quaedam, quae deberes quam maturissime scire. Qua ex causa festinationem tabellarii, quem ad te cum epistulis misit, diplomate adiuui.

LXV. C. Plinivs Traiano Imperatori

(1) Magna, domine, et ad totam prouinciam pertinens quaestio est de condicione et alimentis eorum, quos uocant θρεπτούς. (2) In qua ego auditis constitutionibus principum, quia nihil inueniebam aut proprium aut uniuersale, quod ad Bithynos referretur, consulendum te existimaui, quid obseruari uelles; neque putaui posse me in eo, quod auctoritatem tuam posceret, exemplis esse contentum. (3) Recitabatur autem apud me edictum, quod dicebatur diui Augusti, ad Achaiam pertinens; recitatae et epistulae diui Vespasiani ad Lacedaemonios et diui Titi ad eosdem et Achaeos et Domitiani ad Auidium Nigrinum et Armenium Brocchum proconsules, item ad Lacedaemonios; quae ideo tibi non misi, quia et parum emendata et quaedam non certae fidei uidebantur, et quia uera et emendata in scriniis tuis esse credebam.

LXVI. Traianvs Plinio

(1) Quaestio ista, quae pertinet ad eos qui liberi nati expositi, deinde sublati a quibusdam et in seruitute educati sunt, saepe tractata est, nec quicquam inuenitur in commentariis eorum principum, qui ante me fuerunt, quod ad omnes prouincias sit constitutum. (2) Epistulae sane sunt Domitiani ad Auidium Nigrinum et Armenium Brocchum, quae fortasse debeant obseruari: sed inter eas prouincias, de quibus rescripsit, non est Bithynia; et ideo nec adsertionem denegandam iis qui ex eius modi causa in libertatem uindicabuntur puto, neque ipsam libertatem redimendam pretio alimentorum.

LXVII. C. Plinivs Traiano Imperatori

(1) Legato Sauromatae regis, cum sua sponte Nicaeae, ubi me inuenerat, biduo substitisset, longiorem moram faciendam, domine, non putaui, primum quod incertum

able to learn at the same moment from Lycormas' and the king's epistles news about which you should perhaps be informed at the same moment.

64. C. Plinius to Traianus Imperator

King Sauromates has written to me that there are some matters about which you ought to be informed as soon as possible. For this reason I have assisted with a pass the speedy journey of a letter-carrier whom he has sent to you with epistles.

65. C. Plinius to Traianus Imperator

(1) Sir, there is an important dispute, and one which affects the whole province, concerning the status and the costs of rearing of those whom they call "foster-children". (2) I myself, after having heard decisions of emperors on this matter read to me, because I could not find any local rule or any general one which should be applied to the Bithynians, decided that I must consult you about what rule you wish to have followed; and I did not think that, on a matter which called for your authority, I could be satisfied with precedents. (3) In fact there was read out in my presence an edict relating to Achaia which was said to be one of the deified Augustus'; there were also read out epistles of the deified Vespasian to the Spartans, and of the deified Titus to the same people and to the Achaeans, and of Domitian to the proconsuls Avidius Nigrinus and Armenius Brocchus, and likewise to the Spartans. I have not sent these texts to you for this reason, because they seemed to me to be both inadequately corrected and, in some cases, of doubtful authenticity, and because I believed that the genuine and corrected texts were in your archives.

66. Traianus to Plinius

(1) That dispute, which is concerned with those persons who, born free, have been put out to die and then rescued by certain individuals and reared in slavery, has often been discussed, and there is no rule to be found in the registers of those who were emperors before me which was laid down for all the provinces. (2) There are, it is true, epistles of Domitian to Avidius Nigrinus and Armenius Brocchus, which ought perhaps to be respected; but Bithynia is not among those provinces about which he wrote in reply; and for that reason I do not think that the right to free status should be refused to those who will be proved to be entitled to freedom on grounds of this kind, nor should they have to buy back their actual freedom by paying for the costs of their rearing.

67. C. Plinius to Traianus Imperator

(1) When the ambassador of king Sauromates had waited of his own accord for two days at Nicaea, where he had found me, I did not think, sir, that he ought to experience a longer delay, in the first place because it was still uncertain when your freedman

adhuc erat, quando libertus tuus Lycormas uenturus esset, deinde quod ipse proficiscebar in diuersam prouinciae partem, ita officii necessitate exigente. (2) Haec in notitiam tuam perferenda existimaui, quia proxime scripseram petisse Lycormam, ut legationem, si qua uenisset a Bosporo, usque in aduentum suum retinerem. Quod diutius faciendi nulla mihi probabilis ratio occurrit, praesertim cum epistulae Lycormae, quas detinere, ut ante praedixi, nolui, aliquot diebus hinc legatum antecessurae uiderentur.

LXVIII. C. Plinivs Traiano Imperatori

Petentibus quibusdam, ut sibi reliquias suorum aut propter iniuriam uetustatis aut propter fluminis incursum aliaque his similia quocumque secundum exemplum proconsulum transferre permitterem, quia sciebam in urbe nostra ex eius modi causa collegium pontificum adiri solere, te, domine, maximum pontificem consulendum putaui, quid obseruare me uelis.

LXIX. Traianvs Plinio

Durum est iniungere necessitatem prouincialibus pontificum adeundorum, si reliquias suorum propter aliquas iustas causas transferre ex loco in alium locum uelint. Sequenda ergo potius tibi exempla sunt eorum, qui isti prouinciae praefuerunt, et ut causa cuique, ita aut permittendum aut negandum.

LXX. C. Plinivs Traiano Imperatori

(1) Quaerenti mihi, domine, Prusae ubi posset balineum quod indulsisti fieri, placuit locus in quo fuit aliquando domus, ut audio, pulchra, nunc deformis ruinis. Per hoc enim consequemur, ut foedissima facies ciuitatis ornetur, atque etiam ut ipsa ciuitas amplietur nec ulla aedificia tollantur, sed quae sunt uetustate sublapsa relaxentur in melius. (2) Est autem huius domus condicio talis: legauerat eam Claudius Polyaenus Claudio Caesari iussitque in peristylio templum ei fieri, reliqua ex domo locari. Ex ea reditum aliquamdiu ciuitas percepit; deinde paulatim partim spoliata, partim neglecta cum peristylio domus tota collapsa est, ac iam paene nihil ex ea nisi solum superest; quod tu, domine, siue donaueris ciuitati siue uenire iusseris, propter opportunitatem loci pro summo munere accipiet. (3) Ego, si permiseris, cogito in area uacua balineum collocare, eum autem locum, in quo aedificia fuerunt, exedra et porticibus amplecti

Lycormas was going to arrive, in the second because I was myself on the point of setting out for a distant part of the province at the pressing call of my duties. (2) I considered that I must bring these facts to your attention, because I had only just written that Lycormas had asked me to detain any embassy which might have come from the Bosporus until his arrival. No satisfactory reason has presented itself to me for doing so any longer, especially since it seemed likely that Lycormas' epistles, which, as I told you earlier, I did not want to hold back, would arrive from here several days in advance of the ambassador.

68. C. Plinius to Traianus Imperator

Certain persons have asked me to allow them, in accordance with the precedent set by the proconsuls, to transfer the remains of their relatives to some site or other either because of damage caused by the passage of time or because of the flooding of a river and other reasons similar to these. Because I knew that in our city it is the custom for application to be made to the college of pontiffs in a case of this kind, I decided that I must consult you, sir, as supreme pontiff, about what course you wish me to follow.

69. Traianus to Plinius

It is harsh to enforce upon provincials an obligation to apply to the pontiffs, should they wish to move the remains of their relatives from one site to another for some proper reasons. It is therefore the precedents set by those who have governed that province before you which ought rather to be followed by you, and permission ought to be granted or refused in accordance with the reason each person gives.

70. C. Plinius to Traianus Imperator

(1) When I was investigating whereabouts in Prusa the bath-house for which you had given permission could be built, the best site seemed to be one on which there was once a house, a beautiful one, so I am told, but which is now unsightly with ruins. For by this means we shall ensure that a most foul blot upon the city is beautified and that at the same time the city itself is enhanced without any buildings being demolished, but that those which have crumbled away with age are enlarged and improved. (2) Now the circumstances of this house are as follows: Claudius Polyaenus had bequeathed it to Claudius Caesar and directed that a temple to him should be built in the courtyard, while the rest of the house was to be let. For a while the city collected income from it; then, little by little, in part through being looted, in part through being neglected, the whole house along with the courtyard fell into ruin, and by now almost nothing of it is left except the ground. Whether you, sir, make a gift of it to the city or give orders for it to be sold, the city will consider it a very great service because of the convenience of the site. (3) I myself, if you give your permission, am thinking of siting the bath-house on the unoccupied ground, but of enclosing the actual place where the buildings stood with a recess and colonnades and dedicating them to

atque tibi consecrare, cuius beneficio elegans opus dignumque nomine tuo fiet. (4) Exemplar testamenti, quamquam mendosum, misi tibi; ex quo cognosces multa Polyaenum in eiusdem domus ornatum reliquisse, quae ut domus ipsa perierunt, a me tamen in quantum potuerit requirentur.

LXXI. Traianvs Plinio

Possumus apud Prusenses area ista cum domo collapsa, quam uacare scribis, ad exstructionem balinei uti. Illud tamen parum expressisti, an aedes in peristylio Claudio facta esset. Nam, si facta est, licet collapsa sit, religio eius occupauit solum.

LXXII. C. Plinivs Traiano Imperatori

Postulantibus quibusdam, ut de agnoscendis liberis restituendisque natalibus et secundum epistulam Domitiani scriptam Minicio Rufo et secundum exempla proconsulum ipse cognoscerem, respexi ad senatus consultum pertinens ad eadem genera causarum, quod de iis tantum prouinciis loquitur, quibus proconsules praesunt; ideoque rem integram distuli, dum ⟨ tu⟩, domine, praeceperis, quid obseruare me uelis.

LXXIII. Traianvs Plinio

Si mihi senatus consultum miseris quod haesitationem tibi fecit, aestimabo an debeas cognoscere de agnoscendis liberis et natalibus ueris restituendis.

LXXIV. C. Plinivs Traiano Imperatori

(1) Appuleius, domine, miles qui est in statione Nicomedensi, scripsit mihi quendam nomine Callidromum, cum detineretur a Maximo et Dionysio pistoribus, quibus operas suas locauerat, confugisse ad tuam statuam perductumque ad magistratus indicasse, seruisse aliquando Laberio Maximo, captumque a Susago in Moesia et a Decibalo muneri missum Pacoro Parthiae regi, pluribusque annis in ministerio eius fuisse, deinde fugisse, atque ita in Nicomediam peruenisse. (2) Quem ego perductum ad me, cum eadem narrasset, mittendum ad te putaui; quod paulo tardius feci, dum requiro gemmam, quam sibi habentem imaginem Pacori et quibus ornatus fuisset subtractam indicabat. (3) Volui enim hanc quoque, si inueniri potuisset, simul

you, through whose favour a handsome building, and one worthy of your name, will be put up. (4) I have sent you a copy of the will, although it is defective: from it you will learn that Polyaenus bequeathed many items for the embellishment of the same house, which, like the house itself, have disappeared, but which will be hunted out by me as far as will be possible.

71. Traianus to Plinius

We can use that ground at Prusa with the ruined house, which you say in your letter is unoccupied, for the building of the bath-house. You did not however make this quite clear, whether a temple was put up to Claudius in the courtyard. For, if it was put up, even though it may have fallen down, its religious influence has filled the site.

72. C. Plinius to Traianus Imperator

Certain persons are requesting that I should myself exercise jurisdiction in cases of children being acknowledged and having their freeborn status restored, in accordance with an epistle of Domitian written to Minicius Rufus and with the precedents set by the proconsuls. I have looked at the resolution of the Senate relating to the same kinds of cases, which talks only about those provinces which have proconsuls as governors; and for that reason I have left the matter undecided until you, sir, direct me about the principle you wish me to follow.

73. Traianus to Plinius

If you send me the resolution of the Senate which has given you pause, I shall judge whether you ought to exercise jurisdiction in cases of children being acknowledged and having their true birth-status restored.

74. C. Plinius to Traianus Imperator

(1) Appuleius, sir, the soldier who is stationed at the military post in Nicomedia, wrote to me that an individual named Callidromus, when he was being kept under duress by Maximus and Dionysius, bakers to whom he had hired out his services, had taken refuge at your statue, and that, when he was brought before the magistrates, he had revealed that he had at one time been the slave of Laberius Maximus and been taken prisoner by Susagus in Moesia and sent by Decibalus as a gift to Pacorus the king of Parthia, and that he had been in his service for many years, and then escaped, and so had come to Nicomedia. (2) I had him brought before me; when he had told the same story, I decided that he should be sent to you; I have done so somewhat belatedly, while I sought to find a jewel bearing a likeness of Pacorus and the things which he was wearing, which he claimed had been taken away from him. (3) For I wished to send this also at the same time, if it could be found, just as I have sent the small lump of

mittere, sicut glebulam misi, quam se ex Parthico metallo attulisse dicebat. Signata est anulo meo, cuius est aposphragisma quadriga.

LXXV. C. Plinivs Traiano Imperatori

(1) Iulius, domine, Largus ex Ponto nondum mihi uisus ac ne auditus quidem (scilicet iudicio tuo credidit) dispensationem quandam mihi erga te pietatis suae ministeriumque mandauit. (2) Rogauit enim testamento, ut hereditatem suam adirem cerneremque, ac deinde praeceptis quinquaginta milibus nummum reliquum omne Heracleotarum et Tianorum ciuitatibus redderem, ita ut esset arbitrii mei utrum opera facienda, quae honori tuo consecrarentur, putarem an instituendos quinquennales agonas, qui Traiani adpellarentur. Quod in notitiam tuam perferendum existimaui ob hoc maxime, ut dispiceres quid eligere debeam.

LXXVI. Traianvs Plinio

Iulius Largus fidem tuam quasi te bene nosset elegit. Quid ergo potissimum ad perpetuitatem memoriae eius faciat, secundum cuiusque loci condicionem ipse dispice et quod optimum existimaueris, id sequere.

LXXVII. C. Plinivs Traiano Imperatori

(1) Prouidentissime, domine, fecisti, quod praecepisti Calpurnio Macro clarissimo uiro, ut legionarium centurionem Byzantium mitteret. (2) Dispice an etiam Iuliopolitanis simili ratione consulendum putes, quorum ciuitas, cum sit perexigua, onera maxima sustinet tantoque grauiores iniurias quanto est infirmior patitur. (3) Quidquid autem Iuliopolitanis praestiteris, id etiam toti prouinciae proderit. Sunt enim in capite Bithyniae, plurimisque per eam commeantibus transitum praebent.

LXXVIII. Traianvs Plinio

(1) Ea condicio est ciuitatis Byzantiorum confluente undique in eam commeantium turba, ut secundum consuetudinem praecedentium temporum honoribus eius praesidio centurionis legionarii consulendum habuerimus. (2) ⟨Si⟩ Iuliopolitanis succurrendum eodem modo putauerimus, onerabimus nos exemplo; plures enim eo quanto infirmiores erunt idem petent. Fiduciam ⟨eam⟩ diligentiae ⟨tuae⟩ habeo, ut

ore which he said he had brought from a Parthian mine. It has been sealed with my ring, the device on which is a four-horse chariot.

75. C. Plinius to Traianus Imperator

(1) Iulius Largus, sir, from Pontus, a man I had never seen and not even heard of (no doubt he put his faith in your good judgment) has entrusted me with the disposal and management of an act of devotion towards you. (2) For in his will he has asked me to accept and enter upon his estate, and then, after fifty thousand sesterces have been set aside as a prior legacy, to hand over all the residue to the cities of Heraclea and Tium, with the provision that it should be in my power to decide whether I thought buildings should be put up which would be dedicated in your honour or quinquennial competitions should be founded which would be known as the Trajanic. I decided that this should be brought to your attention, mainly for this purpose, that you may consider which I ought to choose.

76. Traianus to Plinius

Iulius Largus settled upon your good faith as if he had known you well. So choose for yourself what will particularly conduce to the perpetuation of his memory, in accordance with the circumstances of each place, and follow the course which you decide is the best.

77. C. Plinius to Traianus Imperator

(1) You acted with the greatest forethought, sir, in that you instructed that most distinguished man Calpurnius Macer to send a legionary centurion to Byzantium. (2) Consider whether you think the interests of the people of Iuliopolis should also be provided for by a similar plan. Their city, although it is very small, bears very heavy burdens and suffers injuries which are the more serious by reason of its greater weakness. (3) Moreover, whatever help you give to the people of Iuliopolis will also be of advantage to the entire province. For they lie at the edge of Bithynia, and provide passage for very many persons who travel through it.

78. Traianus to Plinius

(1) The situation of the city of the Byzantines, with a throng of travellers flooding into it from every direction, is such that we thought it right, following the practice of earlier periods, that its magistrates should be supported by the protection of a legionary centurion. (2) If we decide that the people of Iuliopolis should be helped in the same way, we shall be burdening ourselves with a precedent: for more cities will seek the same help to the extent that they are weaker ones. I have such confidence in your conscientiousness that I feel sure you will employ every means to ensure that they are

credam te omni ratione id acturum, ne sint obnoxii iniuriis. (3) Si qui autem se contra disciplinam meam gesserint, statim coerceantur; aut, si plus admiserint quam ut in re praesenti satis puniantur, si milites erunt, legatis eorum quod deprehenderis notum facies aut, si in urbem uersus uenturi erunt, mihi scribes.

LXXIX. C. Plinivs Traiano Imperatori

(1) Cautum est, domine, Pompeia lege quae Bithynis data est, ne quis capiat magistratum neue sit in senatu minor annorum triginta. Eadem lege comprehensum est, ut qui ceperint magistratum sint in senatu. (2) Secutum est dein edictum diui Augusti, quo permisit minores magistratus ab annis duobus et uiginti capere. (3) Quaeritur ergo an, qui minor triginta annorum gessit magistratum, possit a censoribus in senatum legi, et, si potest, an ii quoque, qui non gesserint, possint per eandem interpretationem ab ea aetate senatores legi, a qua illis magistratum gerere permissum est; quod alioqui factitatum adhuc et esse necessarium dicitur, quia sit aliquanto melius honestorum hominum liberos quam e plebe in curiam admitti. (4) Ego a destinatis censoribus quid sentirem interrogatus eos quidem, qui minores triginta annis gessissent magistratum, putabam posse in senatum et secundum edictum Augusti et secundum legem Pompeiam legi, quoniam Augustus gerere magistratus minoribus annis triginta permisisset, lex senatorem esse uoluisset qui gessisset magistratum. (5) De iis autem qui non gessissent, quamuis essent aetatis eiusdem cuius illi quibus gerere permissum est, haesitabam; per quod effetctum est ut te, domine, consulerem, quid obseruari uelles. Capita legis, tum edictum Augusti litteris subieci.

LXXX. Traianvs Plinio

Interpretationi tuae, mi Secunde carissime, idem existimo: hactenus edicto diui Augusti nouatam esse legem Pompeiam, ut magistratum quidem capere possent ii, qui non minores duorum et uiginti annorum essent, et qui cepissent, in senatum cuiusque ciuitatis peruenirent. Ceterum non capto magistratu eos, qui minores triginta annorum sint, quia magistratum capere possint, in curiam etiam loci cuiusque non existimo legi posse.

LXXXI. C. Plinivs Traiano Imperatori

(1) Cum Prusae ad Olympum, domine, publicis negotiis intra hospitium eodem die exiturus uacarem, Asclepiades magistratus indicauit adpellatum me a Claudio Eumolpo. Cum Cocceianus Dion in bule adsignari ciuitati opus cuius curam egerat

not exposed to injuries. (3) If any individuals conduct themselves in violation of my discipline, let them be punished at once; or, if they commit acts too serious for it to be enough for them to be punished summarily, if they are soldiers, you shall make it known to their commanding officers that you have arrested them, or, if they are persons on their way back to the city, you shall write to me.

79. C. Plinius to Traianus Imperator

(1) It is prescribed, sir, in the Pompeian law which was laid down for the Bithynians, that no one should hold a magistracy or be a member of a senate who was under thirty years of age. In the same law it was provided that those who had held a magistracy should be members of a senate. (2) Next there followed an edict of the deified Augustus in which he allowed men to hold lesser magistracies from the age of twenty-two. (3) The question is therefore raised whether a man under thirty years of age who has held a magistracy can be enrolled in a senate by the censors, and, if he can, whether those who have not held a magistracy can also, under the same construction, be enrolled as senators from that age at which they have been allowed to hold a magistracy; furthermore this is asserted to have been the practice hitherto and to be necessary, because it is far better that the sons of honourable men should be admitted to the senate-house than that commoners should be. (4) I myself, when asked what my opinion was by the censors-elect, thought that men under thirty years of age who had held a magistracy could indeed be enrolled in a senate both according to the edict of Augustus and according to the Pompeian law, since Augustus had allowed men under thirty years of age to hold a magistracy and the law had wanted anyone who had held a magistracy to be a senator. (5) But about those who had not held one, although they were of the same age as those who had been allowed to hold one, I was in doubt. Hence I have been led to consult you, sir, about what principle you wish to have followed. I have appended to this letter the chapters of the law, and the edict of Augustus.

80. Traianus to Plinius

I agree with your construction, my dearest Secundus: that the Pompeian law was amended to this extent by the edict of the deified Augustus, that men who were not younger than twenty-two years of age could indeed hold a magistracy and that those who had held one might enter the senate of each city. However, I do not think that those who are under thirty years of age can be enrolled in the senate of each place without having held a magistracy, just because they can hold a magistracy.

81. C. Plinius to Traianus Imperator

(1) While I was attending to official business, sir, in my lodgings at Prusa by Olympus, on the same day that I was intending to leave, the magistrate Asclepiades reported that an appeal had been made to me by Claudius Eumolpus. When Cocceianus Dion at a session of the council requested that a building, the supervision of which he

62

uellet, tum Eumolpus adsistens Flauio Archippo dixit exigendam esse a Dione rationem operis, ante quam rei publicae traderetur, quod aliter fecisset ac debuisset. (2) Adiecit etiam esse in eodem positam tuam statuam et corpora sepultorum, uxoris Dionis et filii, postulauitque ut cognoscerem pro tribunali. (3) Quod cum ego me protinus facturum dilaturumque profectionem dixissem, ut longiorem diem ad struendam causam darem utque in alia ciuitate cognoscerem petiit. Ego me auditurum Nicaeae respondi. (4) Vbi cum consedissem cogniturus, idem Eumolpus tamquam si adhuc parum instructus dilationem petere coepit, contra Dion ut audiretur exigere. Dicta sunt utrimque multa, etiam de causa. (5) Ego cum dandam dilationem et ⟨ te⟩ consulendum existimarem in re ad exemplum pertinenti, dixi utrique parti ut postulationum suarum libellos darent. Volebam enim te ipsorum potissimum uerbis ea quae erant proposita cognoscere. (6) Et Dion quidem se daturum dixit. Eumolpus respondit complexurum se libello quae rei publicae peteret, ceterum quod ad sepultos pertineret non accusatorem se sed aduocatum Flaui Archippi, cuius mandata pertulisset. Archippus, cui Eumolpus sicut Prusae adsistebat, dixit se libellum daturum. At nec Eumolpus nec Archippus quam⟨ quam⟩ plurimis diebus exspectati adhuc mihi libellos dederunt; Dion dedit, quem huic epistulae iunxi. (7) Ipse in re praesenti fui et uidi tuam quoque statuam in bibliotheca positam, id autem in quo dicuntur sepulti filius et uxor Dionis in area collocatum, quae porticibus includitur. (8) Te, domine, rogo ut me in hoc praecipue genere cognitionis regere digneris, cum alioqui magna sit exspectatio, ut necesse est in ea re quae et in confessum uenit et exemplis defenditur.

LXXXII. Traianvs Plinio

(1) Potuisti non haerere, mi Secunde carissime, circa id de quo me consulendum existimasti, cum propositum meum optime nosses, non ex metu nec terrore hominum aut criminibus maiestatis reuerentiam nomini meo adquiri. (2) Omissa ergo ea quaestione, quam non admitterem etiam si exemplis adiuuaretur, ratio totius operis effecti sub cura Cocceiani Dionis excutiatur, cum et utilitas ciuitatis exigat nec aut recuset Dion aut debeat recusare.

LXXXIII. C. Plinivs Traiano Imperatori

Rogatus, domine, a Nicaeensibus publice per ea, quae mihi et sunt et debent esse

had undertaken, should be handed over to the city, at that moment Eumolpus, acting as counsel for Flavius Archippus, said that the accounts of the building should be demanded from Dion before it was transferred to the community, because he had behaved otherwise than he ought to have done. (2) He further added that your statue had been placed in the same building as well as the bodies of persons who had been buried, the wife and the son of Dion, and he requested that I should hear the case in open court. (3) When I had said that I would do this at once and that I would postpone my departure, he asked me to give him a longer period to put his case together, and to hold the hearing in another city. I answered that I would hear the case at Nicaea. (4) When I had taken my place on the bench there in order to hold the hearing, this same Eumolpus began to apply for an adjournment on the grounds that he was not fully prepared, while Dion in response demanded that the case should be heard. Many things were said on either side, some of them also about the case. (5) When I had decided that an adjournment should be granted and that you must be consulted on a matter which involved a precedent, I told both sides to supply memoranda of their pleadings. For I wanted you to learn the arguments which had been advanced as far as possible from their own words. (6) And Dion in fact said that he would supply this. Eumolpus replied that he would include in a memorandum the claims he was making for the community, but that, as far as the buried bodies were concerned, he was not the plaintiff but counsel for Flavius Archippus whose instructions he had been carrying out. Archippus, for whom Eumolpus was acting as counsel just as he had at Prusa, said that he would supply a memorandum. However, neither Eumolpus nor Archippus, despite being waited for for very many days, has yet supplied me with the memoranda; Dion has supplied one which I have attached to this epistle. (7) I have been to the spot myself and seen your statue also which has been placed in the library, and the site where Dion's son and wife are said to be buried, which lies in open ground which is enclosed by colonnades. (8) I ask you, sir, to deign to guide me especially in this kind of case, since there is in addition great public interest, as is inevitable with an issue which is both not contested and is defended by precedents.

82. Traianus to Plinius

(1) You could have been in no uncertainty, my dearest Secundus, about that matter on which you decided that I should be consulted, since you were very well aware of my determination not to obtain respect for my name through inspiring men with fear or terror or through charges of treason. (2) Accordingly that charge which I should not allow even if it were supported by the precedents should be dropped; rather let the accounts of the building carried out under the supervision of Cocceianus Dion be examined, since the interest of the city requires it and Dion does not object, nor ought he to object.

83. C. Plinius to Traianus Imperator

Having been requested, sir, by the people of Nicaea as a community, in the name of those things which are and ought to be most sacred to me, that is in the name of your

sanctissima, id est per aeternitatem tuam salutemque, ut preces suas ad te perferrem, fas non putaui negare acceptumque ab iis libellum huic epistulae iunxi.

LXXXIV. Traianvs Plinio

Nicaeensibus, qui intestatorum ciuium suorum concessam uindicationem bonorum a diuo Augusto adfirmant, debebis uacare contractis omnibus personis ad idem negotium pertinentibus, adhibitis Virdio Gemellino et Epimacho liberto meo procuratoribus, ut aestimatis etiam iis, quae contra dicuntur, quod optimum credideritis, statuatis.

LXXXV. C. Plinivs Traiano Imperatori

Maximum libertum et procuratorem tuum, domine, per omne tempus, quo fuimus una, probum et industrium et diligentem ac sicut rei tuae amantissimum ita disciplinae tenacissimum expertus, libenter apud te testimonio prosequor, ea fide quam tibi debeo.

LXXXVIA. C. Plinivs Traiano Imperatori

Gauium Bassum, domine, praefectum orae Ponticae integrum probum industrium atque inter ista reuerentissimum mei expertus, uoto pariter et suffragio prosequor, ea fide quam tibi debeo.

LXXXVIB. ⟨ C. Plinivs Traiano Imperatori⟩

. . . quam ea quae speret instructum commilitio tuo, cuius disciplinae debet, quod indulgentia tua dignus est. Apud me et milites et pagani, a quibus iustitia eius et humanitas penitus inspecta est, certatim ei qua priuatim qua publice testimonium perhibuerunt. Quod in notitiam tuam perfero, ea fide quam tibi debeo.

LXXXVII. C. Plinivs Traiano Imperatori

(1) Nymphidium Lupum, domine, primipilarem commilitonem habui, cum ipse tribunus essem ille praefectus: inde familiariter diligere coepi. Creuit postea caritas ipsa

eternal fame and your well-being, to pass on to you their petition, I did not think it right to refuse and I have attached to this letter the memorandum which I have received from them.

84. Traianus to Plinius

You will be obliged to give a hearing to the people of Nicaea who maintain that the right to claim the property of their fellow-citizens who die intestate was conceded to them by the deified Augustus. Collect together all the persons involved in this same business and summon as your advisers the procurators Virdius Gemellinus and Epimachus my freedman, in order that, after also assessing the arguments which are maintained on the opposite side, you may jointly reach the decision which you will jointly believe to be the best.

85. C. Plinius to Traianus Imperator

Having found by experience, sir, that your freedman and procurator Maximus, during the whole period we have been together, is upright, hardworking and conscientious, and as completely devoted to your interests as he is faithful in observing your discipline, I am very pleased to send him on his way with my recommendation to you, in that good faith which I owe to you.

86A. C. Plinius to Traianus Imperator

Having found by experience, sir, that Gavius Bassus the prefect of the Pontic shore is honourable, upright, hardworking, and besides this most respectful towards myself, I send him on his way with my prayers as well as my support, in that good faith which I owe to you.

86B. ⟨C. Plinius to Traianus Imperator⟩

. . . a man trained by his military service in your company, to whose discipline he is indebted for the fact that he is deserving of your generosity. Both soldiers and civilians, by whom his fairness and his kindness have been closely examined, have vied with each other in bearing witness to him before me, both as individuals and as communities. I bring this fact to your attention, in that good faith which I owe to you.

87. C. Plinius to Traianus Imperator

(1) I had Nymphidius Lupus, the former chief centurion, as a comrade in arms, sir, when I was a tribune and he a prefect: then I began to feel a close affection for him. Later these feelings strengthened with the long duration of our mutual friendship.(2)

66

mutuae uetustate amicitiae. (2) Itaque et quieti eius inieci manum et exegi, ut me in Bithynia consilio instrueret. Quod ille amicissime et otii et senectutis ratione postposita et iam fecit et facturus est. (3) Quibus ex causis necessitudines eius inter meas numero, filium in primis, Nymphidium Lupum, iuuenem probum industrium et egregio patre dignissimum, suffecturum indulgentiae tuae, sicut primis eius experimentis cognoscere potes, cum praefectus cohortis plenissimum testimonium meruerit Iuli Ferocis et Fusci Salinatoris clarissimorum uirorum. Meum gaudium, domine, meamque gratulationem filii honore cumulabis.

LXXXVIII. C. Plinivs Traiano Imperatori

Opto, domine, et hunc natalem et plurimos alios quam felicissimos agas aeternaque laude florentem uirtutis tuae gloriam . . .quam incolumis et fortis aliis super alia operibus augebis.

LXXXIX. Traianvs Plinio

Agnosco uota tua, mi Secunde carissime, quibus precaris, ut plurimos et felicissimos natales florente statu rei publicae nostrae agam.

XC. C. Plinivs Traiano Imperatori

(1) Sinopenses, domine, aqua deficiuntur; quae uidetur et bona et copiosa ab sexto decimo miliario posse perduci. Est tamen statim ab capite paulo amplius passus mille locus suspectus et mollis, quem ego interim explorari modico impendio iussi, an recipere et sustinere opus possit. (2) Pecunia curantibus nobis contracta non deerit, si tu, domine, hoc genus operis et salubritati et amoenitati ualde sitientis coloniae indulseris.

XCI. Traianvs Plinio

Vt coepisti, Secunde carissime, explora diligenter, an locus ille quem suspectum habes sustinere opus aquae ductus possit. Neque dubitandum puto, quin aqua perducenda sit in coloniam Sinopensem, si modo et uiribus suis adsequi potest, cum plurimum ea res et salubritati et uoluptati eius collatura sit.

Therefore I made my claim on his retirement and required him to help me with his advice in Bithynia. This he in a most friendly way has already done and will continue to do, having set aside the usual consideration of leisure and old age. (3) For these reasons I count his relatives as my own, especially his son, Nymphidius Lupus, an upright, hard-working young man, and most worthy of an excellent father. He will be well qualified to receive your generosity, as you can learn from the first trials you have made of him, since he has earned as prefect of a cohort the fullest commendation of those most distinguished men Iulius Ferox and Fuscus Salinator. You will crown my happiness and my satisfaction, sir, by conferring an honour on the son.

88. C. Plinius to Traianus Imperator

I pray, sir, that you may celebrate both this and very many other birthdays in as much happiness as possible and that with eternal fame . . . the flourishing glory of your merit . . . [probable lacuna] which, safe and strong, you will increase by achievements upon achievements.

89. Traianus to Plinius

I acknowledge your prayers, my dearest Secundus, in which you beg that I may celebrate very many most happy birthdays with our commonwealth in a prosperous condition.

90. C. Plinius to Traianus Imperator

(1) The people of Sinope, sir, are short of water; this, it appears, both good and plentiful, can be brought to them from the sixteenth milestone. However, there is ground which is suspect and soft, just by the source, a little more than a mile away. In the meantime I have given orders for it to be investigated, at little expense, to see whether it can take and support a structure. (2) Money, collected under our supervision, will not be wanting, if you, sir, permit this kind of building which will contribute both to the health and the attractiveness of a very thirsty colony.

91. Traianus to Plinius

Investigate thoroughly, dearest Secundus, just as you have begun to do, whether the ground which you consider suspect can support the structure of an aqueduct. And I do not think there should be any hesitation about bringing water to the colony of Sinope, provided only that it can in fact carry the work through out of its own resources, seeing that this project will contribute very greatly both to its health and its pleasure.

XCII. C. Plinivs Traiano Imperatori

Amisenorum ciuitas libera et foederata beneficio indulgentiae tuae legibus suis utitur. In hac datum mihi libellum ad ἐράνους pertinentem his litteris subieci, ut tu, domine, dispiceres quid et quatenus aut permittendum aut prohibendum putares.

XCIII. Traianvs Plinio

Amisenos, quorum libellum epistulae tuae iunxeras, si legibus istorum quibus beneficio foederis utuntur, concessum est eranum habere, possumus quo minus habeant non impedire, eo facilius si tali collatione non ad turbas et ad inlicitos coetus, sed ad sustinendam tenuiorum inopiam utuntur. In ceteris ciuitatibus, quae nostro iure obstrictae sunt, res huius modi prohibenda est.

XCIV. C. Plinivs Traiano Imperatori

(1) Suetonium Tranquillum, probissimum honestissimum eruditissimum uirum, et mores eius secutus et studia iam pridem, domine, in contubernium adsumpsi, tantoque magis diligere coepi quanto nunc propius inspexi. (2) Huic ius trium liberorum necessarium faciunt duae causae; nam et iudicia amicorum promeretur et parum felix matrimonium expertus est, impetrandumque a bonitate tua per nos habet quod illi fortunae malignitas denegauit. (3) Scio, domine, quantum beneficium petam, sed peto a te cuius in omnibus desideriis meis indulgentiam experior. Potes enim colligere quanto opere cupiam, quod non rogarem absens si mediocriter cuperem.

XCV. Traianvs Plinio

Quam parce haec beneficia tribuam, utique, mi Secunde carissime, haeret tibi, cum etiam in senatu adfirmare soleam non excessisse me numerum, quem apud amplissimum ordinem suffecturum mihi professus sum. Tuo tamen desiderio subscripsi et dedisse me ius trium liberorum Suetonio Tranquillo ea condicione, qua adsueui, referri in commentarios meos iussi.

92. C. Plinius to Traianus

The free and allied city of the Amiseni employs its own laws through the benefit of your generosity. I have appended to this letter a memorandum concerning *eranoi* which was handed to me in this city, in order that you, sir, may consider what you think should be forbidden and to what extent they should be allowed.

93. Traianus to Plinius

If the Amiseni, whose memorandum you had attached to your epistle, are permitted by their own laws, which they employ through the benefit of a treaty, to have an eranus, we cannot stand in the way of their having one, all the more readily if they use contributions of this kind not on crowds and unlawful assemblies, but to support the poverty of the humbler people. In the other cities, which are bound by our law, anything of this kind is forbidden.

94. C. Plinius to Traianus Imperator

(1) I have long, sir, included that most upright, honourable and learned man, Suetonius Tranquillus, among my friends, having admired both his character and his learning, and I have begun to love him all the more now that I have had a closer insight into his character. (2) Two reasons make it necessary for him to be awarded the rights of a parent of three children; for he both earns the good opinion of his friends and has had rather an unfortunate experience of marriage, and he must obtain from your kindness through our agency that which the hostility of fortune has denied him. (3) I know, sir, how great is the favour for which I apply, but I am applying to you, and I have experience of your generosity in all my requests. For you can infer how greatly I want this from the fact that I should not be asking for it when not face to face with you if I only wanted it to a moderate degree.

95. Traianus to Plinius

You are certainly aware, my dearest Secundus, of how sparing I am in granting these favours, since I am in the practice of stating in the Senate itself that I have not exceeded the number which I declared in the presence of that most noble order would be large enough for me. However, I have agreed to your request and have given orders for an entry to be made in my registers that I have given Suetonius Tranquillus the rights of a parent of three children, subject to that proviso which I have been in the habit of making.

XCVI. C. Plinivs Traiano Imperatori

(1) Sollemne est mihi, domine, omnia de quibus dubito ad te referre. Quis enim potest melius uel cunctationem meam regere uel ignorantiam instruere? Cognitionibus de Christianis interfui numquam: ideo nescio quid et quatenus aut puniri soleat aut quaeri. (2) Nec mediocriter haesitaui, sitne aliquod discrimen aetatum, an quamlibet teneri nihil a robustioribus differant; detur paenitentiae uenia, an ei, qui omnino Christianus fuit, desisse non prosit; nomen ipsum, si flagitiis careat, an flagitia cohaerentia nomini puniantur. Interim, ⟨in⟩ iis qui ad me tamquam Christiani deferebantur, hunc sum secutus modum. (3) Interrogaui ipsos an essent Christiani. Confitentes iterum ac tertio interrogaui supplicium minatus: perseuerantes duci iussi. Neque enim dubitabam, qualecumque esset quod faterentur, pertinaciam certe et inflexibilem obstinationem debere puniri. (4) Fuerunt alii similis amentiae, quos, quia ciues Romani erant, adnotaui in urbem remittendos.

Mox ipso tractatu, ut fieri solet, diffundente se crimine plures species inciderunt. (5) Propositus est libellus sine auctore multorum nomina continens. Qui negabant esse se Christianos aut fuisse, cum praeeunte me deos adpellarent et imagini tuae, quam propter hoc iusseram cum simulacris numinum adferri, ture ac uino supplicarent, praeterea male dicerent Christo, quorum nihil cogi posse dicuntur qui sunt re uera Christiani, dimittendos putaui. (6) Alii ab indice nominati esse se Christianos dixerunt et mox negauerunt; fuisse quidem sed desisse, quidam ante triennium, quidam ante plures annos, non nemo etiam ante uiginti. ⟨Hi⟩ quoque omnes et imaginem tuam deorumque simulacra uenerati sunt et Christo male dixerunt. (7) Adfirmabant autem hanc fuisse summam uel culpae suae uel erroris, quod essent soliti stato die ante lucem conuenire, carmenque Christo quasi deo dicere secum inuicem seque sacramento non in scelus aliquod obstringere, sed ne furta ne latrocinia ne adulteria committerent, ne fidem fallerent, ne depositum adpellati abnegarent. Quibus peractis morem sibi discedendi fuisse rursusque coeundi ad capiendum cibum, promiscuum tamen et innoxium; quod ipsum facere desisse post edictum meum, quo secundum mandata tua hetaerias esse uetueram. (8) Quo magis necessarium credidi ex duabus ancillis, quae ministrae dicebantur, quid esset ueri, et per tormenta quaerere. Nihil aliud inueni quam superstitionem prauam et immodicam.

(9) Ideo dilata cognitione ad consulendum te decucurri. Visa est enim mihi res digna consultatione, maxime propter periclitantium numerum. Multi enim omnis aetatis, omnis ordinis, utriusque sexus etiam uocantur in periculum et uocabuntur. Neque ciuitates tantum, sed uicos etiam atque agros superstitionis istius contagio

96. C. Plinius to Traianus Imperator

(1) It is my custom, sir, to bring before you everything about which I am in doubt. For who can better guide my uncertainty or inform my ignorance? I have never been present at trials of Christians; for that reason I do not know what the charge usually is and to what extent it is usually punished. (2) I have been in no little uncertainty about whether any distinction should be made between different ages or whether, however young they may be, they should be treated no differently from the more mature ones; whether pardon should be granted for repentance or whether it is of no help to the man who has been a Christian at all to have given it up; whether it is the name itself, if it is free from crimes, or the crimes associated with the name which are being punished. Meanwhile, in the case of those who were prosecuted before me on the charge of being Christians, I followed this procedure. (3) I asked the people themselves whether they were Christians. Those who admitted that they were I asked a second and a third time, warning them of the punishment; those who persisted I ordered to be executed. For I was in no doubt that, whatever it might be that they were admitting to, their stubbornness and unyielding obstinacy certainly ought to be punished. (4) There were others of a similar madness whom I have listed as due to be sent on to the city, because they were Roman citizens.

Subsequently, through the very course of dealing with the matter, as usually happens, the charge spread widely and more forms of it turned up. (5) An anonymous pamphlet containing the names of many persons was posted up. Those who denied that they were or had been Christians, after they had called upon the gods when I dictated the formula, and after they had made offerings of incense and wine to your statue which I had ordered to be brought in along with the cult-images of the gods for this purpose, and had in addition cursed Christ, none of which acts, it is said, those who are truly Christians can be compelled to perform, I decided should be discharged. (6) Others, named by an informer, said that they were Christians and then denied it; they said that they had in fact been Christians but had given it up, some three years before, some more years earlier than that, and a few even twenty years ago. All these also both paid homage to your statue and to the cult-images of the gods and cursed Christ. (7) Moreover they maintained that this had been the sum of their guilt or error, that they had been in the habit of gathering together before dawn on a fixed day, and of singing antiphonally a hymn to Christ as if to a god, and of binding themselves by oath, not to some wickedness, but not to commit acts of theft or robbery or adultery, not to break faith, not to refuse to return money placed in their keeping when called upon to do so. When these ceremonies had been completed, they said it had been their custom to disperse and to meet again to take food, but food that was ordinary and harmless; they said that they had given up doing even this after my edict, in which, in accordance with your instructions, I had banned secret societies. (8) So I believed it to be all the more necessary to ascertain what the truth was from two slave women, who were called deaconesses, and under torture. I found nothing other than a depraved and extravagant superstition.

(9) Accordingly I postponed the hearing and hastened to consult you. For the matter seemed to me to be worthy of your consideration, especially on account of the number of people who are endangered. For many persons of every age, of every rank, of both sexes, are being brought and will be brought into danger. The infection of this

peruagata est; quae uidetur sisti et corrigi posse. (10) Certe satis constat prope iam desolata templa coepisse celebrari, et sacra sollemnia diu intermissa repeti passimque uenire ⟨carnem⟩ uictimarum, cuius adhuc rarissimus emptor inueniebatur. Ex quo facile est opinari, quae turba hominum emendari possit, si sit paenitentiae locus.

XCVII. Traianvs Plinio

(1) Actum quem debuisti, mi Secunde, in excutiendis causis eorum, qui Christiani ad te delati fuerant, secutus es. Neque enim in uniuersum aliquid, quod quasi certam formam habeat, constitui potest. (2) Conquirendi non sunt; si deferantur et arguantur, puniendi sunt, ita tamen ut, qui negauerit se Christianum esse idque re ipsa manifestum fecerit, id est supplicando dis nostris, quamuis suspectus in praeteritum, ueniam ex paenitentia impetret. Sine auctore uero propositi libelli ⟨ in⟩ nullo crimine locum habere debent. Nam et pessimi exempli nec nostri saeculi est.

XCVIII. C. Plinivs Traiano Imperatori

(1) Amastrianorum ciuitas, domine, et elegans et ornata habet inter praecipua opera pulcherrimam eandemque longissimam plateam; cuius a latere per spatium omne porrigitur nomine quidem flumen, re uera cloaca foedissima, ac sicut turpis immundissimo adspectu, ita pestilens odore taeterrimo. (2) Quibus ex causis non minus salubritatis quam decoris interest eam contegi; quod fiet si permiseris curantibus nobis, ne desit quoque pecunia operi tam magno quam necessario.

XCIX. Traianvs Plinio

Rationis est, mi Secunde carissime, contegi aquam istam, quae per ciuitatem Amastrianourm fluit, si intecta salubritati obest. Pecunia ne huic operi desit, curaturum te secundum diligentiam tuam certum habeo.

C. C. Plinivs Traiano Imperatori

Vota, domine, priore anno nuncupata alacres laetique persoluimus nouaque rursus certante commilitonum et prouincialium pietate suscepimus, precati deos ut te remque

superstition has spread, not only through the towns, but also through the villages and the countryside; it seems possible for it to be checked and put right. (10) At any rate it is well established that temples which just now were almost abandoned have begun to be thronged, and customary rites which had long been suspended to be renewed, and the flesh of sacrificial victims, for which until recently very few buyers were to be found, to be sold far and wide. From this it is easy to conjecture what a host of people could be reformed, if room were given for repentance.

97. Traianus to Plinius

You followed the procedure which you ought to have followed, my dear Secundus, in examining the cases of those who were being prosecuted before you as Christians. For no rule with a universal application, such as would have, as it were, a fixed form, can be laid down. (2) They should not be sought out; if they are prosecuted and proved to be guilty, they should be punished, provided, however, that the man who denies that he is a Christian and makes this evident by his action, that is by offering prayers to our gods, shall obtain pardon for his repentance, however suspect he may be with regard to the past. However, pamphlets posted up without an author's name ought to have no place in any criminal charge. For they both set the worst precedent and are not in keeping with the spirit of our age.

98. C. Plinius to Traianus Imperator

(1) The elegant and finely built city of the Amastrians, sir, has among its outstanding structures a most beautiful and also very long street; by the side of this, along its entire length, there stretches, what is by name a stream, but in reality a most foul sewer, and, just as it is disgusting in its most filthy appearance, so it is injurious to health in its most revolting stench. (2) For these reasons it is just as much in the interest of health as of beauty that it should be covered over; this will be done, if you permit it, and we will ensure that money also is not lacking for a project both grand and necessary.

99. Traianus to Plinius

There is good reason, my dearest Secundus, for that stream which flows through the city of the Amastrians to be covered over, if, left uncovered, it is a danger to health. I feel certain that with your usual diligence you will ensure that money is not lacking for this project.

100. C. Plinius to Traianus Imperator

The vows, sir, undertaken last year, we have eagerly and joyfully fulfilled and we have again undertaken new ones, with my fellow-soldiers and the provincials vying

publicam florentem et incolumem ea benignitate seruarent, quam super magnas plurimasque uirtutes praecipua sanctitate obsequio deorum honore meruisti.

CI. Traianvs Plinio

Soluisse uota dis immortalibus te praeeunte pro mea incolumitate commilitones cum prouincialibus laetissimo consensu et in futurum nuncupasse libenter, mi Secunde carissime, cognoui litteris tuis.

CII. C. Plinivs Traiano Imperatori

Diem, quo in te tutela generis humani felicissima successione translata est, debita religione celebrauimus, commendantes dis imperii tui auctoribus et uota publica et gaudia.

CIII. Traianvs Plinio

Diem imperii mei debita laetitia et religione commilitonibus et prouincialibus praeeunte te celebratum libenter cognoui litteris tuis.

CIV. C. Plinivs Traiano Imperatori

Valerius, domine, Paulinus excepto Paulino ius Latinorum suorum mihi reliquit; ex quibus rogo tribus interim ius Quiritium des. Vereor enim, ne sit immodicum pro omnibus pariter inuocare indulgentiam tuam, qua debeo tanto modestius uti, quanto pleniorem experior. Sunt autem pro quibus peto: C. Valerius Astraeus, C. Valerius Dionysius, C. Valerius Aper.

CV. Traianvs Plinio

Cum honestissime iis, qui apud fidem tuam a Valerio Paulino depositi sunt, consultum uelis mature per me, iis interim, quibus nunc petisti, dedisse me ius Quiritium referri in commentarios meos iussi idem facturus in ceteris, pro quibus petieris.

with each other in devotion. We prayed to the gods that they would keep you and the commonwealth prosperous and safe with that kindness which you have earned, apart from your great and numerous merits, by your outstanding purity and reverence and honour to the gods.

101. Traianus to Plinius

I was delighted to learn from your letter, my dearest Secundus, that my fellow-soldiers in most joyful unanimity with the provincials have fulfilled, with you dictating the formula to them, the vows to the immortal gods for my preservation, and renewed them for the future.

102. C. Plinius to Traianus Imperator

We have celebrated with due observance the day on which guardianship of the human race was passed on to you in a most happy succession, recommending both our public vows and our rejoicings to the gods who are the authors of your rule.

103. Traianus to Plinius

I was delighted to learn from your letter that the day of my accession was celebrated with due joy and observance by my fellow-soldiers and the provincials, with you dictating the formula to them.

104. C. Plinius to Traianus Imperator

Valerius Paulinus, sir, having excluded Paulinus, has bequeathed to me his rights over his Latin freedmen; for the time being I ask you to grant three of these the rights of Roman citizens. For I fear that it may be presumptuous to appeal on behalf of all of them at once to your generosity which I am obliged to use the more sparingly, the fuller my experience of it is. Those for whom I am making the request are in fact C. Valerius Astraeus, C. Valerius Dionysius, C. Valerius Aper.

105. Traianus to Plinius

Since you most honourably wish to make prudent provision through me for the interests of those who were entrusted to your good faith by Valerius Paulinus, I have in the mean time given orders for an entry to be made in my registers that I have granted the rights of Roman citizens to those on whose behalf you have made a request this time, and I shall do the same in the case of all the others on whose behalf you make a request.

CVI. C. Plinivs Traiano Imperatori

Rogatus, domine, a P. Accio Aquila, centurione cohortis sextae equestris, ut mitterem tibi libellum per quem indulgentiam pro statu filiae suae implorat, durum putaui negare, cum scirem quantam soleres militum precibus patientiam humanitatemque praestare.

CVII. Traianvs Plinio

Libellum P. Accii Aquilae, centurionis sextae equestris, quem mihi misisti, legi; cuius precibus motus dedi filiae eius ciuitatem Romanam. Libellum rescriptum, quem illi redderes, misi tibi.

CVIII. C. Plinivs Traiano Imperatori

(1) Quid habere iuris uelis et Bithynas et Ponticas ciuitates in exigendis pecuniis, quae illis uel ex locationibus uel ex uenditionibus aliisue causis debeantur, rogo, domine, rescribas. Ego inueni.a plerisque proconsulibus concessam iis protopraxian eamque pro lege ualuisse. (2) Existimo tamen tua prouidentia constituendum aliquid et sanciendum per quod utilitatibus eorum in perpetuum consulatur. Nam quae sunt ab illis instituta, sint licet sapienter indulta, breuia tamen et infirma sunt, nisi illis tua contingit auctoritas.

CIX. Traianvs Plinio

Quo iure uti debeant Bithynae uel Ponticae ciuitates in iis pecuniis, quae ex quaque causa rei publicae debebuntur, ex lege cuiusque animaduertendum est. Nam, siue habent priuilegium, quo ceteris creditoribus anteponantur, custodiendum est, siue non habent, in iniuriam priuatorum id dari a me non oportebit.

CX. C. Plinivs Traiano Imperatori

(1) Ecdicus, domine, Amisenorum ciuitatis petebat apud me a Iulio Pisone denariorum circiter quadraginta milia donata ei publice ante uiginti annos bule et ecclesia consentiente, utebaturque mandatis tuis, quibus eius modi donationes uetantur. (2) Piso contra plurima se in rem publicam contulisse ac prope totas facultates erogasse dicebat. Addebat etiam temporis spatium postulabatque, ne id, quod pro multis

106. C. Plinius to Traianus Imperator

Having being asked, sir, by P. Accius Aquila, centurion of the sixth mounted cohort, to send on to you a petition in which he appeals to your generosity on behalf of the status of his daughter, I thought it harsh to refuse, since I knew how much patience and kindness you were in the habit of showing to the appeals of soldiers.

107. Traianus to Plinius

I have read the petition of P. Accius Aquila, centurion of the sixth mounted cohort, which you sent on to me; moved by his appeal, I have granted Roman citizenship to his daughter. I have sent you the petition with its rescript, for you to hand over to him.

108. C. Plinius to Traianus Imperator

(1) I ask, sir, that you write back about what rights you wish the cities both of Bithynia and of Pontus to have in recovering sums of money which are owed to them from leases or from sales or for other reasons. I have discovered that the right of prior claim was granted to them by very many of the proconsuls, and that this has come to have the force of law. (2) I think, however, that by your forethought some rule ought to be decided upon and laid down through which their interests may be safeguarded for ever. For the practices which have been introduced by them, even though they may have been wisely conceded, are nevertheless short-lived and precarious, if your authority does not uphold them.

109. Traianus to Plinius

What rights the cities of Bithynia or Pontus ought to exercise in respect of those sums of money which, for whatever reason, will be owed to the community, must be determined in accordance with the law of each city. For, if they have a privilege by which they take priority over all the other creditors, it should be protected, but if they do not have one, it will not be appropriate for this to be granted by me to the detriment of private persons.

110. C. Plinius to Traianus Imperator

(1) The public advocate of the city of the Amiseni, sir, was suing Iulius Piso before me for around forty thousand denarii which had been granted to him from public funds twenty years ago with the agreement of the Council and the Assembly, and he cited in support your instructions in which grants of this kind are forbidden. (2) Piso in response said he had made very many gifts to the community and had nearly spent his entire fortune. He also pointed out the lapse of time and begged that he should not

et olim accepisset, cum euersione reliquae dignitatis reddere cogeretur. Quibus ex causis integram cognitionem differendam existimaui, ut te, domine, consulerem, quid sequendum putares.

CXI. Traianvs Plinio

Sicut largitiones ex publico fieri mandata prohibent, ita, ne multorum securitas subruatur, factas ante aliquantum temporis retractari atque in inritum uindicari non oportet. Quidquid ergo ex hac causa actum ante uiginti annos erit, omittamus. Non minus enim hominibus cuiusque loci quam pecuniae publicae consultum uolo.

CXII. C. Plinivs Traiano Imperatori

(1) Lex Pompeia, domine, qua Bithyni et Pontici utuntur, eos, qui in bulen a censoribus leguntur, dare pecuniam non iubet; sed ii, quos indulgentia tua quibusdam ciuitatibus super legitimum numerum adicere permisit, et singula milia denariorum et bina intulerunt. (2) Anicius deinde Maximus proconsul eos etiam, qui a censoribus legerentur, dumtaxat in paucissimis ciuitatibus aliud aliis iussit inferre. (3) Superest ergo, ut ipse dispicias, an in omnibus ciuitatibus certum aliquid omnes, qui deinde buleutae legentur, debeant pro introitu dare. Nam, quod in perpetuum mansurum est, a te constitui decet, cuius factis dictisque debetur aeternitas.

CXIII. Traianvs Plinio

Honorarium decurionatus omnes, qui in quaque ciuitate Bithyniae decuriones fiunt, inferre debeant necne, in uniuersum a me non potest statui. Id ergo, quod semper tutissimum est, sequendam cuiusque ciuitatis legem puto, sed uerius eos, qui inuitati fiunt decuriones, id existimo acturos, ut praestatione ceteris praeferantur.

CXIV. C. Plinivs Traiano Imperatori

(1) Lege, domine, Pompeia permissum Bithynicis ciuitatibus adscribere sibi quos uellent ciues, dum ne quem earum ciuitatium, quae sunt in Bithynia. Eadem lege sancitur, quibus de causis e senatu a censoribus eiciantur. (2) Inde me quidam ex censoribus consulendum putauerunt, an eicere deberent eum qui esset alterius ciuitatis. (3) Ego quia lex sicut adscribi ciuem alienum uetabat, ita eici e senatu ob hanc causam

be compelled to repay what he had received in return for many gifts and a long time ago, to the ruin of what was left of his standing. For these reasons I thought that the case should be left undecided, in order that I might ask your advice, sir, about what course you think should be followed.

111. Traianus to Plinius

Although the instructions do forbid gifts to be made from public funds, yet, in order that the security of many persons may not be undermined, those that were made some time ago must not be reconsidered or claimed to be invalid. Let us therefore disregard whatever was done for this reason twenty years ago. For I wish the interests of individuals in each place to be safeguarded, no less than those of public funds.

112. C. Plinius to Traianus Imperator

(1) The Pompeian law, sir, which the people of Bithynia and Pontus observe, does not order those who are enrolled in a council by censors to pay money; but those whom your generosity has allowed some of the cities to add over and above the lawful number have paid one or two thousand denarii each. (2) Later the proconsul Anicius Maximus ordered those who were enrolled by censors to pay as well, but only in a very few cities, and different sums in different cities. (3) So it remains for you yourself to consider whether in all the cities all those who will henceforward be enrolled as councillors ought to pay some fixed sum for their admission. For it is fitting that that which will remain permanently in force should be determined by you to whose deeds and words eternal fame is due.

113. Traianus to Plinius

No general rule can be laid down by me about whether or not all those who become decurions in every city in Bithynia should pay a fee for their decurionate. So I think that the law of each city should be followed, something which is always the safest course, but indeed I am sure that those who become decurions by invitation will so act that they oututstrip all the rest in generosity.

114. C. Plinius to Traianus Imperator

(1) Under the Pompeian law, sir, the Bythinian cities are allowed to enrol any persons they choose as honorary citizens, provided that none of them come from those cities which are in Bythinia. In the same law it is laid down for what reasons men may be expelled from a senate by censors. (2) And so some of the censors decided that they should consult me about whether they ought to expel a man who came from another city. (3) I myself, because the law, although it forbade a foreigner to be enrolled as a citizen, yet did not order a man to be expelled from a senate for that reason, and because,

non iubebat, praeterea, quod adfirmabatur mihi in omni ciuitate plurimos esse buleutas ex aliis ciuitatibus, futurumque ut multi homines multaeque ciuitates concuterentur ea parte legis, quae iam pridem consensu quodam exoleuisset, necessarium existimaui consulere te, quid seruandum putares. Capita legis his litteris subieci.

CXV. Traianvs Plinio

Merito haesisti, Secunde carissime, quid a te rescribi oporteret censoribus consulentibus, an ⟨manere deberent⟩ in senatu aliarum ciuitatium, eiusdem tamen prouinciae ciues. Nam et legis auctoritas et longa consuetudo usurpata contra legem in diuersum mouere te potuit. Mihi hoc temperamentum eius placuit, ut ex praeterito nihil nouaremus, sed manerent quamuis contra legem adsciti quarumcumque ciuitatium ciues, in futurum autem lex Pompeia obseruaretur; cuius uim si retro quoque uelimus custodire, multa necesse est perturbari.

CXVI. C. Plinivs Traiano Imperatori

(1) Qui uirilem togam sumunt uel nuptias faciunt uel ineunt magistratum uel opus publicum dedicant, solent totam bulen atque etiam e plebe non exiguum numerum uocare binosque denarios uel singulos dare. Quod an celebrandum et quatenus putes, rogo scribas. (2) Ipse enim, sicut arbitror, praesertim ex sollemnibus causis, concedendum ius istud inuitationis, ita uereor ne ii qui mille homines, interdum etiam plures uocant, modum excedere et in speciem διανομῆς incidere uideantur.

CXVII. Traianvs Plinio

Merito uereris, ne in speciem διανομῆς incidat inuitatio, quae et in numero modum excedit et quasi per corpora, non uiritim singulos ex notitia ad sollemnes sportulas contrahit. Sed ego ideo prudentiam tuam elegi, ut formandis istius prouinciae moribus ipse moderareris et ea constitueres, quae ad perpetuam eius prouinciae quietem essent profutura.

moreover, I was assured that in every city there were very many councillors from other cities and that the result would be that many men and many cities would be thrown into confusion by that part of the law which had long since become a dead letter by a kind of general agreement, thought it necessary to consult you about what course you think should be followed. I have appended the chapters of the law to this letter.

115. Traianus to Plinius

You had good reason to be uncertain, dearest Secundus, about what you ought to write in response to the censors who consulted you about whether those who were citizens of other cities, but came from the same province, ought to remain in a senate. For the authority of the law and a custom which had been long established in violation of the law could have pulled you in different directions. I have decided on the following resolution of this issue, that we should make no change in respect of what was done in the past, but that citizens of whatever cities, although they were enrolled in violation of the law, should remain; for the future, however, the Pompeian law should be observed. Should we wish to maintain the force of the law retrospectively as well, it is inevitable that many things would be thrown into confusion.

116. C. Plinius to Traianus Imperator

(1) Those who put on the toga of manhood or celebrate a wedding or enter upon a magistracy or dedicate a public building are in the habit of inviting the whole council and no small number from the commons as well and to give them two denarii or a single denarius apiece. I ask you to write to say whether you think this celebration should be held and on what scale. (2) For my own part, while I believe that this kind of right of invitation should be allowed, especially for the customary reasons, yet I am afraid that those who invite a thousand people, and sometimes even more, may be thought to be going beyond the bounds and to fall into a type of bribery.

117. Traianus to Plinius

You have good reason to fear that an invitation would turn into a type of bribery, if it is one which goes beyond the bounds in the matter of numbers and gathers people together for customary gifts in organised bodies, as it were, not as separate individuals on the basis of personal acquaintance. But it was for this purpose that I chose a man of your wisdom, that you might exercise control over shaping the habits of that province and lay down those rules which would be of benefit for the permanent tranquillity of the province.

CXVIII. C. Plinivs Traiano Imperatori

(1) Athletae, domine, ea quae pro iselasticis certaminibus constituisti, deberi sibi putant statim ex eo die, quo sunt coronati; nihil enim referre, quando sint patriam inuecti, sed quando certamine uicerint, ex quo inuehi possint. Ego contra uehementer addubitem an sit potius id tempus, quo εἰσήλασαν, intuendum. (2) Iidem obsonia petunt pro eo agone, qui a te iselasticus factus est, quamuis uicerint ante quam fieret. Aiunt enim congruens esse, sicut non detur sibi pro iis certaminibus, quae esse iselastica postquam uicerunt desierunt, ita pro iis dari quae esse coeperunt. (3) Hic quoque non mediocriter haereo, ne cuiusquam retro habeatur ratio dandumque, quod tunc cum uincerent non debebatur. Rogo ergo, ut dubitationem meam regere, id est beneficia tua interpretari ipse digneris.

CXIX. Traianvs Plinio

Iselasticum tunc primum mihi uidetur incipere deberi, cum quis in ciuitatem suam ipse εἰσήλασεν. Obsonia eorum certaminum, quae iselastica esse placuit mihi, si ante iselastica non fuerunt, retro non debentur. Nec proficere pro desiderio athletarum potest, quod eorum, quae postea iselastica non esse constitui, quam uicerunt, accipere desierunt. Mutata enim condicione certaminum nihilo minus, quae ante perceperant, non reuocantur.

CXX. C. Plinivs Traiano Imperatori

(1) Vsque in hoc tempus, domine, neque cuiquam diplomata commodaui neque in rem ullam nisi tuam misi. Quam perpetuam seruationem meam quaedam necessitas rupit. (2) Vxori enim meae audita morte aui uolenti ad amitam suam excurrere usum eorum negare durum putaui, cum talis officii gratia in celeritate consisteret, sciremque te rationem itineris probaturum, cuius causa erat pietas. Haec tibi scripsi, quia mihi parum gratus fore uidebar, si dissimulassem inter alia beneficia hoc unum quoque me debere indulgentiae tuae, quod fiducia eius quasi consulto te non dubitaui facere, quem si consuluissem, sero fecissem.

118. C. Plinius to Traianus Imperator

(1) The athletes, sir, think that the rewards which you established for triumphal games are due to them from the very day on which they were crowned; for, they say, it is not the date on which they made a triumphal entry into their native city which matters, but the date when they were victorious in the games, as a result of which they can make a triumphal entry. I myself, on the other hand, seriously doubt whether it should not rather be the time at which they made their entry which ought to be observed. (2) These same men are applying for allowances in respect of that contest which was made triumphal by you, although they won their victories before it was so made. For they say that it is fitting that, just as allowances are not paid to them in respect of those games which ceased to be triumphal after they won their victories, they should likewise be paid in respect of those which began to be triumphal (after they won their victories). (3) On this point also I have the gravest doubts, whether consideration should be given to anyone retrospectively and whether that which was not due to them when they won their victories should be paid to them. So I ask you to deign to guide my uncertainty yourself, that is to clarify your own benefactions.

119. Traianus to Plinius

It seems to me that a triumphal reward first begins to be due at that time when any man himself has made his entry into his own city. The allowances in respect of those games which I have decided are to be triumphal are not due retrospectively, if they were not triumphal previously. Nor does the fact that they have ceased to receive allowances in respect of those games which I decided should not be triumphal after they won their victories support the claim of the athletes. For, although the status of the games has been changed, the allowances which they had collected before that are nevertheless not being reclaimed.

120. C. Plinius to Traianus Imperator

(1) Up to this time, sir, I have not provided anyone with passes nor have I sent anyone off on any business but yours. A kind of necessity has broken down this permanent rule of mine. (2) For I thought it harsh to deny the use of these passes to my wife who, after hearing of her grandfather's death, was anxious to hasten to her aunt's side, since the value of a service of this kind depends on speed, and I knew that you would approve of the reason for a journey the motive for which was family affection. I have written to you about this, because I considered that I should be quite ungrateful, if I had concealed the fact that, in addition to your other kindnesses, I was also indebted to your generosity for this particular fact, that I did not hesitate, in my confidence in that generosity, to take action as if I had consulted you, since, if I had consulted you, I should have acted too late.

CXXI. Traianvs Plinio

Merito habuisti, Secunde carissime, fiduciam animi mei nec dubitandum fuisset, si exspectasses donec me consuleres, an iter uxoris tuae diplomatibus, quae officio tuo dedi, adiuuandum esset, cum apud amitam suam uxor tua deberet etiam celeritate gratiam aduentus sui augere.

121. Traianus to Plinius

You were right to feel confidence in my attitude, dearest Secundus, nor should there have been any doubt whether you should have waited until you could consult me about whether your wife's journey ought to be expedited by the passes which I provided for your official duties, seeing that your wife was under an obligation to enhance the gratitude felt by her aunt for her arrival by its promptness as well.

COMMENTARY

Epistles 15–16
P. reports his arrival at Ephesus at the end of his voyage from Italy; T. acknowledges the report.

Epistle 15
Written, probably in late August, 110, from Ephesus. (SW, 580, dates 15 to "after 17 September", which would mean it was written after P. had reached BP. But it is clear from the second sentence that P. is announcing his future plans after his arrival in Ephesus; thus Merrill, 415).

sir. See Introd. VI (B).

all my people. Elsewhere in P. 'my people' and 'your people' commonly refer to household slaves and freedmen (Merrill, 252), but here it must also include his wife Calpurnia (120) and personal friends whom he had recruited as *comites* (official 'companions') such as Nymphidius Lupus (87) and Suetonius (94).

Ephesus. The most important city on the east coast of the Aegean; presumably P. decided to disembark from his seagoing ship there, instead of sailing north to the Hellespont, because of the opposing winds (see below).

"rounding Malea". P. uses a Greek phrase in the original language. Malea, the headland at the tip of the south-eastern peninsula projecting from the Peloponnese, was regarded in antiquity much as Cape Horn has been in modern times, because of the danger to sailing ships from strong winds and violent storms. A Greek proverb said, "go round Malea and forget your home" (Strabo 8,6,20); and a merchant from Hierapolis proudly recorded on his tombstone the total of 72 safe voyages to Italy "rounding Malea" (W. Dittenberger, *Sylloge Inscriptionum Graecarum*, no.1229).

coastal vessels. These would be smaller and more lightly built than the ship in which P. had sailed from Italy, and hence unsuitable for the open sea (L. Casson, *Ships and Seamanship in the Ancient World*, 337).

carriages. Provincial cities had, since the time of Augustus, been obliged to provide transport through their territory for official travellers: see 45 nn.

Etesian winds. *Etesios* is a Greek adjective meaning "yearly". "The Etesians" was used especially of northerly or north-easterly winds which blew in the Aegean regularly every summer: according to P.'s uncle (*Hist. Nat.* 3,123–4) they blew steadily for 40 days from July 21st (see Casson, *Ships and Seamanship*, 270–3). So P. probably reached Ephesus in August, which would also explain the "oppressive heat".

Epistle 16
You were right to report. No more was called for from T. than a polite acknowledgment. The reply reproduces much of P.'s language, with two adverbs of approval placed emphatically at the beginning of each sentence: "rightly you reported"; "wisely you decided".

my dearest Secundus. See Introd., VI(B)

Epistles 17A, 17B, 18
P. reports his arrival in BP and on his inspection of the finances of Prusa (17A), and in another epistle probably sent off soon afterwards (17B) P. repeats the news of his arrival and suggests the despatch of a surveyor from Rome to BP; T. acknowledges the receipt of both epistles and declines to send a surveyor (18).

Epistle 17A
Written soon after 18 Sept., 110, from Prusa. For the dating of P.'s epistles, see Introd. VI (A).

17A, 1

slight attacks of fever. In view of Lucian's rhetorical question to Roman officials in his essay "On error in greeting" (section 13, 736), "is this not the first command in the book of instructions which you always receive from the emperor, that you should take care of your own health?", it was entirely appropriate for P. to report that he had interrupted his journey in order to recover from the fever.

I halted at Pergamum. Clearly for a respite to recover from the effects of heat and fever. SW, 581–2, argues from Pergamum's situation, 25 miles inland, that P.'s original intention had been to continue his journey overland from Pergamum to Prusa in BP (or to Cyzicus in Asia), but that at Pergamum he changed his mind and came down to the coast to take ship at Elaeus. However, in 15 he had declared his intention of making his journey partly by ship, and this sentence implies that he had come all the way from Ephesus to Pergamum by land: had he continued north overland he would have had no real opportunity to use ships. So it is probable that he had decided at Ephesus to go by the well-travelled roads to Pergamum, and then take ship at Elaeus so as to avoid crossing the mountainous routes through Mysia to the border of BP (on which, see L. Robert, *Bulletin de Correspondence Hellenique,* Vol.102, 1978, 442f.).

17A,2

held back by opposing winds. The Etesians must still have been blowing as he sailed north past the coast of the Troad and north-east through the Hellespont into the Propontis (Sea of Marmara).

I entered Bithynia. The first city P. reached after his entry was an inland one, Prusa, so that he must have travelled overland from a port in Asia (probably Cyzicus: thus Hardy, 108), crossing the border of BP on his way; had he come by ship all the way to BP, he would have landed at the city of Apamea (see SW, 582).

to celebrate your birthday. September 18th, the day after his entry. P.'s *Panegyric* 92,4, reveals that T.'s birthday was on the same day as Domitian's murder, which is recorded by Suetonius as September 18 (*Domitianus* 17, 3). How P. celebrated the occasion is not clear: he does not refer here, or a year later (88–9), to any public ceremonies such as those at the New Year (35) and on the anniversary of T.'s accession (52).

17A,3

I am examining expenditures etc.. The most important part of P.'s mission (18.3 and Introd. IV C).

under different pretexts. P. gives no examples. Administrators of public works (17B.2) may have delayed handing back any surplus moneys after a building was finished (see also 81.1).

wholly unlawful outlays. Again no examples, and P. is referring to unlawful expenditure, not mere extravagance (see 43): see 110 for a payment to an individual which violated T.'s *mandata.*

Epistle 17B

The text of this letter is printed as a continuation of 17A by Aldus, but it is clear that it must have been sent off as a separate letter, because P. repeats the date of his entry; this would be a very curious thing to do in the same letter (as it would be to repeat "sir" only nine words after its appearance in 17A,4). Hence the heading "Pliny to Trajan" has to be restored after 17A.4. 17B must have been sent off soon after 17A, since P., in repeating the date, anticipates the possibility that 17B may reach T. first. P.'s motive for sending a second letter was that he had suddenly had the bright idea of getting a surveyor from Rome.

a surveyor. Not a "land surveyor" (Radice):   although land-surveying is the best known aspect of Roman surveying, because a corpus of technical works survives (see O.A.W. Dilke, *The Roman Land Surveyors*), it is clear that what P. needs is a quantity surveyor ("building surveyors" is how Dilke (p. 42) describes the ones in P.'s letters).

could be recovered from the administrators of public works. These *curatores* are not the private contractors who put up the buildings, but wealthy citizens of Prusa obliged as a compulsory service to their city (in Greek a "liturgy", in Latin a *munus*) to supervise on behalf of the city construction work carried out by private contractors (see Jones, *GC*, 237–8). There were no responsible permanent officers such as a Town Clerk (see 19) and the elected magistrates served only for a year, too short a period for most such projects. *Curatores* were both conscripts and wealthy because, as P.'s words show, they were liable to make up any financial loss incurred by the city out of their own pockets. SW, 584, discusses the possible reasons why P. was only proposing to recover money and not to prosecute the *curatores* on criminal charges (to which Roman magistrates were liable, but possibly not those of non-Roman communities). However, P. does not explicitly charge the *curatores* with fraud: it is possible that they had been negligent and had been deceived by dishonest contractors and surveyors acting in collusion.

if measurements were carried out honestly. A whole title in the Digest is headed "if a surveyor has reported a false measurement" (11,6):   in it Ulpian envisages a surveyor who may have "deceived in the measurement of a building" (*id.*,5,2), and Paulus one who may have "lied in measuring the site or the timber or the stone" (*id.*,6).

Epistle 18

17A and 17B must have reached T. within a short time of each other, for he was able to respond in this letter to P.'s news about his fever (from 17A) and to his request for a surveyor (from 17B). Apart from this last, this letter, like 16, merely acknowledges what P. has reported.

18,1

physical condition. The literal meaning of the Latin is "your little body". Elsewhere T. uses a diminutive form with indulgent contempt (40,2:"Greeklings"), but here he may be attempting to unbend a little.

18,3

it is an established fact (or "there is general agreement"). T. does not specify his sources of information. SW, 585, rules out revelations at the trials of proconsuls (Introd. IVC) and suggests that the procurators of imperial estates in BP were T.'s sources. There were also natives of the province in the highest circles at Rome (e.g. the historian Arrian of Nicomedia, who may have been entering on his senatorial career at this time: Syme, *RP*, Vol.4, no.2).

works which are in progress at Rome. T.'s Forum, with his Basilica and covered markets next to it, was dedicated in 113; his Baths were finished by 109 (Ward-Perkins, 84–95).

or nearby. New harbours at Ostia (Ward-Perkins, *ibid.*), Centum Cellae (VI,31,15–17) and Ancona (*ILS*.298), and a new aqueduct for Rome (*ILS*.290).

if only you are willing to search for them. Instead of expressing regret that Rome must have priority, T. makes a grand generalisation, which P. clearly believed did not apply in BP (39,6).

Epistles 19–20

P. suggests replacing public slaves with soldiers as guards for prisoners awaiting trial; T. rejects the suggestion.

Epistle 19

Written from Prusa, soon after 18 Sept., 110 (23 shows that P. remained at Prusa while 19 and 21 were written).

19,1

I ask you to guide me. Since it is clear that military discipline and troop-dispositions were close to T.'s heart, P. was clearly wise to consult him before permanently transferring soldiers to new, civilian duties.

to have prisoners guarded . . . or by soldiers. The plural of the Latin abstract noun *custodia* is also used to mean actual 'prisoners' by Seneca (*Epistles* 5,7) and by Suetonius (*Tiberius* 61,5). Imprisonment in a town jail was not used as a criminal penalty in the Roman world but only for the 'remanding custody' of people awaiting trial. On the 'auxiliary' soldiers stationed in BP, see 21,1n.

public slaves owned by the cities. The practice in Greek city-states of buying slaves and using them for public order, as well as clerical, duties goes back to Athens in the 5th century B.C., where Scythian archers kept order at meetings of the democratic Assembly. M.I. Finley argued that, in slave-owning communities in the ancient world, the self-respecting freeborn regarded any form of full-time employment as degrading, so that privately-owned slaves had to be used as secretaries and managers (*The Ancient Economy*, 75–7). It must be for the same reason that cities developed the practice of using slave archivists, policemen and prison warders (see Jones *GC*,213,230,242–3).

Epistle 20

T. appears to ratify the action P. has already taken in stiffening the guards with a few soldiers, because in his first sentence he only rules out the transfer of more soldiers.

20,1

fellow-soldiers. Campbell (37–8) has analysed the use of this term by T. and other emperors to flatter the common soldiers, on whose loyalty, in the last resort, an emperor's power rested. P. in his *Panegyric* had stressed that in 100 many serving soldiers could still call T. their fellow-soldier (or "comrade") because of T.'s 10 years of service as military tribune (Pan. 15,2–5; cf. 19,3). T. himself, in a section of the *mandata* in which he freed soldiers from any need to observe formalities in their wills, referred to his "integrity of purpose towards my best and most loyal fellow-soldiers" (D.29,1,1,pr.). This is the only letter where T. starts by referring to "fellow-soldiers" and then reverts to plain "soldiers": elsewhere he uses the former only in acknowledging messages of loyalty (53;101;103) and plain "soldiers" in business letters (22;28). P. uses only the latter in business letters (cf.18), and the former in his formal messages (52;100).

20,2

as a result of either group relying on the other. T. slightly misinterprets what P. said. T.'s phrase implies that both groups will say "we can skip this job and the other lot will do it", whereas P. had implied that they would say "if anything goes wrong and any-one finds out, we can blame the other lot".

as few of them as possible should be called away from their units. It must have been a great temptation for imperial administrators, with no trained civil servants at their disposal, to detach soldiers to carry out civilian duties: the clerical staffs of imperial legati and other officials were made up of soldiers on secondment from their units (see A.H.M. Jones, *Studies in Roman Government and Law*, Chap.10, on the "clerical and sub-clerical grades" of the Roman civil service). T., the last great Roman conqueror, pre-dictably wanted to check this practice (cf.22,2; 28); under his successors soldiers do seem to have been widely used to guard prisoners (D. 48,3,12 and 14).

Epistles 21–2

P. reports to T. that an equestrian officer has protested against T.'s order to P. to reduce the size of his military escort, and T. informs P. that he has received that officer's letter.

Epistle 21

Written from Prusa, not long after 18 Sept., 110 (cf.19n.).

21,1

Gavius Bassus, the prefect of the Pontic shore. New light has been shed on Bassus by the inscriptions on a statue-base discovered at Ephesus (*Année Epigraphique* 1972, no.573; H. Devijer, *Prosopographia Militiarum Equestrium*, vol. 1, G8). The statue was put up in Bassus' honour by 8 members of his HQ staff (*praetorii*), two of whom were *stratores*, probably the equivalent of the two cavalrymen in P.'s letter. The dedication re-veals that Bassus' first name was Publius, that his place of origin was Rome itself, that he had passed through the usual sequence of three junior officer posts held by equestrians in the emperor's service (cf.87,3 n.), and had been decorated by T. (probably during the Dacian Wars), before becoming "prefect of the Pontic maritime shore", the final post recorded on the stone.

    The precise functions of this officer are unclear. The "Pontic shore" could mean ei-ther the whole coastline of the Black Sea or the southern coast, most of which had been part of the kingdom of Pontus. All of the southern coast lay within P.'s province, except for the most easterly section which came under the legate of Galatia-Cappadocia. That would be the reason for Bassus' prompt courtesy call on the new governor, who, as a sena-tor, was Bassus' superior in rank, although Bassus clearly held an independent appoint-ment directly from T. This prefecture should not be identified with the command of the Black Sea Fleet because the title of recorded holders of this command was *praefectus clas-sis Ponticae* (*ILS* 1327, line 7) and because the fleet's base at this date was at Trapezus, outside P.'s province (C.G. Starr, *The Roman Imperial Navy*, 127 f.).

worthy – and deserving of your generosity. P. uses the vocabulary of letters of recommendation (cf.26 n.) but the "generosity" would presumably involve no more than letting Gavius Bassus keep his present escort.

privileged soldiers. These were soldiers below the rank of centurion who were given ex-tra pay for special duties, such as secondment to a governor's staff (see Watson, 85–6).

cohorts. This implies the presence in the province of at least two such units of auxiliary troops (i.e. units recruited from non-Roman subjects of the emperor), which were normally 500 in number; one of these units is referred to in 106, and was a mixed unit of cavalry and infantry. For how long they had been stationed in the province, and for what purpose (given that BP was not a frontier province), is not known.

22,1

my instructions. This is T.'s first explicit reference to the book of instructions (*mandata*), issued by him to P., as to every governor (see Introd. II (G)iii).

a copy ... to be appended to this letter. Both P. and T. consistently distinguish between having a copy of a document written below the text of a letter on the same sheet of papyrus (Latin *subicere*, here translated as "append": this verb is also used in 56,5; 58,4; 79,5; 114,3) and having the original text of a document fastened to the sheet on which the letter had been written (Latin *iungere*, translated as "attach": this verb is used in 48,1; 60,2; 81,6; 83). Only in one case does P. use "append" in reference to the original of a document, but in his reply T. correctly uses "attach" (92–3). See SW, 591.

Epistles 23–4

P. urges T. to permit the construction of a new bath-house at Prusa, and specifies how the money will be raised. T. sends his permission, with a proviso about the city's finances.

Epistle 23

Written from Prusa, between 18 Sept. and 24 Nov., 110.

23,1

a bath-house. For the spread of this Roman amenity to eastern cities, see Jones,*GC*,219; Ward-Perkins, 292–6; A. Farrington in *Rom.Arch. in Greek World*, 50–59.

you can grant their request. The first of four requests for T.'s approval of a new civic building (see 70,3; 90,2; 98,2), from which SW deduced that T. had included in his *mandata* a ban on any new building by the cities (593).

23,2

that which I have begun to recover: from the administrators of public works, among others (17A,3; 17B,2).

spending on olive-oil. A.H.M.Jones held that this money was spent on oil to be supplied for athletes to rub into their skins at the gymnasium (*GC*,221f. with 351, n.23); but Hardy, 117–8 and SW,594, suggested that it was used for edible oil to be distributed free to the poor. There is no conclusive evidence to settle this issue but, since the bulk of the evidence from other cities in Asia Minor concerns oil for the gymnasia (e.g. J Reynolds, *Aphrodisias and Rome*, p. 196), and since a fund intended to provide one means to physical cleanliness would be appropriately diverted to another means to the same end, Jones' view is the more probable one.

the splendour of your age. P. also invokes the theme of the new age inaugurated by T. in connection with building schemes in 37, 3 (see also 41,5; 70,3).

Epistle 24

T.'s agreement to the request is hedged about with qualifications ("if it is not going to put a burden ...provided that..."), presumably in the belief that the city would squander money, unless T. issued such warnings.

no special tax is imposed. For such a special tax which was permitted by an emperor, see Antoninus Pius' letter to a city in Macedonia, which allows the city to impose a poll tax in order to raise revenue for "necessities" (J.H. Oliver, *American Journal of Philology* 1958, 52–3); it appears that by the time of Severus no city could impose any new tax without the emperor's permission (Cod.Just.4,62,1–2).

Epistle 25

P. reports to T. the delayed arrival of his deputy (no response from T. was called for). Written soon after 24 Nov., 110, from Nicomedia.

my deputy. For his office and functions, see Introd., II(D)i.

Epistle 26

P. asks T. for promotion for his ex-quaestor. Written between 24 Nov., 110 and 3 Jan., 111.
A letter of recommendation for an appointment did not necessarily call for a reply, but T.'s silence may imply that Rosianus did not get an appointment on this occasion. Like 87 (but unlike 85–86b) this letter is written on behalf of someone not actually serving in the province. Six other such letters, probably written to T. during his absences from Italy after his accession or during the Dacian Wars, were collected at the beginning of Book X (4–6; 10–12; 13 is a direct request for a priesthood for P. himself), and books I–IX include numerous such letters to acquaintances in important positions. This practice of pleading for advancement for one's protégés, and the emperor's custom of allowing senior senators to act as "brokers of patronage", is fully studied in R. P. Saller: *Personal Patronage under the early Empire* .

26,1
Rosianus. His full name was T. Prifernius Paetus Rosianus Geminus, and he was the recipient of several of P.'s letters, mainly of fatherly advice (VII, 1; 24; VIII,5; IX,11; 30). See Syme, *RP* Vol.2, 483–7, for his career.

your kindnesses. In fact his appointment of P. as consul suffectus in 100.

the closest of links ... quaestor. The relationship between a quaestor, who was just beginning his senatorial career, and the more senior senator (consul, praetor or proconsul) whose assistant he was, was supposed to be quasi-filial. Cicero says that "we have it handed down from our ancestors that a praetor should be in the place of a father to his quaestor" (*Div. in Caecil.*19,61), and so three would-be prosecutors had been denied the right to prosecute men under whom they had served as quaestors (*id.*,19,63).

26,2
offices ... in the city. Besides the quaestorship, these were probably an aedileship or tribunate 2–3 years later, and a praetorship 2–3 years after that (see Introd., IVB). Syme, *loc.cit.*, suggests Rosianus was now aspiring to a consulship (which in the event he only attained about 15 years later), but SW,596, thinks the request "too loosely worded" for that, and suggests a provincial legateship or a praetorian appointment at Rome.

military service with you. If "shared with you" is to be taken literally, Rosianus had either been a military tribune in a legion on the Rhine or Danube in 97–99, or held a more senior command during the Dacian Wars.

Epistles 27–8

P. reports on his allocation of guards for an imperial procurator on a special mission, and T. approves his decision.

Epistle 27

Written between 24 Nov., 110 and 3 Jan., 111. P. has to secure approval for an allocation of soldiers to the staff of an imperial official which actually violated T.'s instructions (see 21).
your freedman Maximus: assistant to Virdius Gemellinus, the equestrian procurator for the province (see 28; Introd., II(D)ii).

apart from the ten. This implies that T.'s *mandata* ("you ordered)" laid down that the equestrian procurator was to have 10 soldiers on secondment (see 20,2; 21,2 n.) and to distribute as many of these to his freedmen assistants (see 63,67,80) as he thought appropriate.

Paphlagonia. The former client kingdom of Paphlagonia at this date formed part of the province of Galatia-Cappadocia, but, according to Strabo (XII,3,9–10), the coastal tract between the boundary of Bithynia and the mouth of the Halys had once counted as part of Paphlagonia, so Maximus may have been going either to the eastern part of BP, or into the adjoining province. The coastal plain (narrow though it be) seems a more likely place to levy grain than the mountainous interior.

to collect grain. This is described by T. as a "special duty". SW,597–8, rightly points out that the suggestion that the grain was intended to feed the army which T. eventually took east to fight the Parthians is discredited (see B. Levick, *Greece & Rome* 1979,124–5), but SW's own suggestion that it was intended to supplement Rome's food supply seems less likely than the view that the grain was to meet the needs of the permanent garrison either on the Euphrates or on the lower Danube (see S. Mitchell in *Armies & Frontiers*, 132f.)

Epistles 29–30

P. consults T. about the appropriate penalty for slaves found among army recruits. T. rules that only if they were volunteers do they deserve execution.

Epistle 29

Written between 24 Nov., 110 and 3 Jan., 111.

29,1

Sempronius Caelianus. The epithet *egregius* (worthy, excellent) indicates that he was probably an equestrian officer (see Gavius Bassus, 21,1). Since he received his own *mandata* from T. (see 30,1 n.), he probably had an independent commission from T. to recruit men in the province. In Italy and the "public" provinces only men of senatorial rank were appointed to raise recruits (T. Mommsen, *Römische Staatsrecht*, II, 850), but Sempronius could have been sent to BP as soon as it had been made an imperial province, well before P.'s arrival.

slaves ... discovered among the recruits. At Rome, as in other ancient states, slaves were regarded as unfitted for service in the regular army except in the gravest emergency (such as the revolt in Illyricum in A.D.6–9: Dio Cass.55,31,1). The early 3rd century jurist Marcianus wrote that "slaves are banned from any form of military service; otherwise they are to suffer capital punishment" (D.49,16,11).

as founder and upholder of military discipline. Campbell, 266,n.7, plausibly suggests that this phrase was artfully 'planted' by P. to engage T.'s close attention, and deduces that P. obviously expected T. to read his letters himself. P.'s *Panegyric* shows that T. posed as the restorer of discipline in the army after an alleged period of slackness under Domitian (*Panegyricus* 6,2; 18,1).

29,2

the oath. An oath of obedience administered to soldiers on enlistment, and annually on January 3rd (see Watson, 49). The military oath was distinct from the oath of loyalty renewed every year by civilians as well as by soldiers on January 28, the anniversary of T.'s accession (see 52 n.).

not yet enrolled in the ranks. That is, registered in the roll of a specific unit. The same technical language occurs in a papyrus text of a letter of the Prefect of Egypt of A.D.103: "give orders that 6 recruits who have been checked (*probatos* as in 27,2) by me are enrolled in the ranks (*in numeros referri*) of the cohort which you command" (A.S. Hunt and C.C. Edgar, *Select Papyri*, Vol 2 (Loeb Library), no.421, ll.4–6). Men who had sworn the oath but had not been enrolled had a legally debatable status. Ulpian said that "men who are not yet in the ranks, though they may have been picked as recruits and travel at public expense, are not yet soldiers" (D.29,1,42; see Watson, 42–3). Hence P. presumably wondered whether the slaves were really guilty of an offence, if they did not yet count as soldiers. The fact that they had not yet been enrolled in specific units strongly suggests that the recruits were not intended to join the auxiliary units stationed in BP but were to be sent either to legions or to auxilia outside it (see SW, 599, for 25 legionaries of Bithynian origin in Africa in Trajan's reign; and M. Speidel, in *Armies and Frontiers*, p. 17).

Epistle 30

3 0 , 1

my instructions. It would be surprising if this were a reference to P.'s own *mandata* (as SW,601, thinks possible), because P. should not need to be told by T. what was in them. It is more likely that Caelianus was an independent officer with his own *mandata* and that T. is informing P. that Caelianus was only "following orders".

to have deserved the capital penalty. It appears from this sentence that Caelianus was empowered to inflict lesser penalties, but not death. Two offences could be committed by recruits which were punishable by death, resistance to conscription and enrolment by a slave (see 29,2 n.). The fact that Caelianus was required by his *mandata* to send offenders who were liable to the death penalty to be tried before P. confirms the hypothesis that in the provinces only the governors were empowered to impose this (SW, 595, and see Dio Cass. 53,14,5).

volunteers ... or were conscripted. Before 107 B.C Roman legions were manned by conscripts selected from citizens with a minimum property qualification. It used to be generally accepted that after the property qualification was scrapped in 107, and especially from the time of Augustus, the Roman army was recruited from poor men who volunteered for service as an escape from poverty, but this dogma has been overthrown by P.A. Brunt (*Italian Manpower*, chap.22; *Scripta Classica Israelica* Vol.1, 90 f.; see also SW, 601). Brunt accepts that volunteers of suitable quality would be welcomed, but questions whether they came forward in sufficient numbers before the age of the Severi. He points out that T. took it for granted that recruits might belong to either category (although the text provides no evidence about which was the more numerous).

offered as substitutes. There is no other evidence for the offer (and acceptance) of substitutes for men conscripted into the Roman army. One can therefore only conjecture that rich men who happened to be chosen at the levy were allowed to pay for poor men to serve in their place, as happened under systems of selective conscription in other societies (e.g. in the USA during the Civil War). See also Millar, *JRS*. 1968,219.

3 0 , 2

the examination. The abstract noun is presumably a polite way of referring to the "examiner", i.e. Caelianus, who ought to have found out their status before administering the oath.

first approved. The same term (*probati*) is used in the Prefect of Egypt's letter about recruits who had been checked by him (*Select Papyri* Vol.2, no.421, l.4). T. implies that they were questioned by the recruiting officer about their status.

Epistles 31–2

P. asks T. how to deal with convicts who are used as public slaves in the cities, and is told to send those sentenced within the last ten years back to finish their sentence.

Epistle 31

Written between 24 Nov., 110 and 3 Jan., 111, presumably from Nicomedia or Nicaea (see 31,2).

31,1

the privilege of placing before you. P.'s elaborate allusion to what was presumably some explicit encouragement in his *mandata* to consult T., in light of his special mission (thus SW,602), was surely inspired by the suspicion that T. would regard his hesitations as unnecessary (and 32 shows this proved to be the case): P. wanted to be lenient, but T. took a tougher line.

31,2

sentenced to forced labour or to appearing at the games and similar kinds of penalties to these. This is one of the earliest references to the use by Roman courts of what Millar calls "hard-labour sentences", imposed on free persons of low social status, and constituting a form of "custodial penalty" (Millar, *Papers of the British School at Rome* Vol 52,1984, 124 f.). Much of the evidence for these penalties comes from the jurists of around 200, and it "hardly allows us to write an actual history showing how institutions evolved" (Millar, 127): it is thus difficult to decide exactly what P. meant by "labour" here. The jurists refer both to "public labour" (*opus publicum*) and to "labour in the mine" (*opus metalli*). The former was less severe than the latter: it involved being forced to perform for provincial cities the kind of menial tasks listed by T. at the end of 32, was usually imposed for limited periods, and those sentenced to it did not become "slaves of the penalty". Convicts who ran away from "public labour" were sent to do "labour in the mine": this was a life sentence, and the convicted did become "slaves of the penalty". Millar holds that P. is referring to the less severe penalty of "public labour" here. However, the menial tasks for the cities which Millar thinks constituted "public labour" are regarded by T. (32,2) as lenient treatment for the older convicts (a kind of "remission"); but he ordered the rest of the convicts to be sent back "to their punishment", which must therefore have been a more severe one. It appears likely that this was "labour in the mine",' as was suggested by SW,603. This interpretation is supported by the fact that P. puts this penalty on a par with being sentenced "to the games" (*in ludum*), which like "labour in the mine" was a sentence for life. Some of those so condemned had to fight as gladiators, so that it amounted virtually to a delayed death sentence; and it would not be long delayed for the others who were simply exposed to the beasts (Crook,273). Millar argues that those sentenced "to the games" by provincial governors were put at the disposal of provincial dignitaries who paid for such shows to be put on in provincial cities. The spread of the bloodthirsty taste for such spectacles had, by P.'s day, spread from Italy to the Greek East (L. Robert, *Les gladiateurs dans l'Orient grec*, Paris, 1940; and on the topic in general, see K. Hopkins, *Death and Renewal*, chap.1).

public slaves: see 19, 1nn.

a yearly allowance. This is the only evidence for the existence of such allowances cited in Jones *GC*, 357, n.58; he argues that they would have been lower than the salaries paid to free employees, since a proconsul of Asia, Fabius Persicus, rebuked Ephesus for employing free men "at excessive cost" on work which could be done by public slaves (Smallwood, *Documents of Gaius,Claudius and Nero*, no.380, col.6, ll.13–18).

31,3

improper to continue to use convicts. Not all forms of work done by public slaves would be unsuitable for convicts, as T. points out (32,3). SW,604, suggests that P. was thinking of "confidential work, custody of prisoners, keeping records".

dangerous. Presumably because total destitution would drive them to fresh crimes.

31,4

judgments in which they had been sentenced. Such judgments were read aloud by Roman judges at the end of trials, but from texts written out on tablets (see an inscribed text of a proconsul of Achaea's *decreta: decreta ex tabellis recitata*, Smallwood, 447, 1.2). Elsewhere in P.'s letters it is private persons appearing before his tribunal who submit documents, including decisions of proconsuls in criminal cases (56,2; 58,3, where "he produced (*proferebat*) nothing"; 65,2–3), and it is probable that it was enemies of the convicts who "produced" these documents as private prosecutors. The texts must have been copies of the original tablets on which the judgments had been recorded, since an inscription from Sardinia reveals that the original texts of proconsular *decreta* were taken back to Rome for storage in an archive (*ILS*.5947). There is no good reason to suppose that an official archive with copies of proconsuls' decisions existed in the province, so these copies must have been in private possession (most likely, in that of the successful prosecutors in the original cases); for the evidence from papyri, which reveals that such private copies circulated in Roman Egypt, see Williams, *JRS* 64, 1974, 90–93.

31,5

There were, however, some who claimed. It is not clear whether these were some of the convicts, or third parties testifying on their behalf.

at the orders of proconsuls or legates. SW,605, suggests they could have given oral instructions, without any written record being taken of them. "Legates" refers to the single "deputy" with the rank of *legatus pro praetore* to which each proconsul had been entitled (Introd. II(D)i).

Epistle 32

32,1

Let us remember. This solemn injunction is the first real rebuke to P. in the collection. It is not for troubling T. about the subject, but for even suggesting the possibility of leniency in such a case. T. shows himself less humane than P.

32,2

convicts of longer standing and old men sentenced more than ten years ago. This must refer to a single category of people, those whom P. had described as old men who had been released from their penalty a long time before (31,3). T. is prepared to show some leniency to them, although "functions not very different from punishment" is still brutal in tone.

Epistles 33–4

After a serious fire at Nicomedia P. proposes to establish an association of volunteer firemen, but T. rejects the scheme.

Epistle 33

Written not long before 3 Jan., 111, from Nicomedia.

33,1

A distant part of the province. Possibly the visit to Claudiopolis which led P. to write 39,5–6 (thus SW,606).

Gerusia. The building must have served as a headquarters for the local "Association of Older Men" (*gerousia* is the Greek abstract noun derived from *geron*, "old man"). Such associations were common in Greek cities of the Hellenistic and Roman periods: unlike the Gerousia of classical Sparta, which had been the governing council of the state, these were wealthy voluntary associations for social and religious functions, made up of members of the upper classes who had undergone athletic training in the gymnasia; there were similar associations for younger men known as "The Young Men" (*Neoi*). See Jones,*GC*,225-6.

Temple of Isis. The cult of this Egyptian goddess, modified to fit in with Greek and Roman practice, had spread very widely in the Roman empire: see R.E. Witt, *Isis in the Greek and Roman World.*

33,2

any pump. A description of such a 'sipo' in use among 'easterners' is given by Isidore of Seville: "siphons is the name given to a device which pumps water by blowing from below; easterners use it; for when they discover that a house is on fire, they run up with siphons full of water, and put out the fires. But they also clean ceilings by forcing water up to the higher levels" (*Etymologiae* 20,6,9).

33,3

pray consider, sir. P. has to ask T.'s approval for his scheme because in his *mandata* T. had ordered the dissolution of clubs in the cities of the province and P. had announced the ban in his edict (96,7: for T.'s motives see 34, 1n.). Hence P.'s limit on the size of the proposed association and his insistence that he will be able to supervise a body of such a size: he was aware of the need to allay T.'s anxiety.

an association of firemen. *Faber* is the Latin for 'workman' or 'craftsman', more specifically for 'carpenter' or 'blacksmith', but inscriptions from cities in Italy and the western provinces reveal that *collegia* of *fabri* were associations composed of such craftsmen who served as volunteer firemen. P. is proposing to introduce a western institution which would have been wholly new to the eastern provinces, where there are no epigraphic references to any associations with this function. The passage quoted from Isidore suggests that in eastern cities the general public were expected to turn out to extinguish fires.

use the permission ... for any other purpose. P. is clearly thinking of the organisation of political demonstrations and even riots (see 34,1).

Epistle 34

34,1

The example set by very many people. The order of the words in the Latin rules out the interpretation given in the translations of Firth and Radice (the latter has "on the model of those existing elsewhere"): since the phrase is sandwiched between *tibi*, "to you", and in *mentem venit*, "it has come to mind", it must be P. himself who is following the example set by many other *persons* in conceiving such a scheme.

But let us recall. As in 32,1 'us' means 'you and me', and it is a less harsh way of saying "you ought to remember". T. implies that P. should have realised he would never approve of such a scheme for the reason which follows. This is a second rebuke to P. (cf.32,1), not for consulting T., but for not realising that such a plan was out of the question.

troubled by cliques. For the quarrels between cliques in the cities of the province and the troubles they fomented, fully attested in Dio of Prusa's speeches, see Jones, *Dio*, 100-3.

Whatever name we may give etc.. This sweeping, dismissive generalisation reflects the same contemptuous view of "easterners" as "Greeklings" in 40,2.

political clubs. *Hetaeriae* (cf.96,7) is a transliteration of a Greek noun derived from *hetairos* 'companion'. The term had been applied to groups of young aristocrats with political aims in democratic Athens, and carried overtones of secret plotting for subversive ends (Jones, *Dio*, 100, translates it as "cabals"; cf. Dio 45,8, "neither conduct public affairs by *hetaeriae* nor divide the city into pieces").

34,2

to use ... the crowd which gathers. To judge by the passage from Isidore of Seville quoted above, this continued for centuries to be the practice in the eastern provinces.

Epistles 35-6

P. reports that the annual vows for T.'s preservation have been taken; T. acknowledges his report.

Epistle 35

Written on or soon after 3 Jan., 111, from Nicomedia (see 33 and 37).

Customary vows ... undertaken and fulfilled. The vow would be to sacrifice such and such animals to such and such deities in a year's time if the emperor were then alive and well. Every year on Jan. 3rd such sacrifices would be carried out in fulfilment of the previous year's vow and fresh vows undertaken: at Rome this was done on the Capitol by colleges of priests such as the Arval Brethren and in the provinces by the governors (Plutarch, *Cicero* 3,1: "January 3rd, the day on which the governors now pray and sacrifice for the emperor").

perpetually fulfilled and perpetually sealed. P. repeats the words he had used in referring to such vows in his *Panegyric* 67,4: "vows which deserve to be perpetually undertaken and perpetually fulfilled". A written record of the promises made to the gods must have been sealed up like a legal document until it was opened on the next Jan. 3rd.

Epistle 36

you along with the provincials. "You" (plural) must include P.'s entourage (15). The obvious persons to represent the whole population of the province (or at least its Bithynian half) would be the members of the "Council" of Bithynia which had its HQ at Nicomedia (Introd. IIF) where this ceremony must have been held (see 33,1; 37,1).

Epistles 37-8

P. reports on unfinished aqueducts at Nicomedia, to support his request for a technical expert from Rome. T. approves the new project, but orders P. to find out who was responsible for the failure of the earlier projects.

Epistle 37

Written not long after 3 Jan., 111, from Nicomedia.

37,1

3,318,000 sesterces on an aqueduct. To judge from this letter and 90,1, aqueducts of the kind which had long been in use in Italy were a novelty in P.'s province in this period, even for wealthy cities like Nicomedia and Sinope; likewise Alexandria Troas in Asia was still dependent on wells and rainwater cisterns until the reign of Hadrian (Philostratus, *Lives of the Sophists* (Loeb ed), p. 143): at that city Herodes Atticus had already spent 7 million drachmas (= 28 million sesterces) when Hadrian intervened (i.e., over 8 times the cost of Nicomedia's first project). SW,613, suggests that the inexperience of eastern builders with aqueducts "may be one reason for the failure". P. had presumably had his interest aroused by an inspection of the city accounts (see 17A,B). On Roman aqueducts in Asia Minor, see J.J. Coulton in *Rom.Arch. in Greek World*, 72-82.

37,2

so that it may not reach just the flat and low-lying parts of the city. This presupposes that the water would be brought in an open channel, not under pressure in a closed pipe (thus SW, 614). The advantage of an open channel would be that it could supply as much water as several closed pipes (Coulton, *art.cit.* 76)

dressed stone. Literally "squared stone", i.e. cut blocks of stone, usually referred to as "ashlar" in modern textbooks (see Ward-Perkins, 491).

brickwork. Whether P. intends this to mean solid brickwork or concrete faced with brick (as envisaged by P. in 39,4) is unclear.

37,3

A water-engineer or an architect. Although the basic sense of *aquilex* is "dowser", P. clearly means an expert at constructing aqueducts (of the kind clearly lacking in BP). This is the only explicit request made in the letter (see below), and, after his failure over the surveyor (18,3), P. has tried to arouse the interest of T., the great builder, by his description of the technical problems.

Epistle 38

T. deals with P.'s actual request very briefly and, typically, seizes on an aspect of the situation which had provoked his anger and which he clearly felt had not aroused sufficient concern in P.

I am truly confident. A more polite form of rejection than T. used in 20,3: "you won't need an architect, because your own abilities are up to it"!

But, by heaven, etc. With an oath T. expresses his anger at evidence of possible corruption (this sentence at any rate must be the emperor's own), and rather unfairly implies that P. has been neglecting his duty of tracing the culprits.

doing each other favours: see 17Bnn.

bring to my attention. P. never does so in the existing collection (see 40,1; 57,1). It may be that the collection is incomplete (Introd. I (D)ii), or that P. never did establish who was responsible, or that he just forgot to report.

Epistles 39–40

P. describes unfinished buildings at Nicaea and Claudiopolis to support another request for an architect to be sent from Rome. T. tells P. to decide for himself and refuses the request.

Epistle 39

Written between 3 and 27 Jan.,111, from Nicaea or Claudiopolis. or possibly Nicomedia. All the details of the buildings in this long letter are just used to support P.'s request for an architect in section 6: as in 37, P. must have hoped to arouse T.'s personal interest in grand buildings.

39,1

Nicaea See Introd., III(C)i.

the stone itself is soft and crumbling. It is not clear whether the theatre was built entirely of ashlar (a practice which did survive in Asia Minor in the Roman period: see Ward-Perkins,273), or whether the "stone" referred to is rubble included in a form of concrete (see 4 n. below).

supports and substructures. The superimposed half-circles of vaults on which the tiers of seats in the auditorium (*cavea*) were supported when a theatre was built on a level site instead of against a hillside (see D.S. Robertson, *Handbook of Greek and Roman Architecture*, 164 f).

39,3

promised by private persons. A widespread practice by wealthy men seeking popularity (see P. Garnsey and R. Saller, *The Roman Empire*, 378): Dio had made such a promise to build a portico at Prusa (*Or.*40,3: see Jones, *Dio*,111–12). On their legal enforceability see 40,1n.

halls. Literally "basilicas", which were used at Rome for public business, especially courts of justice.

a colonnade. Such a covered walk is preserved at the theatre at Aspendos in southern Asia Minor, above and behind the highest row of seats (Robertson, *Handbook*,276; Ward-Perkins, 302).

39,4

on a much more lavish and extensive scale. Veyne, 744, pointed out that by this period the plan and the facilities of a Greek gymnasium had come to approximate to those of a set of Roman baths. An example is the monumental "gymnasium" built by Vedius Antoninus at Ephesos in the mid 2nd century (see Ward-Perkins, 292–4; and p. 274, pl.173). See also A. Farrington, in *Rom.Arch. in Greek World*, 50–1.

made up of a core of rubble and are not encased in brickwork. "Rubble" (*caementum*) refers to "lumps of aggregate" which, combined with a mortar made up of lime and volcanic sand, produced Roman "concrete" (*opus caementicium*): see Ward-Perkins, 98. The concrete made in Italy from the volcanic sand known as *pulvis puteolanus* could be used for large, vaulted structures which would stand up without any casing of brick or stone: in Italy the latter were only used to enhance the external appearance (see Ward-Perkins, chap.4). In most areas of Asia Minor, however, "a material which closely resembles, and patently derives from, the concrete of Roman Italy --- did not have the strength --- which Roman engineers derived from their use of dark volcanic sands" (*id.*273); and, in particular, "the mortar lacked the strength needed for the creation of vaulting" (*id.*,275). Presumably the architect of the gymnasium was unaware that this local variety of "concrete" was not as strong as Italian concrete, and his rival held that a facing of brickwork was needed to strengthen it. In fact there appeared in Asia Minor in the second century A.D.a style of building "in which bands of brickwork alternate with wider bands of mortared rubble" (*id.*,277), but this can hardly be what is referred to here since "bound in front" (*praecincti*) must refer to a facing of brick. In the auditorium of the theatre eventually built at Nicaea "a facing of ashlar masking a concrete core was used for the exterior walls and vaults" (*Rom. Arch. in the Greek World*, p. 98; and see pp.94–114 for building techniques and brickwork in Asia Minor).

39,5

Claudiopolis. See Introd. III(C)i.

the money which those members who were added to their council through your favour etc. See 112,1 n.

Epistle 40

All but the last two sentences of this letter are irrelevant as a response to P.'s direct request. T. tells P. in two cases to take decisions which P. clearly intended to take, provided he could get reliable advice. One gets the impression that T. is a little embarrassed at turning P. down yet again and feels obliged to use up some space expressing a polite interest in P.'s report before doing so.

40,1

It will be enough for me to be informed. No such report survives: see 38n.

make the private individuals add the embellishments ... promised. P. had given no hint that the Nicaeans who had made such promises were dragging their feet (39,3: it was simply that the actual theatre had to be finished first), but he *had* indicated that he was going to force councillors at Claudiopolis to pay their entrance fees (39,6). SW,621, comments: "T. or his secretary has been inattentive"; but it is surely more likely to have been the hard-pressed emperor who got in a muddle.

Such promises were often made by newly-elected city magistrates (possibly after making an informal pledge while still only candidates): 39,3n., and Garnsey cited below. T. himself made such a promise to put up a building, undertaken "for the sake of an honour" (i.e a magistracy), legally binding on the individual *and* on his heirs (D.50,12,14). See P. Garnsey, '*Taxatio* and *pollicitatio* in Roman Africa', *JRS* 1971, 116f.; Jones,*GC*,237; 247.

40,2

The Greeklings do enjoy their gymnasia. On the diminutive cf.18,12 n. The sentence is clearly the emperor's own expression of a personal prejudice (he would presumably not voice such sentiments in more public correspondence, with Greek cities for example). It is the construction of a gymnasium which will have aroused the traditional Roman prejudice, shared by the "soldier emperor", against the training in athletics given there to the younger members of the Greek upper-classes: in Roman eyes the only physical training appropriate for the young was for warfare (H.I. Marrou, *History of Education in Antiquity*, part 3, chs 1–2). P. himself had approved of T.'s banning of an athletic festival at Vienne (IV,22,7, with SW's note).

40,3

There is no province etc. P. had not questioned the skill, but, by implication, only the impartiality of the men available in the province: his adviser was the business rival of the architect of the gymnasium (39,4; at Prusa he had been more explicit, "if measurements were carried out honestly", 17B,2). T. disregards P.'s point, possibly not through inadvertence, but because he had no answer to it.

accustomed to come from Greece to us. There is not enough evidence about the identity of the architects of buildings in Italy to make it possible to assess the truth of this (see M. Henig, ed, *Handbook of Roman Art*, 50–1). T. may be generalising from the case of his own favourite architect, Apollodorus of Damascus (Dio Cass.79,4,1).

Epistles 41–2

P. describes a scheme to link a lake to the Gulf of Nicomedia and asks for a surveyor to be sent. T. expresses interest and promises to send one.

Epistle 41

Written between 3 and 28 Jan., 111, possibly from Nicomedia.

41,2

A very large lake in the territory ... of Nicomedia. The town of Nicomedia lay on the coast ("to the sea", below) at the head (and eastern end) of a long, narrow gulf which extends due east from the Sea of Marmara. 18 miles east of the town lies a lake, known in antiquity as Sophon (modern Sapanca Göl); a stream (ancient Melas) runs NE from the eastern end of the lake to join the river Sangarius which itself runs into the Black Sea; another stream flowing west into the Gulf of Nicomedia was separated from the lake by a watershed (see 41,4; 61,1–2).

Marble, grain, firewood, and timber. A considerable body of evidence (especially from inscriptions) shows that large quantities of marble and timber were shipped out of Nicomedia by sea: it is collected by L. Robert, in *Bulletin de Correspondence Hellénique* Vol.102, 1978, 415 f. (see also Mitchell, *Armies and Frontiers*, 138).

This project calls for many hands. The *OCT* follows earlier editors in suggesting that some part of P.'s original text must have been lost before "this project ..": in the text as it stands P. has not yet defined "this project" (a canal between the lake and the river flowing west into the Gulf of Nicomedia: see 61, 1–2).

they would all most gladly take part. Cutting a canal through 18 miles of land without modern earth-moving machines would clearly involve an enormous amount of labour and P. envisages obtaining this by extracting forced labour from the local population as a public duty to their community (thus SW, 623: one can reasonably take P.'s "most gladly" with a pinch of salt). The newly-published text of a charter of the Spanish municipality of Irni dating from the Flavian period provides that every male resident between 15 and 60 could be required to perform five days' work in any one year on construction (*opus*) or road-work (*munitio*) (*JRS* 1986,175,195,ch 83); there was a similar provision for road-work in the charter of the Spanish colony of Urso (*ILS* 6087, ch 98). See Crook, 202.

41,3
A surveyor. The Latin *librator* is a technical term for an expert in determining water levels (Vitruvius 8,6; Frontinus, *De aq.* 2,105). This is the only direct request made to T. (but see n. to 5 below) in the letter, and the description of the project is neatly characterised by SW,622, as "bait" for T. (see 37 and 39 nn.).
the experts in this district claim it is 40 cubits higher (than sea-level). See SW,614: "the lake is today about 120 feet, twice P.'s estimate, above sea-level." Since these experts had no particular motive for dishonesty (contrast 17B,2; 39,4,) in this case it is their technical competence which P. doubts.

41,4
by one of the kings. One of the Bithynian dynasty which ended in 74 B.C. (Introd.III(A)i).
to link the lake to the river. The river flowing west into the Gulf of Nicomedia(41,2n).

41,5
to see what the kings had merely begun completed by your agency. P. apparently implies that the cost of the project (apart from labour: see above) will be met by the imperial government: (i) there is no request to T. to "indulge the wishes" of the Nicomedians (contrast 23–24; 90); (ii) the project is presented as entirely P.'s own idea; (iii) T.'s personal role is stressed here, and in 42 T. says that "the lake can incite us" (i.e. T. and P.). On imperial building schemes in the provinces see R. MacMullen, *Harvard Studies in Classical Philology* Vol.64,207; S. Mitchell, in *Rom.Arch. in the Greek World*, 18–25.

Epistle 42
T. expresses cautious approval: he has taken the 'bait' and actually promises a technical expert from Rome (but see 62).
Calpurnius Macer. P. Calpurnius Macer Caulius Rufus (*consul suffectus*, 103) was the imperial *legatus* of Moesia Inferior, probably from 110 to 113 (Eck, 349–55; see Introd.IV(A)). This was the nearest province to BP to have legions stationed in it. For *libratores* serving in, or retired from, a legion, see *ILS*. 2422 and 5795, and for the use of the army on civilian projects, R. MacMullen, *Soldier and Civilian in the later Roman Empire*, 32f.

Epistles 43–4
P. asks, and gets, T.'s approval for his plan to cancel an annual embassy from Byzantium to T. and to reduce the expenses of a similar embassy to the governor of Moesia.

Epistle 43
Written between 3 and 28 Jan., 111, possibly from Byzantium.
43,1
When I was examining. See 17A,3; 18,3.
the Byzantines. See Introd.III(C)i.

an envoy. Many Greek cities had originally been sovereign states (including Byzantium) and, when they passed under the overlordship of Hellenistic kings or of Rome, they continued to conduct their "relations with the suzerain" (, title of Part 2) through formal embassies. Many inscriptions from the Greek cities record visits of ambassadors to the emperors and show that the frequency of embassies from Byzantium to the emperor was by no means unusual: e.g. one citizen of Ephesus is recorded as having travelled as ambassador, on behalf of his city, to the emperors Severus and Caracalla, to Rome, Britain, Upper Germany, Sirmium, Nicomedia, Antioch, Mesopotamia (*Supplementum Epigraphicum Graecum* 17, no.505). See Jones,*GC*, 243; Millar, 363–4, 380–85.

with a resolution. *Psephismate* is a Latin ablative form of the 3rd declension used with a transliterated Greek noun; *psephisma* is derived from *psephos* (a "pebble", and by derivation a "vote"), and the noun had been used since the 5th century B.C. to refer to the "decrees" or "resolutions" voted upon by the assemblies of citizens. Although by P.'s day the initiative for such decrees will always have come from the Councils of the cities, inscriptions show that *psephismata* were still formally ratified by the Assemblies (see Introd. II(E))

to bring you greetings. Some embassies to the emperor were concerned with matters of substance, especially the defence or enhancement of a city's privileges, but others were, like these, simply acts of homage. These were common on occasions such as an emperor's accession, a major victory, or the elevation of a "junior emperor" (see Millar, 410–20); but there is no other evidence of a city sending a regular annual embassy. Byzantium at least restricted itself to a single envoy: most embassies had several members (see G. Souris, *ZPE*, 48,235–44).

twelve thousand sesterces. P. explains, in connection with the embassy to the governor of Moesia, that this sum was "under the heading of travelling-expenses". The Latin word, like its Greek equivalent *ephodion*, incorporates the root "road"; hence it was literally "road-money". Envoys were not usually paid their expenses by their city until they had completed their mission (but see Millar, 383): many imperial letters to Greek cities in the second century end with a standard formula, "the ambassadors were so-and-so, to whom the *ephodion* should be paid unless they promised to serve at their own expense" (see Williams, *Historia* 16,472–4).

43,2

Mindful of your policy. The policy was that extravagance by the cities should be curbed (18,3).

the envoy ... kept at home, but ... the resolution ... sent on. Provincial communities, like individual petitioners, could only get their messages delivered to the emperor if they sent someone to Rome to carry them, because there was no public post in the Roman Empire (see Williams, *JRS* 1976,97); and it would not have been appropriate for a city to send a humble letter-carrier to carry a civic decree to the emperor. Only governors and other imperial officials could use the official system of requisitioned transport (see 45–6 nn.). Here P. indicates that he has promised the Byzantines that he will send their annual messages by this means, along with some of his own letters. This does not seem to have become a common procedure for handling civic messages to the emperor, except in the reign of Antoninus Pius (see Williams, *Historia* 16,470–83). There is other evidence of concern over the scale of civic expenditure on embassies: Vespasian laid down that no embassy should have more than 3 members (D.50,7,5,6) and the historian Cassius Dio advocated banning them except for litigation, and having governors screen civic requests (52,30,9).

43,3

the person who is governor of Moesia. In fact, of Moesia Inferior (Moesia had been divided into two provinces in 86). For that province's trade links with Byzantium, see 77,1 n. (they explain the need for the city to keep on good terms with the governor of the province); for the governor at this date see 42 n. The use of "cut down", rather than "abolished", and T.'s phrase "in a less expensive way" (44), show that the embassy to Moesia was to be allowed to continue, but with reduced expenses: P. would not normally have any occasion to send a courier, who could also take the city's message, to the governor (61,5, is exceptional).

43,4

I ask you, sir, etc. A rather elaborate request, when P. is quite clear in his own mind about what needs to be done, and his proposal is certainly in accordance with T.'s general policy. However, it would affect the emperor's own standing, and, to a lesser extent, that of a fellow governor.

Epistle 44

A straightforward response, approving P.'s scheme, and making that approval clear by the emphatic "you acted quite correctly" at the beginning. There is surely a hint of irony, at the Byzantines' expense, in the last sentence.

Epistles 45-6

P. asks whether he should respect passes for the use of requisitioned transport whose expiry date has passed, and T. replies emphatically that he should not do so.

Epistle 45

Written between 3 and 28 Jan., 111.

45,1

Passes. *Diplomata* is the Greek plural form of a noun *diploma*, which originally meant anything that was double. In Latin the word had been used since Republican times for an official document, and in particular for a "pass" which entitled the bearer to make use of the official transport system (see below). It is commonly used in Latin prose in its Greek form (see 64,120–1; Suetonius, *Divus Augustus* 50). It is probable that such *diplomata* consisted of a pair of wooden tablets fastened together, with wax panels on their interior surfaces to carry a written text. Suetonius describes Augustus' institution of a system for rapid communication between himself and the provinces (49,3): "in order that he could more rapidly be informed . . . of what was going on in every province, he stationed at short distances along the military roads, first young men, later carriages. The latter seemed more convenient, in order that the same persons who brought letters from a place could also be questioned if the situation called for it." The second system became permanent, and it was by this means that P. and T. exchanged letters. The local city authorities had to provide carriages and horses, as well as lodgings, free of charge, for travellers through their territories who carried *diplomata*. Travellers on official business could also requisition, against payment, transport for baggage, and an edict of a governor of Galatia of circa A.D.13–15 reveals that this placed a particularly heavy burden on the cities: the edict laid down maximum numbers of waggons and animals which could be demanded by persons of different rank and a scale of payments (see S. Mitchell, *JRS* 1976,106 f.). A long series of official documents preserved on inscriptions or papyri show emperors and governors trying to check abuse of the system, especially by soldiers (a list is given by Mitchell, *art.cit.*111–12; see 77–8 below). T.'s close control over the issue of *diplomata* forms part of this continuing effort, which seems to have had little success. The philosopher Epictetus told his audience c.A.D.108 to treat their bodies like a donkey: "if there is a requisition and a soldier takes it, let it go, do not resist or grumble. Otherwise you'll get beaten up and still lose your donkey" (Epictetus,*Discourses* 4,1,79). Epictetus takes such treatment as a matter of course.

their expiry date. Literally, "whose day has passed by" (see 46). These two letters provide the only evidence that *diplomata* had an expiry date, so it is not known whether this was an innovation by T. There is no evidence to show what the date was and for how long a *diploma* was valid, but it is a plausible view that it was for one year and that December 31 was the expiry date, especially since P. is writing in the middle of January.

sanction what is unlawful. It is probable that P. is referring to *diplomata* carried by travellers coming from other provinces. They would have presented their expired passes to the city authorities on their route, and the latter would have asked P. whether they were obliged to meet their demands. In that case the "essential business" he feared to impede might have included messages from other governors or officials to T. himself, and it was this risk which led him to consult T. For a different intepretation, that the words referred to *diplomata* distributed by P. himself, see S. Mitchell, *art.cit.* 126,n.132.

Epistle 46

It is for that reason that I lay it upon myself etc. Presumably each governor or official who was entitled to distribute *diplomata* received a fixed allocation for, probably, one year, and these had to be used within the year; by this time only *diplomata* which carried the imperial seal (Suet.,*Divus Augustus* 50; Plutarch, *Galba* 8,4) were valid (Mitchell, 125–6, argues that until A.D.69 governors could issue their own *diplomata*, but that either Vespasian or Domitian had put a stop to this). These rules were clearly intended to put a limit to the burdens imposed on the cities and on abuse of the system. "I lay it upon myself as one of my first duties" is an emphatic personal statement, and indeed an expression of indignation: T. is implying, "I go to a great deal of trouble to ensure that people do not have to distribute out of date *diplomata*, but here they are still doing so". Despite the indignation, there is no direct rebuke for P., which confirms the view taken above, that P. was enquiring about *diplomata* issued by others (as does the phrase "through all the provinces").

Epistles 47–8

P. passes on to T. a memorandum from Apamea about its privileges, and T. tells P. to reassure the colony.

Epistle 47

Written between 3 and 28 Jan., 111, possibly from Apamea.
47,1
To investigate the public debtors, etc. See 17A,3; 18,3; 43,1.
Apamea. See Introd. III(C)i.
the privilege and long-established custom. As the only community of Roman citizens (colony) in Bithynia proper Apamea enjoyed a special cachet and that would help to explain why proconsuls had left it to its own devices; its immunity from imperial taxation (the *ius Italicum*: D.50,15,1,10) meant that the proconsuls lacked one important motive for investigating a city's finances. But colonies were not 'free cities' (see 92) and cannot have enjoyed as of right complete freedom from intervention by the governors. What Apamea claims is only a special status of its own (a *privilegium*), and one based only on

"long-established custom"; G.P. Burton (*JRS* 1975,104) is right to detect in 48,2 T.'s scepticism about even this claim.

47,2

the precedents they were quoting. Documents which the colony's spokesmen read out before P.'s tribunal (see 85,2-3). They surely included epistles from some of the proconsuls.

in a memorandum. A *libellus* is literally a "booklet", and in the language of Roman administration it came to be used specifically of any document addressed to the emperor by a petitioner or petitioners of humble status (see 106-7); but a city would have addressed the emperor directly in an epistle, so here *libellus* must refer to a memorandum (Williams, *JRS* 1974,95 and *ZPE* 66, 181, n.3).

47,3

For I am concerned not to be thought etc. P.'s motive for referring the question to T. is an apparent conflict between P.'s own chief mission and local custom, which it is usually T.'s policy to respect (see 113).

Epistle 48

48,1

Which you had attached. Although P. had only said "I have sent to you", this statement shows that the memorandum (an original document) was glued to P.'s own epistle (see 22,1n.)

has relieved me of the need to weigh. This statement is one of the most striking pieces of evidence that the emperor himself handled P.'s enquiries (see SW,631). He saves himself time and trouble in reading through the memorandum and making up his mind about the Apameans' claim by evading the issue: since they were willing to let P. check their accounts on this occasion, he would lay it down that this was not to count as a precedent which could be used to challenge their privilege in the future. T. is not himself accepting the validity of the claim but takes the view, "let one of my successors find the time to assess their claim". If P.'s enquiry had been handled by a "civil servant", he would surely have read the memorandum and produced a recommendation about the claim.

the kind of reasons they had for wishing it to be seen. This language does indicate that T. was sceptical about the validity of the claim (Burton, cited on 47,1), but that he did not want to spend time pursuing the point.

48,2

they should now know. P. could supply the Apameans with a copy of T.'s letter for use as a precedent in any future dispute about the issue: in Hadrian's reign a proconsul of Asia, Avidius Quietus, sent the city of Aezani in Asia a copy of a Latin epistle from Hadrian to Quietus about land rights (Smallwood, no. 454b). T. may have composed his answer with this possibility in mind.

without prejudice to the privileges which they now possess. Literally, "the privileges being safe (or undamaged)", a common usage in Latin legal language (*OLD, salvus* 8b). Since Roman administration operated very much on the basis of precedents, it was dangerous to allow even one exception to a "custom", so the Apameans had perhaps been angling for just this guarantee.

Epistles 49-50

P. consults T. about the propriety of moving a temple to a new site, and is reassured by T.

Epistle 49
Written between 3 and 28 Jan., 111; possibly from Nicomedia.
49,1
Before my arrival. P. needs to explain that the new forum is a project already in progress, since he was apparently expected to get T.'s consent for any new building (23,1 n.)
the Great Mother. Called the Mother of the Gods by T. (50). The name by which she was most commonly known in the Roman world was Cybele. The original centre of this cult was western Anatolia, but it spread very widely in the Greek and Roman world, and an official cult had been instituted at Rome during the crisis of the Second Punic War (Livy 29,11). See J. Ferguson, *The Religions of the Roman Empire*, pp.26–31.
49,2
Any foundation charter. P. was thinking in terms of Roman religious law (not only was he an augur (Introd. IVB), but he had himself paid for a temple near one of his estates: IV,1,5–6; X,8,2). When a new temple was founded, a written charter (the *lex dicta*) regulated its future administration, and elaborate rituals would be required to alter its provisions.

Epistle 50
land in an foreign state is incapable . . of consecration . . under our law. This exemplifies the Roman view that *religio*, i.e. the cult of supernatural powers, was a matter of the inherited traditions of different peoples: the Roman people had their own ancestral laws, regulating their relations with their own national deities, but other peoples could be expected to have their quite different traditions and Roman sacred law only applied within the territory of the Roman state. Veyne, 745–6, pointed out that at Magnesia on the Maeander in the province of Asia a simple resolution of the Council and People was enough to sanction the transfer of the shrine of Artemis to a new site (W. Dittenberger, *Sylloge Inscriptionum Graecarum* 695, ll.10–23).

Epistle 51
P. thanks T. for transferring a relative of his mother-in-law's to BP. Written not long before 28 Jan., 111.
51,1
mother-in-law. This must be Pompeia Celerina, mother of P.'s former wife, since his current wife Calpurnia's closest living female relative was an aunt (SW, 92; 633; see 120,2n.).
Caelius Clemens. There is no evidence to show what his post was, but, if he was a young man on his way up, it is likely to have been an equestrian officer's post, in command of one of the auxiliary units in the province. "Transferring" implies he had already been holding such a post in another province. There is no surviving letter of application for this favour: P. may have raised it with T. in person before leaving Rome (see 94, 3 n).
51,2
I also comprehend profoundly the scope of your kindness etc. As 26 also shows, P. thought much more elaborate language appropriate for requesting and acknowledging personal favours from T. than for official reports. See Saller's work cited in 26 n.

Epistles 52-3
P. reports the renewal of the oath of loyalty by the soldiers and the provincials on the anniversary of T.s accession; T. acknowledges the report.

Epistle 52

Written on or soon after 28 Jan., 111, probably from Nicomedia (see 35).

The day on which you saved the empire. January 28, 98 was the probable date of the death of Nerva (SW,558), who had adopted T. as his son a few months earlier. Despite this relationship between the two emperors, the official line of the new régime, expressed in Pliny's *Panegyric*, was that T.'s accession had saved the empire from civil war which might have resulted from indiscipline among the soldiers after Domitian's murder (R. Syme, *Tacitus*, Vol.1, p. 12).

praying to the gods. See 35 n.

the oath. This oath of personal loyalty to the emperor, taken by the whole population of the empire, civilians as well as soldiers, at the accession of a new emperor, and apparently renewed annually on the anniversary of the accession, is quite distinct from the soldier's military oath taken on enlistment and renewed on January 3rd (29,2 n.). The former originated in the oath of loyalty to the future Augustus taken in 32 B.C., before his war with Antony, by the people of Italy and the western provinces, allegedly on their own initiative; this was subsequently extended to the inhabitants of provinces controlled by Antony in 32, and to provinces annexed later. See P.A. Brunt and J.M. Moore, *Res Gestae Divi Augusti*, 67–8 (with a translation of one of several inscribed texts of this oath).

fellow-soldiers. See 20 n.

the provincials. Possibly the members of the "Council" of Bithynia (36 n.).

Epistles 54–5

P. suggests finding borrowers for city funds by lowering the rate of interest and coercing city councillors; T. accepts the former proposal but rejects the latter, with some asperity.

Epistle 54

Written between 28 Jan. and 18 Sept., 111.

54,1

Moneys ... are still being recovered. See 17A,3; 17B,2; 23,2, for the process at Prusa; P. has presumably been doing the same in the other cities he has visited.

idle. I.e. not yielding revenue from rents or interest payments (see below).

no opportunity ... of buying estates. In the ancient world, in an economy with no stock exchanges or investment banks etc, land was the main source of 'investment income'. Ownership of land also conferred social status and political 'weight' in one's own city, so large estates would usually pass by inheritance, and large landowners would be reluctant to alienate their land (M.I. Finley, *The Ancient Economy*, chap.4; but see also J. Crook and E. Rawson in M.I. Finley (ed), *Studies in Roman Property*, chaps.4–5).

men .. willing to become debtors to the community. Loans to private individuals were the second main source of "investment income", not only for public corporations such as cities, but also for wealthy individuals such as P. himself, who in a private letter had said, " I am almost wholly in land, but I do have some money out on loan" (III,19,8; see M.I. Finley, *The Ancient Economy*, 115 and 203 n.56 on this passage)

at twelve asses. I.e., at an interest rate of 12% a year. P. here calculates an annual interest rate as is done at the present day, although in antiquity it was usually the monthly rate which was quoted (which in this case would have been plain *assibus*). SW,635, lists evidence for legal interest rates of between 5 and 12% a year in this period (see also R.P. Duncan-Jones: *The Economy of the Roman Empire*, 132f.)

the rate at which they borrow from private persons. Potential borrowers might prefer raising loans from private persons to raising them from the cities: see 55,2 and SW, 635.

54,2

the rate of interest should be lowered. Since this appears merely to have been the "going rate" in the province, and P. mentions no rule that city funds could not be lent below the "going rate", P. could surely have taken this decision on his own initiative; it is his "last resort" proposal which really led him to consult the emperor.

the money should be allocated among the decurions. As P. admits, this will involve coercing ("they may be unwilling and refuse") city councillors ("decurions" was the term used for members of city councils in Italy and the western provinces) into borrowing money for which they might have no need or use (as T. points out in his reply): in effect it would impose a kind of annual tax upon them. This would indeed have been a drastic novelty, when it is far from certain whether qualified persons were obliged to become councillors at all, and whether all councillors had to pay an entrance fee (see 112–113 nn.).

they provide their community with proper security. The jurist Ulpian was to lay it down that the governor of a province "ought to ensure that civic funds are not lent without suitable pledges" (D 22,1,33,1).

Epistle 55

I myself also see no other remedy. An emphatically personal admission by T. and a fairly polite expression of agreement with P.'s first proposal.

not in accordance with the justice of our age. An equally emphatic and personal rejection of the second proposal, with an implied rebuke to P. for even considering it: T. uses very similar language in 97,2 when criticising P. for taking notice of anonymous denunciations. "Our age" is specifically "my régime", which from its beginning had been presented as a contrast to the alleged tyranny of Domitian (as in P.'s *Panegyric*). P.'s proposal is classed as the kind of thing Domitian might have done. For assessing the attitude of the Roman imperial administration to the obligations of the governing classes of the cities in this period, T.'s response is surely far more significant than P.'s proposal; as SW,636, argues, this is a very long way from the situation in the fourth century when the imperial government imposed heavy burdens on conscripted councillors (see Appendix).

Epistles 56–7

P. consults T. about what to do with men who were convicted by proconsuls but who are still living in the province: T. postpones judgment in one case, but in the other orders P. to impose a harsher sentence.

Epistle 56

Written between 28 Jan. and 18 Sept., 111.

56,1

I offer you my .. thanks. An even more elaborate apology for troubling T. than 31,1; since T. had had to deal with seven enquiries in the month of January alone (37–50), P. may well have felt nervous about his reaction to even more.

56,2

his opponents. I.e., persons he was suing or being sued by before P.'s tribunal: this case, like that in sections 3–5 and Archippus' in 58, would have come to P.'s attention in the course of holding judicial assizes, and to prove that your adversaries were runaway convicts would be a most effective gambit.

(Publius) Servilius Calvus (see 57,1): clearly a recent proconsul of the province, not otherwise attested. "Most distinguished man" (*vir clarissimus*) was an informal title of respect for a senator (Talbert, 493). Eck (346) dates Calvus' term to 108/9.

banished for three years. The classical Roman jurists indicate that governors were free to sentence criminals to reside outside the province, but such "relegation" neither deprived those sentenced of civil rights nor confined them to one place (as "deportation" did): see SW,165 and Crook,272–3.

they asserted in rebuttal. I.e., before P.'s tribunal, when face to face with their accuser.

they had had their status restored. For convicted criminals to undergo "restitution" is not so much to be pardoned as to have the original sentence cancelled, so as to be restored to their civil rights, if the type of penalty had involved loss of these rights (which "relegation" in fact did not): D.48,23. Hence the clumsy paraphrase "to restore their status" is used to translate *restituere* in this context.

they read out his edict. Again before P. in court. See 31,4 n. on the source of the text of the edict.

56,3

laid down in your instructions. P. has a good reason to consult T. about the precise interpretation of a point on which T. had laid stress in his *mandata* . From P.'s emphatic reference to himself (that I should not restore), and the fact that Servilius Calvus' action in doing what P. was forbidden to do passes without any hostile comment in T.'s reply (57,1), we may reasonably deduce that this was a novel provision by T., at least as far as BP was concerned. T.'s ruling may have been inspired by the knowledge that such "restorations" had been frequent in the province and the suspicion that they had been the result of corruption or undue influence.

56,4

brought before me. I.e. charged before P.'s tribunal by private prosecutors.

the proconsul Iulius Bassus. His trial and conviction by the Senate in 103 for corruption while proconsul in BP is described in IV,9 (P. had been one of the defence counsel), but the part of the Senate's decree mentioned here is not referred to in that letter.

56,5

any others. Iulius Bassus will have convicted a number of people and P. reasonably suspected there would be others who had taken the Senate's vote in 103 as an occasion to disregard Bassus' judgments. Hence the need to consult T., because the decision in this case might well serve as a precedent.

I have appended. The texts of these documents were copied at the bottom of the letter from the copies in the possession of the litigant (see 22,1 and 31,4 nn.)

Epistle 57

57,1

After I have ascertained from Calvus. No later letter about this survives (see 38 n; 40,1). Either (a) the collection is incomplete or (b) T. never did write, whether he (i) forgot to pursue the matter or (ii) was satisfied with Calvus' reasons, but omitted to inform P. In the case of (b) one might expect P. to have raised the matter but P. may have been chary of prodding T. (see 56,1).

57,2

to be sent in chains to the Prefects of my Praetorian Guard. This would be in order for him to be kept in custody until T. himself had time to hear the case. T.'s motive was clearly anger at what he regarded as the man's "insubordination" (*contumacia*, an impudent disregard for established authority) and presumably the wish to make an example of him (reimposing the same penalty is not enough).

Epistles 58–60

P. consults T. about the philosopher Archippus who is accused of being an escaped convict, and forwards the pleas of Archippus and his accuser;   T. takes the more charitable view of Archippus' past.

Epistle 58

Written between 28 Jan. and 18 Sept., 111; possibly from Prusa.

58,1

While I was calling out the names of Jurors. *Iudices* ("judges" or "jurymen") were
  used in two capacities in Roman Italy: (a) in civil cases a single *iudex* was chosen by the
  parties or appointed by the praetor, usually to determine questions of fact after the questions of law had been defined in a formula drawn up by the praetor; (b) in criminal cases
  which could be brought under a number of statutes, a large panel of *iudices* decided the accused's guilt or innocence by a majority vote, the penalties being fixed by the statutes. In
  their own provinces governors had always had a wide discretion about how to exercise
  their jurisdiction. In civil cases a governor could either give judgment himself or "give a
  iudex". In this case, however, SW,640, argues that there was no need to keep a list of local *iudices* for civil cases (*citarem* implies a roll-call; see note on section 2), since any
  governor could find enough "single judges" among his own entourage. An inscribed text
  of an edict of Augustus from Cyrene has revealed the existence of juries which gave ver-
  dicts in criminal cases in the province of Cyrene (translated in R.K. Sherk, *Rome and the
  Greek East* no.102, edict 1). It is probable that the present text reveals the existence of a
  similar system in BP. On the functions of *iudices* see Crook, Chap. 3.

as I was about to begin the assizes. P.'s main civil duty as governor: Introd. IICii.
  SW,639, deduces that this took place at Prusa, Archippus' native city (81,1), which had
  been made an assize-centre by T. (Introd. III(C)i).

exemption as a philosopher. The jurist Ulpian wrote that "a man who does not have
  exemption is forced to serve as a *iudex* even against his will" (D 50,5,13,2). Such service,
  like *tutela* (the administration of an orphan's property) and *munera* (compulsory services
  owed to one's city), was an onerous burden imposed by the imperial government on the
  wealthier sections of the population, but one from which successive emperors granted
  immunity to whole categories of people (see Millar, 491–506). Archippus claimed that
  the category to which he belonged was entitled to this immunity. An edict of the emperor
  Vespasian had granted such immunity to physicians and teachers (Greek *paideutai*): part of
  the Greek text is preserved on an inscription (McCrum and Woodhead, *Documents of the
  Flavian Emperors*, no.458; trans. in Lewis and Reinhold, 2, p. 295). In the reigns of later
  emperors, "the question (of whether philosophers could claim immunity in the same way
  as teachers of grammar and rhetoric) remained a disputed area of case-law, in which immunity could be asserted or denied" (Millar, *JRS* 1983, 78; see also V. Nutton, *JRS*. 1971,
  52f.) But in this case P. shows no sign of any doubt that Archippus would have been entitled to exemption.

58,2

from the ranks of Jurymen. *Numerus* ("number") was used to refer to the whole membership of a military unit (see 29,2 above), and, by extension, to that of any distinct body or
  group of people (see *OLD numerus* 5a,6). Its use here implies that a permanent register of
  men qualified for service as *iudices* was kept in BP, which resembled the five *decuriae*
  (panels) at Rome, whose members were drawn from all Italy (see A.H.M. Jones, *The
  Criminal Courts of the Roman Republic and Principate*, 88–9).

by breaking out of his fetters. This must be meant literally, since Ulpian asserts that "being burdened with chains" was part of the punishment of men sent to the mines (as Archippus had been (sect.3): D 48,19,8,6).

58,3

A judgment was read out. The allegation was first dealt with as a formal accusation before P.'s tribunal, with the relevant document being entered in evidence by Archippus' accusers (see 31,4 n., and 56,2).

Velius Paullus. His term as proconsul must have preceded that of Lappius Maximus (if Archippus was being truthful in asserting that Domitian's letters were written after Velius' judgment), and Lappius' term preceded his first consulship in A.D.86 (see sect.6 below). Thus Archippus had been living as a respectable citizen at Prusa for at least 25 years, which makes it all the more plausible that he was being honest and that his accusers were just harassing him with vexatious charges. Eck (302) dates Velius' term to circa 79/80.

a charge of forgery. This was a crime for which a special jury-court had been set up at Rome under one of Sulla's statutes: it originally covered tampering with wills, but it had been extended to a wide variety of types of "misrepresentation" (see Crook,270).

condemned to the mines. The jurist Callistratus regarded this as the next worst penalty to death (D 48,19,28, praef.): like condemnation "to the games" (see 31,2,n.) it involved reduction to the status of a slave, and was a kind of delayed death sentence. See Millar, *Papers of the British School at Rome* 1984, 138–40.

he was unable to produce. See 31,5 n., for a possible innocent explanation.

his status had been restored. See 56,2 n.

a resolution of the people of Prusa. For the content, see 60,1.

58,4

which seemed to me to be worthy of your decision. There was no great question of principle to be decided; it was just a matter of Archippus' credibility. It must have been the fact that Archippus was evidently held in esteem by T. himself and had been honoured by being the recipient of epistles from T. which made P. hesitant about dealing with the charge himself.

I have appended ... the documents. On "appended", see 22,1 n. This is the only case where texts of such appended documents were included in the published text of Book X (contrast 22,56,79,114), but not all of those listed by P. were reproduced: Velius' judgment, Archippus' petition, the resolution of Prusa, and T.'s epistles are missing.

58,5

Terentius Maximus. This man must have been the equestrian procurator in charge of the imperial estates in BP, and not a proconsul, because he is instructed to use Domitian's own funds: see SW, 643.

Archippus ... has prevailed upon me. Archippus' petition (sect.3) must have begged for financial help, presumably on the grounds of his importance as a philosopher (for similar imperial gifts, see Millar, 496–8); he will have had to travel to Rome to deliver it in person (id., 474).

Prusa, his native city. For Archippus' connection with Prusa, see 81,1 (as well as the resolution cited in sect.3 above). For the arguments for adopting the correction *Prusam* (printed here but not in the *OCT*), see SW, 643, and 81,6n.

58,6

Lappius Maximus. In older texts he appears as L(ucius) Appius Maximus, but epigraphic evidence has revealed his full name, Aulus Bucius Lappius Maximus Norbanus (see SW, 643). This epistle must have been addressed to him as proconsul of BP, and therefore dates from before Lappius' first consulship in 86. On his later career, see *PIR*, Vol.5, L.84. It is probable that Domitian wrote to Lappius at the suggestion of Archippus, made in his petition, and not in response to any epistle from Lappius (see Millar, 323). Eck (307) dates his proconsulship to circa 83/84.

58,7

Edict of the deified Nerva. Since a copy of this edict was available in BP, it was certainly intended to be of universal application and copies must have been distributed for publication throughout the empire. On imperial edicts see IIGiii(a).

citizens. The Latin word *Quirites* was an archaic name used in addressing, face to face, Roman citizens assembled in a civilian capacity (Julius Caesar quelled a band of mutinous soldiers simply by addressing them as *Quirites* instead of *milites*: Suetonius, *Divus Iulius* 70). Hence SW, 644, suggested that the text was "an extract, it seems, from a general statement of Nerva, issued to or even before an assembly of the Roman people". However, an edict by this date was essentially a written text with a heading in the form "Imperator Caesar Nerva Augustus edicit", and the first sentence of this text is a play on words echoing that heading: "Nerva says" was followed by, and contrasted with, "the happiness of the age says". Such a conceit would not have worked, had this been the first sentence of a speech addressed to the People, and hence had not been preceded by such a heading. The use of *Quirites* probably indicates that the edict had originally been composed for publication in Rome itself, although it must subsequently have circulated throughout the empire (see above).

58,8

the reputation of him who conferred them. A reference to Domitian, whose murder had been followed by the destruction of statues and arches in his honour (Dio Cassius 68,1,1) and a vote of the Senate to erase all records of his name (Suetonius, *Domitianus* 23,1). The Senate's resolutions must have led to "such widespread uncertainty about the validity of his (Domitian's) measures that Nerva felt compelled to issue reassurances" (Talbert, 357–8).

58,9

whether as an individual or as a member of a community. The two adverbs *privatim* and *publice* are used in this sense to distinguish between dealing with people as private individuals and as members of communities: e.g. by Tacitus, when describing Agricola's efforts to encourage the Britons to live in towns ("he exhorted them as individuals, he helped them as communities"; *hortari privatim, adiuvare publice*; see Tacitus, *Agricola* 21,1, with the note in Ogilvie and Richmond's edition, p. 222).   SW,644, appears to interpret the adverbs as describing two aspects of the emperor's activity: "personal gifts .. and favours .. involving the rights of the Roman state" (see Radice's translation, "any public or private benefactions"). But any attempt to distinguish between personal and official acts of an emperor would be highly unreal.

Let these favours be confirmed and secure. Suetonius records of Titus that "whereas all the emperors hitherto, following the precedent of Tiberius, had not held favours conferred by earlier emperors to be valid unless they themselves had also granted the same favours to the same persons, he was the first emperor to confirm all earlier grants in one edict and to prevent applications being made to himself" (Suetonius, *Divus Titus* 8,1). Domitian at his accession followed his brother's example (Dio Cassius 67,2,1), so Nerva, who presented his own régime as such an improvement on Domitian's, could hardly have done less. It is reasonable to assume that T. and his successors also followed this precedent.

58,10

Epistle of the same person to Tullius Iustus. Iustus, who is not otherwise known, is more likely to have been proconsul than procurator of BP in 96/7 or 97/8, (see Eck 327, n.184), and must have written to ask Nerva whether to treat as a binding precedent some decision contained in an epistle of Domitian (his doubts being aroused by the Senate's resolutions: see above).

Epistle 59

the memorandum which he has given me. The same word, *libellus*, has been translated as "memorandum" in this letter and the next, but as "petition" in 58,3. Archippus' *libellus* addressed to Domitian contained requests (*preces*) and was probably answered by an imperial subscript (cf.106–107), whereas the *libelli* in these letters were statements of their respective cases by the two parties to a dispute (cf. that of Apamea, 47,2, with n.), and did not evoke imperial subscripts from T.

I have attached to these epistles. Being original texts, these were "attached", not "appended" (unlike those of 58): see 22,1 n. The plural "epistles" indicates that P.'s courier has not yet set off to take 58 to Rome. Had P. not given Archippus and his adversary Furia (see 60,2) this access to the "imperial post", they would have had to go to Rome if they wanted to present their cases directly to T. (see 43,2 and 45,1 nn.).

Epistle 60

60,1

the status Archippus was in. I.e.,a convict and a slave (see 58,3,n.). T. does not propose consulting Velius Paulus (as he did Servilius Calvus: 57,1): perhaps Velius was dead.

it is more in accordance with my character to believe. An emphatic assertion of the wholly personal nature of the decision, which must be T.'s own work. He presumably means that it is his nature to prefer to run the risk of being duped by a crook rather than be ungenerous or risk injuring an innocent man.

Epistles 61–2

P. lists various methods of obviating the risk (raised by T. in 42) that P.'s scheme for linking the lake to the sea (41) would simply result in draining the lake dry, and urges T. to carry out his promise (in 42) to send a surveyor out from Rome. T. commends P.'s efforts and tells him to choose a scheme himself, but implicitly retracts his promise to send a surveyor.

Epistle 61

Written, probably from Nicomedia (in sect. 1, P. describes himself as "being on the spot"), between 29 Jan. and 18 Sept., 111 (SW,646, argues that "the placing of the letter suggests an interval of not many months", after the original exchange on the subject in Jan.: 41–42).

61,1

You are indeed most far-sighted. P. is using flattery, as well as continuing his effort of 41 to engage T.'s well-known interest in engineering projects, in order to try and get a surveyor sent out from Rome (see sect.5).

61,2

easy to transport to the river ... across the very narrow strip of land. F.G. Moore (*American Journal of Archaeology* 54, 1950, 97) suggested that P. had in mind a slipway down which loads "could be lowered or rolled down to boats on the river".

61,4

by means of sluice-gates. Passages in Ammianus Marcellinus (24,1,11; 3,10; 6,2) and Rutilius Namatianus (1,481) show that these *catarractae* were gates set in stone weirs: they were opened by being raised like a portcullis. The passage of boats up and down a descent such as that described by P. appears to require the use of pound locks with gates at either end (the same applies to a canal between the rivers Saône and Moselle in Gaul, which was planned in Claudius' reign: see Tacitus *Annals* 13,53),   as is argued by Moore, *art.cit.*, and by K.D. White, *Greek and Roman Technology*, p. 112. But there is no other clear evidence of the use of pound-locks in antiquity, so SW,647, argues that P.'s sluice-gates were intended to serve as single (or stanch) locks in weirs. Since neither P.'s canal nor the one planned in Gaul was actually built, the debate cannot be resolved. For a discussion of the evidence by a historian of technology, see N.A.F. Smith, in *Transactions of the Newcomen Society* 49, 1977, 75–86.

61,5

surveyor. Here, as in 41–2, used to translate *librator* and not *mensor*. See 41,3 n.

whom you certainly should send out, as you promise. To remind T. of his under-taking and to try to induce him to keep to it must have been P.'s main purpose in writing this epistle.

Calpurnius Macer. See 42 n.

Epistle 62

It is evident etc. The flattery of the first sentence may be intended to soften the blow which is coming in the third.

and those provinces of yours are not lacking in these experts. With these words T. reverts to the unconvincing arguments with which he had justified his rejection of P.'s requests in 18,3 and in 40,3, and by implication T. retracts his promise made in 42. After this failure, after four attempts, to wheedle a surveyor out of T., P. seems to have given up.

Epistles 63–4

P. informs T. about a message he has received from an imperial freedman and that he is sending on to T. the couriers sent to him both by the freed-man and by the king of the Bosporus.

Epistle 63

Written between 28 Jan. and 18 Sept., 111, from Nicaea (see 67,1).

Your freedman Lycormas. Speculation about his function, his whereabouts and his rela-tionship with the king of the Bosporus, is pointless because of lack of information (see B. Levick, *Greece & Rome*, 1979, 124–5).

any embassy which might have come from the Bosporus. The Bosporus was a kingdom in the southern Crimea and in the territory to the east of it across the Straits of Kerch, and had been a "satellite" of Rome since 14 B.C. (see *Cambridge Ancient History* X, 265f, 775f.).

to the city where I am myself staying. Nicaea, as 67,1 shows.

King Sauromates. Tiberius Iulius Sauromates was king of the Bosporus from A.D. 92–3 to 124: his links with the province of BP are revealed by an inscription put up in his honour at his capital of Panticapaeum by the colony of Sinope, in which he is described as "most outstanding friend of the Roman emperor and people" (*ILS* 851). See *PIR* Vol.IV, I.550.

Epistle 64

King Sauromates has written. It is convincingly sugested by Hardy, 172, and SW, 650, that this letter was brought to P. by another letter-carrier, who had been sent off later than the one who was taking the king's epistles to T.: presumably the king has got wind of Lycormas' wish to intercept his messenger.

I have assisted with a pass. On the pass, see 45–46 nn. Here, as in 120, P. writes to notify T. when he issues such a pass to a person to whom he was not strictly entitled to is-sue one (because he was not P.'s own letter-carrier).

Epistles 65–6

P. consults T. about the status of persons who were freeborn, but reared as slaves by those who rescued them when they were put out to die as infants, and T. rules that in BP such people do not have to pay for the costs of their upbringing as a condition of recovering their free status.

Epistle 65

Written between 28 Jan. and 18 Sept., 111, probably from Nicaea (see 67,1).

65,1

one which affects the whole province. I.e., not just the city he was visiting (perhaps Nicaea), where some specific case must have been brought before P. as judge. P.'s enquiries must have led him to the conclusion that the issue was likely to be raised elsewhere and mentions this fact to justify consulting T.

the status and the costs of rearing of those whom they call "foster-children" SW.,650, notes that P. does not frame a specific question for T. to answer, but it must have been clear from this rubric that P. was asking whether he was entitled to recognise these persons as being of free status (*condicio*) even if they could not, or would not, compensate those who had paid the costs of their upbringing (*alimenta*). "Foster-children" is a translation of a Greek word used by P. (*threptous*), a word derived from the Greek verb "to nurse" or "to rear". The term occurs in Greek inscriptions from Asia Minor to refer to at least three different kinds of status (see B.Levick and S.Mitchell, *Monumenta Asiae Minoris Antiqua*, Vol IX, p. lxiv). P. is using it here to refer to a single category of persons, which is clearly defined in T.'s reply: "people who were freeborn (i.e children of free parents), put out (to die of exposure), rescued and reared as slaves" (66,1).

The exposure of newborn infants was a very common method of limiting the size of families in the Greek and Roman world: classical authors were surprised by nations which disapproved of the practice and reared all children, such as the Egyptians (Strabo 17,824), the Jews (Tacitus, *Historiae* 5,5) or the Germans (Tacitus, *Germania* 19,5); a letter from a Greek in Egypt to his wife in 1 B.C., includes, as a remark in passing, a now notorious sentence, "if you do give birth, if it is male, let it live, if it is female, cast it out" (*Select Papyri* (Loeb) I, no.105,8–10). W.V. Harris has shown that some of these infants were rescued before they died of exposure and were brought up as slaves, and that this was one of the main sources of new slaves from the first century A.D. onwards (see J.H. d'Arms and E.C. Kopff (eds), *The Seaborne Commerce of Ancient Rome* (=Memoirs of the American Academy at Rome 36), 123). Roman law held that in principle they retained their status as freeborn persons, but it must have been very unlikely that those who had been shipped far from their place of birth would discover, let alone be able to prove in court, the truth about their origin. The puzzling question of how a considerable number of these people were able to uphold such claims has been solved by Veyne's demonstration that exposure was a cover for one peasant family with surplus children to pass them on to another family which needed additional labour (P. Veyne (ed), *A History of Private Life*, Vol 1,9–11; and, with J. Ramin, in *Historia* 30, 1981,475–8). In such cases the parents or other relatives would be able to demonstrate to a judge that the supposed slaves were freeborn: one must assume that a case of this kind had come before P.'s tribunal. On the whole topic of the abandonment of children, from late Antiquity to the Renaissance, see John Boswell, *The Kindness of Strangers* (Allen Lane, 1989).

65,2

Having heard decisions of emperors on this matter read to me. On imperial "constitutions" see Introd. II(G)iii. The ones quoted in this case, by one of the parties to the suit before P., must have included those listed by P. and referred to by T. below. Since the latter apparently required the payment of the costs of rearing the children who have been exposed,   it must have been counsel for the people who had reared the "foster-children" who quoted them as precedents.

any local rule or any general one. It was in fact rare for emperors to issue general rules which were intended to be applied throughout the empire (see Millar, 252–7).

satisfied with precedents. It is not clear whether P. is referring only to these imperial decisions, or also to judgments made in individual cases by proconsuls of BP.

65,3

An edict relating to Achaia. This would be an example of an imperial edict of local, not general, application.   The Latin text printed here differs from the *OCT* in printing *Achaiam*, instead of *Andaniam*. Avantius and Aldus both printed *Anniam*, which must be wrong, because this is not a place-name but the feminine form of a Roman clan name. The correction *Andaniam* (involving only the insertion of the letters DA) was favoured by SW,652, because there was a shrine of the goddess Demeter at Andania, in the territory of Messene, in the province of Achaia, which had a right of sanctuary "and may have sheltered a community of *threptoi*". However, he adduces no evidence for the existence of such a community. Since imperial edicts of local application usually concerned whole provinces or groups of provinces, one would expect to find the name of a province here; and, since other documents read out to P. concerned communities in the province of Achaia, Mommsen's emendation, *Achaiam* (which involves replacing NN with CHA) is to be preferred to Hardy's *Asiam* (see Williams, *ZPE* 17,48,n.29).

of the deified Titus to the same people and to the Achaeans. These would be two separate epistles to two communities in the province of Achaia. Titus' second epistle was   addressed to the community in the northern Peloponnese officially named "The Achaeans", which was the rump of the much larger federal republic defeated and dismembered by Rome in 146 B.C., and which had given its name to the entire province.

the proconsuls Avidius Nigrinus and Armenius Brocchus. Nigrinus had a brother (Quietus), who became consul in 93, and a more famous son, who was consul in 110 and executed at Hadrian's orders after his accession (*PIR*.A.1407–10). Armenius Brocchus is not otherwise known. As SW,652, pointed out, T. refers to the provinces (plural) about which Domitian responded to these two proconsuls (66,2); so it seems likely that the two men served in two different provinces. One of these is likely to have been Achaia.

inadequately corrected. To "correct" was to check an MS for slips of the pen, presumably in this case against the originals from which the copies derived: see IV, 26,1 "you ask me to see to it that the copies of my little books which you have acquired are read through and corrected (*emendandos*)": see *OLD, emendare* (2).

of doubtful authenticity. P. commented that the edict "was said" to be Augustus': presumably its age (at least 50 years older than the other documents) aroused his suspicions. For examples of forged imperial constitutions, relating to the early Church, see T.D. Barnes, *JRS* 1968,38–9.

in your archives. *Scrinia* were in origin large wooden cases in which a large number of papyrus rolls could be stored . In the present context *scrinia* were the cases used to store what must have been the very extensive imperial registers (67,1n:), for which the imperial freedmen called *scriniarii* (*ILS* 1671,1675) were presumably responsible. P. appears to believe that they held file copies of all imperial edicts and epistles (see Millar, 261; 266).

Epistle   66

66,1

persons who, born free, have been put out to die and then rescued etc. T. spells out very precisely the category of persons he intends his ruling to apply to (in contrast to P.'s use of a single Greek word), presumably because T. was aware that his decision would be used as a precedent, and he wanted to leave no uncertainty about the people to whom it applied.

has often been discussed. This is presumably a reference to the documents which have been traced in the archives.

the registers of those who were emperors before me. A single "register" (*commentarius*) comprised a record of all imperial decisions of a specific type: the title of one such register is preserved on a bronze tablet from Banasa, "the register of those granted citizenship by the deified Augustus etc." (*ex commentario civitate donatorum divi Aug.* etc: *JRS* 1973, 86, line 22; there follow the names of all but two of the emperors down to the reigning ones, Marcus Aurelius and Commodus; see *ZPE* 17,64). Other such registers recorded grants of the privileges of a father of three (see 94–95 nn.), and of full citizen rights to Latins (see 104–105 nn.). From this reply it appears that there was a register with file copies of imperial epistles written to governors. If they were kept in the same format as the files of Roman officials in Egypt (see E.G. Turner, *Greek Papyri*, 138f), each register must have filled numerous papyrus rolls, each of great length (Millar, 262, regards the codex format (i.e that of a modern book) as a possible alternative to the roll).

which was laid down for all the provinces. See 65, 2n.

the right of free status ... who will be proved to be entitled to freedom. T. uses two legal terms associated with the procedure by which a free person held as a slave could get his free status recognised by a court. The abstract noun *adsertio* (right of free status) is related to *adsertor*, the legal term for the free person who acted in court on behalf of the "slave" whose status was in dispute, and the phrase *vindicare in libertatem* (to "reclaim for liberty", here rendered "proved to be entitled to freedom") was the legal term for the procedure followed by an *adsertor* (see Crook,58; and A. Berger, *Encyclopedic Dictionary of Roman Law*, s.v.).

nor should they have to buy back their actual freedom by paying for the costs of their rearing. The masters of the "foster-children" appear not to have contested the facts about their birth, but only to have maintained that they themselves ought to be compensated for paying for the upbringing of the "foster-children". The only earlier imperial rulings T.'s staff could find were those of Domitian concerning a number of provinces (including, presumably, Achaia), but not BP. T.'s sequence of thought is as follows: there is no precedent of universal application; admittedly (*sane*; concessive), there are rulings by Domitian which perhaps should be respected; however (*sed*) BP was not one of the provinces he dealt with; and for that reason (*et ideo*), i.e. because BP was not one of those provinces, T. thought the "foster-children" should not have to pay. The implication in T.'s words is that, if BP had been one of these provinces, T. would not have been able to permit this, and so Domitian must have insisted on such payments in the provinces he was concerned with. SW is therefore mistaken in holding that T. was extending and not reversing T.'s ruling (653).

Epistle 67

P. informs T. of his reasons for not detaining king Sauromates' ambassador, despite the request of T.'s freedman Lycormas.
Written between 28 Jan. and 18 Sept., 111, from Nicaea.

67,1

the ambassador of king Sauromates. The ambassador was presumably empowered to explain Sauromates' case to T. and to answer T.'s questions: it was the arrival of just such an embassy that Lycormas had anticipated (63).

67,2

I must bring these facts to your attention. 63, 64 and 67 were all just written "to keep T. informed", and called for no response from T. (hence the absence of any replies). P. found himself in rather a delicate position, not wishing to cause offence either by interfering with the representative of a client ruler or by disregarding a "request" from an imperial freedman who was evidently engaged in some confidential mission, and so P. was anxious to report and to explain to T. each step he took in the matter.

Epistles 68–9

P. asks T. whether provincials need to obtain the permission of the college of pontiffs before moving the remains of their relatives, and is told that he himself can grant or withold permission.

Epistle 68

Written between 28 Jan. and 18 Sept., 111.

to allow them, in accordance with the precedent set by the proconsuls, to transfer the remains of their relatives. Although under Roman law any site used for interring human remains became sacred (*locus religiosus:* Gaius 2,3–6), T. had declared that "land in an alien state is incapable of consecration under our law" (50; confirmed by the jurist Gaius, 2,7: "most authorities hold that on the soil of the provinces land does not become sacred"), and Dio of Prusa refers to a recent decision of the people of Nicomedia to move tombs (*Or.* 47,16). The proconsuls of BP must have been enforcing the Roman rules on tombs, but themselves exercising the jurisdiction which was exercised by the pontiffs in Italy (see SW, 655–6; Gaius in his commentary on the provincial edict discussed legal problems about moving tombs (D 11,7,7 and 9) and, in 2, 7, he added "however, even if it (provincial soil) is not sacred, it is treated as if it were sacred"; see also Caracalla's subscript quoted below).

because of the flooding of a river. Caracalla in a subscript to one Dionysia in 213 wrote: "if the remains of your son are being affected by the force of a river or some other legitimate and necessary reason is present, you can move them to another site at the discretion of the governor of the province" (Cod.Iust. 3,44,1).

in our city. Rome, not in the sense of a place, but of a state with its own laws (of which T. and P. are citizens), distinct from the cities of BP, each with its own laws.

it is the custom for application to be made to the college of pontiffs. The pontiffs (*pontifices*) were the members of the most prestigious of the four great priestly colleges. Latin inscriptions record that "remains" have been transported "by permission of the college of pontiffs" (V. Arangio-Ruiz, *Fontes iuris Romani*, Vol 3,no.83 e and f.), and Ulpian reports a debate among the jurists about whether the owner of a site was allowed to dig up bones or corpses brought on to his land by another person "without a resolution of the pontiffs or an order of the emperor" (D 11,7,8 praef.). See Crook, 133 ff, for the problems of Roman law about tombs.

I decided that I must consult you, sir, as supreme pontiff, about what course you would wish me to follow. The Pontifex Maximus had exercised great power as head of the state religion under the Republic, and the office had been monopolised by the emperors since Augustus took it over in 12 B.C.

Epistle 69

T. displays no sign of impatience with P.; as in 50 and in 71 he, like P., takes matters of religio *very seriously.*

Epistles 70–1

P. asks T. to give or to sell to the city of Prusa the site of a house once intended for a temple to Claudius; T. agrees, provided that no such temple was built.

Epistle 70

Written between 28 Jan. and 18 Sept., 111.

70,1

When I was investigating whereabouts in Prusa. This must have been during P.'s visit to Prusa referred to in 58: P. is not at this moment in Prusa, since in 67 he was on the point of leaving Nicaea for a distant part of the province and by 77 has reached Iuliopolis (which lay in the opposite direction from Nicaea to Prusa). P. has presumably been informed of the history of the site he chose since he left Prusa.

the bath-house for which you had given permission. See 23–4.

we shall ensure that a most foul blot etc. The stress on the utility and beauty of the project, like the details of P.'s plans in section 3, must have been included by P. to attract the interest and agreement of T. the great builder.

70,2

to Claudius Caesar. Presumably during Claudius' lifetime because (a) only a living person could inherit in a Roman will (see 75,2n.), (b) Claudius had not yet become *divus* as a god of the Roman state. Cults of living emperors were very common in Asia Minor: see S.R.F. Price, *Rituals and Power.*

in the courtyard. A *peristylium* was an internal court of a house which was surrrounded by a colonnade, but in house plans such as that of the "House of the Faun" at Pompeii (see L. Richardson, *Pompeii,* 115–7, 124–6) there was a garden surrounded by a colonnade as well as a courtyard. A "peristyle" on the scale of the former seems more appropriate as a site for a temple.

the city collected income from it. It is clear that the site became imperial property, as the request to T. in sect.3 shows, so how the city came to be collecting the rents from the tenants of the house is puzzling. It was presumably Polyaenus' intention that the city authorities should be responsible for the upkeep of the temple once it was built and use the rents to pay for this.

make a gift of it to the city or give orders for it to be sold. P. must presume that, if sold, it would be bought by the city out of the funds set aside for the new baths, but the first clause is a pretty clear hint to T. to make a gift to the city.

70,3

if you give your permission. SW (658, referring to 593) must be correct in taking this as a request for approval of a new building which was an addition to the original scheme for the bath-house which T. had already approved in 24.

the unoccupied ground. Since this is contrasted with "the actual place where the buildings stood" (i.e. the house), it should refer to the open space in the middle of the *peri-*

stylium. If this land was still unoccupied, this implies that the answer to T.'s query in 71 is that the temple had not been built.

with a recess. An *exedra* was a recess, often opening out of the back wall of a colonnade, and with stone seats. Vitruvius in his description of colonnades surrounding training-fields in the Greek world speaks of "spacious recesses, containing seats on which philosophers, rhetoricians and others who delight in learning can sit and argue" (*De Architectura* 5,11,2). See D.S. Robertson, *Handbook of Greek and Roman Architecture,* p. 384.

and dedicating them to you. There is no need to assume, as Hardy, 179, and SW, 658, do, that P. is using *consecrare* to mean that these buildings will be associated with the cult of T. as a god (by the addition of "an altar or shrine", suggests Hardy) because Veyne, 746, has shown that this is "a 'dedication' or a 'consecration' in the modern sense of the word": it was an old Hellenistic custom to dedicate monuments in honour of important persons, and such homage did not imply deification of the dedicatees.

70,4

I have sent you a copy of the will. Since this was a copy of a document, it was probably written out after P.'s own epistle: see 22, 1 n.

Epistle 71

We can use that ground. By implication T. agrees to make a gift of the site to Prusa.

its religious influence has filled the site. *Religio* in this sense is akin to taboo: once a temple had been built, the ground on which it stood had been taken over by supernatural power, and to put it to some other use might provoke that power. T.'s reply appears to be "in marked contrast with" his own assertion in 50 that "land in an alien state is incapable of consecration under our law" (Hardy, 180). But that assertion only meant that Roman rituals were not required to "deconsecrate" the site of a temple, not that such land could not be consecrated under the rules of local religious law: in that case (and in this, if a temple to Claudius had been put up), it was up to P. to establish what the local rules for deconsecration were and to follow them.

Epistles 72–3

P. enquires whether he is entitled as an imperial legate (and not a proconsul) to give judgment in cases of persons whose claim to be freeborn was contested, and is told to send T. a copy of the resolution of the Senate which had left him in this uncertainty.

Epistle 72

Written between 28 Jan. and 18 Sept., 111.

cases of children being acknowledged and having their freeborn status restored. To "acknowledge children" (*agnoscere liberos*) was the Latin legal phrase for the formal recognition of the parenthood of a child, and especially of paternity by a father (*OLD agnosco* (2a)). "Restoration of birth" (*restitutio natalium*) was the legal term for the recognition that a person who had been held as a slave was freeborn (*ingenuus*): a fictitious "restoration" was used by emperors to confer freeborn status on freed slaves whom they particularly wanted to honour (see Crook, 46–55). The cases to which P. refers appear to be ones in which a plaintiff claims that a slave of the defendant's is in fact the plaintiff's freeborn child, but the defendant denies this claim. In contrast, the masters of the "foster-children" in the cases to which P. referred in 65 did not deny that the persons concerned were freeborn children who had been exposed and reared as slaves. Presumably the same social circumstances that lay behind those cases explain how it was that parents were able to claim that other people's slaves were their own freeborn children (see Veyne cited in 65, 1n.). News of the cases which had come before P. at Nicaea had perhaps encouraged these further applications to his tribunal.

Minicius Rufus. L. Minicius Rufus was *consul ordinarius* as Domitian's colleague in 88, so his praetorian proconsulship in BP should fall at some date between Domitian's accession and 87 (*PIR*, Vol.5,M.627); it is dated to 82/83 by Eck (306).

the resolution of the Senate ... which talks only about those provinces which have proconsuls as governors. There is no other known case in which a resolution of the Senate applied only to the "public" provinces, and not to "imperial" provinces as well (see Millar, 342 and Talbert, 394).

the principle you wish me to follow. P. consults T. because he feels unhappy about exercising as an imperial legate a jurisdiction which, to his knowledge, only proconsuls have hitherto exercised (see 65,2 and 69 nn.). P. does not mention what alternative procedure would be available for the claimants, nor whether they would be expected to apply to the emperor.

Epistle 73

If you send me the resolution of the Senate. Hardy, 181, and SW, 660, are probably right to say that it would have been quicker for P. to send a copy than for T.'s clerks to hunt in the archives for a text which P. had not identified very clearly. Nevertheless, the fact that this procedure was the quicker one is a striking comment on the primitive character of the "system" used for filing senatorial legislation (see Talbert, 304–5).

I shall judge. There is no surviving letter in which T. informs P. of his decision.

Epistle 74

P. explains to T. why he is sending on to him a fugitive slave who claimed to have been a prisoner in Dacia and Parthia.
Written between 28 Jan. and 18 Sept., 111
74,1

Appuleius ... the soldier. He was presumably on secondment from one of the auxiliary units based in BP (see 20,2; 21,1–2 nn.); on his duties, see 77, 1n. His name is a well-attested Roman "clan-name" (*gentilicium*: e.g. Sextus Appuleius, husband of Augustus' half-sister), but SW, 661, rightly holds that "the single *nomen* of Appuleius shows that he was not a legionary soldier" (i.e., had he been a legionary, he would have been a Roman citizen, and P. would have used two names, e.g. Marcus Appuleius).

he was being kept under duress. Callidromus was a fugitive slave passing himself off as a free man (see Crook, 186–7, on the situation of such *fugitivi*), and it may be that his employers had discovered the truth and blackmailed him into working for nothing; on the other hand, they may simply have been keeping him locked up since, as managers of a bakery, they would have had the means of doing so: as early as the 2nd century B.C. the penalty for wicked slaves was despatch to a *pistrinum* (Plautus, *Pseudolus*, 494: see Millar, *Papers of the British School at Rome*, 1984, 143).

he had hired out his services. *Locatio operarum* was legal Latin for the act by which a free man hired himself out as a full-time employee (see Crook, 194–8).

had taken refuge at your statue. Since the deification of Julius (Dio Cassius 47,19,2) this practice had developed, which resembled seeking sanctuary in medieval Europe, and it was the only recourse for slaves who claimed intolerable treatment by their owners (see K. Hopkins, *Conquerors and Slaves*, 222–3).

before the magistrates. I.e., the elected executive officials of Nicomedia. After hearing his story they must have decided to turn him over to Appuleius, in order that the matter should be referred to P.

the slave of Laberius Maximus. Manius Laberius Maximus, consul in 89, was *legatus* of Lower Moesia by 25 October, 100, and was one of T.'s generals in the First Dacian War of 101–2, before holding a second consulship as T.'s colleague in 103; he was later exiled for alleged conspiracy (*PIR*, vol.5, L.9).

Susagus in Moesia. The very brief epitome of Dio Cassius' narrative of the First Dacian War (68,6,1–2; 8–9) makes no reference to such a raid nor is there any other record of a Dacian general of this name. Even if Callidromus invented the story of his capture and the raid (see below), he is likely to have used the name of a real person (as with Decibalus and Pacorus) as "corroborative detail to add verisimilitude to an otherwise bald and unconvincing narrative." An invasion of Moesia by Sarmatians may be depicted on Trajan's Column: see F. Lepper and S. Frere, *Trajan's Column*, 78–85.

Decibalus. King of the Dacians since the reign of Domitian; eventually he killed himself at the end of the Second Dacian War in 106 (see *JRS* 1970, 142 f.).

sent as a gift. If the story was true, this must have happened in the period between the two Dacian Wars, c.103–105.

Pacorus. King of Parthia c.80–c.110 (*Cambridge History of Iran*, Vol 3(i), pp.86–8; 99).

74,2

I decided that he should be sent to you. Presumably, if the story were true, T. could be expected to be interested in an additional source of information about the internal situation in Parthia (which he was to invade in 114). SW, 662–3, rightly pointed out how fishy this story was: (i) the length of Callidromus' "escape" route from Iran to Nicomedia; (ii) on the other hand, Nicomedia, as a large Greek town with close shipping links with Lower Moesia, would have been an obvious haven for a runaway slave who, to judge by his name, was a Greek; (iii) no precious metals were mined in the western parts of the Parthian Empire, from which the *glebula* of section 3 could have been brought. One could add that Callidromus could not produce the ring (section 2) which would have been the best piece of evidence for this story, and the *glebula* which he did produce could have been a lump of ore rather than a "nugget" (Radice's translation of *glebula*) of precious metal. Of course, a runaway slave had a strong incentive to fabricate such a story, if only to put off the evil hour of being sent back to his owner. P. gives no indication that he believes Callidromus: note his expressions, "when he had told the same story", "he claimed", "he said". Perhaps P. thought he might as well be sent to T. for interrogation, just in case his story were true, because he would have to be sent back to Italy to his owner, in any case (assuming that Laberius had not yet been exiled).

a likeness of Pacorus and the things which was wearing. I.e. a bust of the king wearing his regalia (including the upright tiara which was the Persian "crown").

74,3

from a Parthian mine. See note on section 1.

Epistles 75–6

P. informs T. about the will of a man from Pontus who left money either to put up buildings or to establish a quinquennial festival in T.'s honour, and asks T. which he would prefer. T. tells P. to choose for himself.

Epistle 75

Written between 28 Jan. and 18 Sept., 111.

75,1

Iulius Largus. His name shows that he was a Roman citizen, and he was presumably a native of either Heraclea or Tium (sect.2). He would have been obliged to draw up his will in Latin according to the rules of Roman law, whatever difficulties this might present in relation to local practices in Pontus (sect.2): in the next reign it was only as an act of special favour that T.'s widow Plotina prevailed upon Hadrian to permit the head of the school of Epicurean philosophy at Athens to make his will in Greek and name a non-Roman as his heir, and thus as the next head of the school (see Lewis and Reinhold, 2, p. 297).

75,2

to accept and enter upon his estate. Certain categories of heir could not legally refuse to accept an inheritance, but others were free to refuse; these latter, if they wanted to accept the inheritance, had to make a formal declaration within a time limit (see Crook, 124–5). Such a declaration was known as a *cretio* (from *cernere*, "to decide"), and a papyrus text of such a declaration of A.D. 170 includes the same Latin verbs as P. uses here: "*hereditatem ... adiisse crevisseque*" (V. Arangio-Ruiz, *Fontes iuris Romani*, Vol 3, no.60,4–7).

after fifty thousand sesterces have been set aside as a prior legacy. A "prior legacy" was a legal device by which a testator could set aside from the estate some specific sum which was to be paid to his heir or to one of the joint heirs before any liabilities had been deducted from the total (see SW, 330, on V,7,1, and Crook, 120). In this case Largus is leaving this sum to P. in return for his trouble in acting as the purely nominal heir to the estate (see next note).

to hand over all the residue to the cities of Heraclea and Tium. On these cities, see Introd.III(C)i. Under Roman law Largus could not bequeath his estate directly to these cities. To make a valid will a Roman testator had to institute an heir or joint-heirs to act as "universal successor(s)" to the property, although the testator could direct his heir(s) to pay out legacies to other people. Heirs had to be living persons, and *incertae personae*, such as unborn children or corporations (including cities), were excluded. Cities had in the past also been excluded from receiving legacies, but by Ulpian's day this had been changed: "legacies can be left to all cities under the rule of the Roman people; and this was brought in by the deified Nerva, subsequently more carefully laid down by the Senate at the proposal of Hadrian" (*Tituli ex corpore Ulpiani* 24,28). Possibly Largus did not know about Nerva's ruling or it applied only to municipalities (i.e., communities of Roman citizens): see SW, 663–4. At any rate, the device which Largus adopted was the *fideicommissum*, a request made by the testator to his heir(s), which originally had no legal force, although the law gave increasing protection to *fideicommissa* from the time of Augustus. On the Roman law of inheritance, see Crook, 118–128.

quinquennial competitions. In music, poetry and athletics: see 118, 1n.

to be known as the Trajanic. In the original Latin the nominative plural of the adjective formed from T.'s name is used (*Traiani*). Since in English neither "Trajanian" nor plain "Trajan" can be used as an adjective, the equivalent of the Greek adjective formed from T.'s name has been used in the translation.

Epistle 76

So choose for yourself. P.'s courteous enquiry to T. about his preference, whether for buildings or for competitions, leads to an equally courteous direction for P. to make the choice for himself.

in accordance with the circumstances of each place. I.e., which of the two things Heraclea or Tium needs the more. Similar language is used by T. in 109, 111 and 113.

Epistles 77–8

P. suggests to T. the establishment of a military post at Iuliopolis similar to one T. has set up at Byzantium, and T. rejects the proposal because it would create an inconvenient precedent.

Epistle 77

Written between 28 Jan. and 18 Sept., 111, perhaps from Iuliopolis.

77,1

You acted with the greatest forethought etc.   P. himself had made no such proposal and SW, 666, must be right in suggesting that Byzantium had made a direct request to T. (possibly before P. reached the province). P. could have learned about it on the spot (see 43) and he only refers to it here, with lavish praise for T.'s forethought, because it is a useful precedent to cite.

Calpurnius Macer.   See 42 n.

to send a legionary centurion to Byzantium.   This centurion, like the soldier Appuleius at Nicomedia (74,1), was being seconded to a *statio*, a military post with the function of supporting the local city magistrates in dealing with disturbances caused by travellers (see below): other functions of such *stationarii* recorded in later sources include hunting bandits (Tertullian, *Apology* 2,8) and recapturing runaway slaves (D 11,4,1,2). See R. MacMullen, *Soldier and Civilian in the later Roman Empire*, 55–9.

77,2

Their city, although it is very small, bears very heavy burdens.   For Iuliopolis' history see Introd. III(C)i. S. Mitchell in *Armies and Frontiers*, 141, points out that the city had a large, mountainous, forested and thinly-populated territory, and that the city authorities would be responsible for providing facilities for official travellers along the entire stretch of main road which passed through that territory (see 45–46 nn.). That road ran east from the Bosporus and Nicomedia to Iuliopolis and thence to Ancyra in Galatia: it was the main route linking both Italy and the Danube frontier with the eastern frontier.

and suffers injuries.   T. assumes (78,3) that this will be mainly at the hands of soldiers and others travelling on official business, and there is a large body of evidence which reveals abuse of official status and imperial "passes" (see 45–46 nn.).

at the edge of Bithynia.   Literally "in the head of" (*in capite*): i.e., on the most eastern section of the road before it crossed the frontier between Bithynia and Galatia.

78,1

The situation of the city of the Byzantines.   On the city's history, see Introd. IIICi. Its geographical situation would bring in travellers by sea passing between the Aegean and the Black Sea and by land between Europe and Asia; it lay at the eastern end of the *Via Egnatia*, the road taking travellers to and from Italy and the eastern provinces, and also on the main route between the Danube and eastern frontiers. In Claudius' reign Byzantium had protested to the Senate about its burdens and secured, with the emperor's support, a remission of tribute for 5 years: "they occupied a site which was convenient for generals and armies travelling by land and sea and for the transport of supplies", and the emperor explained that they were worn out from the wars in Thrace and the Bosporus (Tacitus, *Annals* 12,62–63; see Mitchell in *Armies and Frontiers*, 131).

that its magistrates should be supported.   City magistracies were commonly referred to as *honores*, and the abstract noun is used here to refer to the holders of the office (see *OLD honor*, 5b).

we shall burden ourselves with a precedent. This anxiety is consistent with T.'s concern not to divert too many soldiers away from their units, despite the pressures on him to do so (as here from P.): see 20 n. and 22 and 27.

78,2

I have such confidence in your conscientiousness. SW, 667, takes the use of the plural "we" in the preceding sentences as a sign of "the somewhat pompous chancellery manner of the Secretary", which he contrasts with "the crisp intervention of the Princeps on a point that interests him in section 3". However, if T. had himself begun by using the plural of the first person, he would have had to switch to the singular at this point, when he addressed himself directly to P. The earlier use of the plural can better be explained as a polite show of associating P. in his decisions, even if, in the case of Byzantium, P. had nothing to do with it.

78,3

in violation of my discipline. For *disciplina*, one of T.'s favourite words, cf.29,1 n. T. is mainly concerned with travellers on official business (and they were no doubt the main offenders: see 45–46 nn.). T. distinguishes first between lesser and graver offences: P. is directed to inflict summary punishment for the former. Secondly, T. distinguishes, in the case of graver offences, between soldiers, who are to be reported to their commanding officers, and civilian officials, who are to be reported to T. himself.

Persons on their way back to the city. "The city"(*urbs*) on its own refers to Rome. T. is presumably referring to civilians on official business.

Epistles 79–80

P. asks whether men under 30 may be enrolled in the city councils of the province, and is told by T. that such men may only be enrolled if they have already held a magistracy.

Epistle 79

Written between 28 Jan. and 18 Sept., 111, possibly from Nicomedia (section 4).

79,1

the Pompeian law. See Introd. II(G)i.

be a member of senate. In the Latin West the term *senatus* was usually reserved for the Roman Senate, and the council of a municipality was called *ordo* or, later, *curia* (section 3). In the Greek cities of BP before the *lex Pompeia* the members of the councils were subject to popular election every year (see Jones, *GC*, 165). This epistle shows that Pompeius remodelled these councils on the pattern of the Roman senate, so that councillors were enrolled for life by censors (section 3), and it was presumably he who first referred to these remodelled councils as "senates" in the Latin text of his law.

under thirty years of age. At the time of the Pompeian law 30 was still the minimum age for election to the quaestorship at Rome, although it was to be lowered to 25 by Augustus (see Talbert, 17–18); once again Pompeius was following the Roman pattern closely (cf. the same minimum age for municipal magistrates and decurions in Italy laid down by Julius Caesar: *ILS* 6085, 89f.).

those who had held a magistracy should be members of a senate. At Rome until 81 B.C. the censors had in principle had freedom of choice in enrolling new senators but in practice had given preference to men who had been elected to junior magistracies (see note on section 2) since the previous census; in 81 Sulla as dictator had laid down that henceforth the 20 men elected as quaestors each year should automatically become senators (see Jolowicz-Nicholas, 33). Pompeius again followed the most recent Roman rule.

79,2

an edict of the deified Augustus. This would have been an imperial edict of restricted application (see 65, 2 n.), restricted in fact to this one province. It is likely to have been issued in response to a request from the cities for an amendment of the Pompeian law (this is implied in *permisit*, "allowed" or "gave permission"). This request was presumably made because of difficulty in finding enough candidates who were over 29. Augustus himself at some point lowered the minimum age for the quaestorship at Rome from 30 to 25 (see Talbert, 17–18), and it could well be their knowledge of this change which prompted the provincials' request to him.

lesser magistrates. At Rome, from about 197 B.C. onwards, candidates for the consulship had already to have held the praetorship, and Sulla in 81 B.C. made it obligatory for candidates for the praetorship to have held the quaestorship (A.E. Astin, *The lex annalis before Sulla* (1958), and his article, "cursus honorum", in *Oxford Classical Dictionary*). The use of the word "lesser" here by P. indicates that Pompeius had introduced a similar ladder of promotion for candidates to city magistracies in BP; inscriptions reveal, however, that a variety of Greek titles were retained for their magistracies by different cities (see SW, 671).

79,3

enrolled in a senate by the censors. This shows that Pompeius introduced into the cities of BP an office alien to the Greek world. Under the Roman republic censors were elected every five years and usually took 18 months to fulfil their duties of registering the citizens, letting state contracts and revising the roll of the Senate (see C. Nicolet, *The World of the Citizen in Republican Rome*, chap 2). Inscriptions reveal the existence of an officer called *timetes* in Greek in some cities of BP, and this is the term used in Greek literary works to refer to Roman censors (Liddell-Scott-Jones, *Greek-English Lexicon*, timetes II); see SW, 672–3, with discussion of the officer called politographos (registrar of citizens) found at Prusias.

better that the sons of honourable men should be admitted to the senatehouse than that commoners should be. The name of the building where the city council met (*curia*) is used to refer to the council as an institution, the earliest example of what became a common usage (see *OLD curia* 4, 5b). SW, 673, points out that P. reports this as the opinion of those who consulted him, not his own. Neither he nor T. express any open disapproval of this prejudice. Among later emperors, Hadrian wrote a letter to the council of Ephesus supporting the application of a ship's captain (presumably a "commoner") for membership of the council (trans. in Lewis-Reinhold 2, p. 328), but Marcus Aurelius in an edict about the affairs of Athens exclaimed "would that there were an abundance of illustrious families for it to be possible for me even now to maintain our earlier ruling" (a ruling that only men who could prove three generations of free birth in their ancestry should enter the Areopagus: see C.P. Jones, *ZPE*, Vol.6, p. 179). This last rule suggests that an important element in the prejudice against commoners who were "new rich" may have been the suspicion or knowledge that most such men were descendants of freed slaves: see P. Garnsey, in *The Ancient Historian and his materials*, ed. B. Levick, 167–80.

79,4

When asked what my opinion was by the censors-elect. It is highly probable that these censors were elected every five years, as at Rome under the Republic (and like the *duoviri quinquennales* who performed the same functions in western municipalities), and it appears from the use of the plural here that the elections in all the cities took place about the same time (presumably as part of a cycle initiated by Pompeius). SW,673, suggests they were elected in the summer of P.'s second calendar year and would be taking up their duties the following January. P.'s words imply a joint approach by the censors from several cities: a meeting of the council of Bithynia at Nicomedia would provide an occasion for arranging such a joint approach. Presumably it was P.'s own mission as the special deputy of the emperor which led these censors to apply for approval of a practice in which their predecessors had engaged without interference from the proconsuls.

79,5
I have been led to consult you. P. expresses no opinion about the desirability of the wider extension of a lower age limit, but is certain that it would involve, not a mere modification of the Pompeian law, but a drastic change which only the emperor could sanction.
I have appended. See 22, 1 n.

Epistle 80
I agree with your construction. This is T.'s response to section 4 of P.'s letter.
However, I do not think. In response to section 5 T. again agrees with P. about what the present state of the law is, and, typically, shows no desire to change it. He makes no comment on the problem of finding enough candidates who were "honourable men" (79, 3).The whole letter spells out the issues with great precision, and repeats much of what P. said, perhaps because T. anticipated that copies of this epistle would be passed on to the censors by P. and that it would serve as a binding precedent (see 66, 1 n.).

Epistles 81–2
P. consults T. about a charge of treason brought against Dio of Prusa for burying his wife and son in a building containing T.'s statue, and is told by T. to dismiss such a charge.

Epistle 81
Written between 28 Jan. and 18 Sept., 111, from Nicaea (sect.3–4).
81,1
in my lodgings at Prusa by Olympus on the same day that I was intending to leave. For Prusa, see 17A–B, 23. P.'s "lodgings" (*hospitium*) would probably be a private house requisitioned for his use. P. stresses that he was not conducting assizes in public (*pro tribunali*: sect.2), but clearing up his business in private ready for departure, either to show T. his zeal in dealing with a matter involving T.'s dignity, or to indicate how ready he had been to give Eumolpus every latitude.
the magistrate Asclepiades. Prusa had a single chief magistrate known in Greek as the First Ruler (protos archon: see Jones, *Dio*, 4).
Coccelanus Dion. The Greek orator from Prusa, a large number of whose orations survive, commonly known by his nickname of "golden-mouthed", Dio "Chrysostom". At this date he would probably be in his fifties or sixties. For his career and writings see Jones, *Dio*.
a session of the council. P. uses the Greek term for the institution he called a senate in 79.
a building, the supervision of which he had undertaken. The building is described by P. in sect.7: a library next to a courtyard enclosed by colonnades. In a number of orations delivered at Prusa Dio refers to a building put up at Prusa partly at his expense, described as a colonnade (Greek *stoa*) in which one could promenade (Dio *Or.* 47, 17, 19–20). Jones, *Dio*, 114, holds that it is that stoa which is being referred to here. However, as SW points out, 676, the stoa described in the orations is more likely to have been a colonnaded street; furthermore,there is no reference in them to the library which is a central feature of the building described by P. In that case this was a quite different project, and Dio had been required to serve as its curator as a compulsory service to the city (see

17B, 2 n.). His request for the council to "take delivery" of the building and so discharge him from his duties as curator enabled his enemies in the aristocracy at Prusa to pursue their vendetta by charging him both with misappropriation of public funds and with treason against T.

acting as counsel for Flavius Archippus. On Archippus see 58–60. The verb adsistere, "to stand next to", is used here (as in VII, 3, 6) to mean "support in a lawsuit", i.e. act as a barrister.

81, 2

your statue had been placed in the same building as well as the bodies of persons who had been buried, the wife and son of Dion. The circumstances of the burial of Dio's wife and son are untangled by Veyne, 748–9. SW, 677, suggested that Pompeius would have enforced in BP the Roman ban on burials within the walls of cities (see Crook, 135), but Veyne pointed out that such burials were also forbidden in the Greek world, except in the case of heroes, city-founders and, occasionally, benefactors. Dio claimed the right to bury his wife and son in the building as a civic benefactor (in this same period, at Ephesus, the ex-consul Iulius Celsus was buried in the library put up in his memory by his son: see Ward-Perkins, 288–90). Dio's pretensions provoked the jealousy of other leading families, especially since the library was probably not the building for which Dio had helped to pay but one of which he had only been curator (see above). Eumolpus may have claimed that Dio was committing treason in burying them next to the emperor's statue.

in open court. Literally "on a platform": the tribunal was the raised platform on which Roman officials took their seats to conduct public business. Eumolpus asks for a formal hearing in public, not an informal enquiry by P. in his lodgings.

81, 4

some of them also about the case. It is tempting to detect irony in P.'s words here (some of these many arguments were actually relevant to the matter in hand), but SW, 678, is probably right: P. is just distinguishing arguments about the adjournment from ones about the substance of the case.

81, 5

a matter which involved a precedent. Presumably to treat the kind of action Dio had taken as treason would set the precedent, and SW, 678, suggests that the great public interest mentioned in section 8 was aroused by the prospect of many other such accusations being brought if Dio lost the argument.

81, 5

memoranda of their pleadings. See 47, 2 n; 59 n.

81, 6

at Prusa. The *OCT* prints *Prusiade*, but this should be emended to *Prusae* (see 58, 5 n): in sect.1 P. used *Prusae*, "at Prusa".

81, 8

especially in this kind of case. A case which involves an allegation of an insult to T. himself. P. does not venture to dismiss this element in the accusation on his own initiative, and he does not express his own opinion directly, but the unusually detailed narrative is clearly designed to convey the message that Eumolpus and Archippus with their delaying tactics (two requests for adjournments, one for a change of venue, and complete failure to deliver the promised memoranda) were, in P.'s view, just harassing Dio with vexatious accusations which they had no serious hope of being able to prove.

Epistle 82

82,1
**You could have been in no uncertainty ... since you were very well aware
....** A direct rebuke to P., not for troubling T. with an unimportant issue, but for implying that T. might be willing to treat Dio's act as one of treason. He gives the impression
of being offended because P.'s failure to dismiss the charge out of hand implies mistrust of
T.'s publicly declared attitude (*propositum meum*) on such matters. T.'s sensitivity is to be
explained in part by the propaganda put out after T.'s accession, as revealed in P.'s own
Panegyric (34–35; 42, 1): there were to be no more accusations of treason against the emperor based on trivial acts or words, such as there had been under Domitian.

Epistles 83–4

*P. passes on to T. a memorandum from Nicaea, and is instructed by T. to
investigate that city's claim to the goods of its citizens who die intestate.*

Epistle 83

Written not long before 18 Sept., 111 (see 88), from Nicaea.
**Having been requested by the people of Nicaea ... to pass on to you their
petition.** In this epistle P. is not himself asking for guidance but explaining in a cover-
ing note why he is sending on a document from Nicaea. It is not clear what prompted
Nicaea to make the request, but it can hardly have been any action taken by P. himself, for
in that case he would have informed T., as he did in the case of Apamea (47).
I did not think it right to refuse. P. is making rather an elaborate apology, probably
not so much for giving Nicaea access to the official "post" (he had done this for
Byzantium, 43), as for swelling the emperor's "in-tray": if governors were simply to pass
on every appeal from provincial communities, the emperor would soon be overwhelmed
(see Williams, *JRS* 1974, 97). Nicaea would normally have had to send a deputation to
Rome: the news of P.'s action at Byzantium may have deterred the city from doing so on
this occasion.
I have attached. See 22, 1 n.
memorandum. See 47, 2 n.

Epistle 84

to give a hearing to. *Vacare* means literally "to be empty", hence "to keep one's time
free" and so "to attend to" (see 81, 1, where P. was "attending to" public business); but the
rest of the epistle makes it clear that T. is ordering P. to hold a formal judicial hearing.
the right to claim the property of their fellow-citizens who die intestate.
Under Roman law there were elaborate rules about which relatives had first claim upon such
property (see Crook,118–119), and only if were no such heirs did the estate (as "empty
property", *bona vacantia*) escheat to the state (see Millar, 158–63). It seems incredible
that Augustus should have sanctioned a rule of the local law of Nicaea which excluded even
the children of a person who died intestate from any claim to their parent's property; so
SW, 680, wonders whether a qualifying phrase such as "who have no heirs" may have
dropped out of the text, or should be taken as implied. The latter hypothesis is the more
probable, since T. knew P. had read the memorandum and would know the details of the
dispute.
was conceded to them by the deified Augustus. As Millar points out, 397, "the
expression (viz."was conceded") makes perfectly clear that they (the Nicaeans) had taken
the initiative in requesting this privilege from the emperor" (see 79, 2 n.). What remains
unclear is at whose expense Nicaea acquired the privilege and against whom they were de-

fending it at this moment. The alternative possibilities are (a) the kindred of the intestate, probably only those whose relationship was a remote one (see above); (b) the Roman state. Since this was a privilege conceded to them by Augustus (rather than an existing rule of local Nicaean law confirmed by him), (b) appears to be the more probable. However, (b) also assumes that by the time of Augustus the general principle was already established that *bona vacantia* of provincial subjects as well as of Roman citizens escheated to the Roman treasury, and that provincial communities could only lay claim to such property as a special privilege. Such was the situation 300 years later when Diocletian in effect withdrew all such privileges claimed by individual cities (see Millar, 160). But one piece of evidence does indicate that by the middle of the first century A.D. the situation outlined above already prevailed: in the reign of Claudius the municipality of Volubilis in Mauretania obtained among a number of grants from the emperor "the goods of their fellow-citizens killed in the war who had no surviving heirs" (Smallwood, *Documents of Gaius Claudius and Nero*, no. 407b, ll.14–16; trans. Millar, 404).

all the persons involved in this same business. This phrase indicates that the dispute was between the city authorities and private individuals, not between the city and the agents of the Roman treasury (the latter are to act as P.'s assessors). If Augustus' grant included some phrase similar to Claudius' "who had no surviving heirs" (*quorum heredes non extabant*), the dispute could be about which relatives counted as "heirs" under Nicaea's law of intestate succession.

summon as your advisers the procurators. *Adhibere* is the technical term for the act of a Roman magistrate in empanelling advisers to sit with him in a judicial hearing (see VI, 11, 1;15, 3–4). P. would normally have drawn such advisers from among his own *comites* and subordinates, since the imperial procurators had their own separate sphere of activity. Why T. should order P. to empanel them in this case is unclear: perhaps to bring to bear their specialised knowledge of the law of escheat (see Millar, 162–3); in the same way Hadrian ordered a proconsul of Achaea to empanel surveyors when deciding a boundary dispute (Smallwood no.447, ll.2–5).

Virdius Gemellinus. See 27–28.

Epimachus my freedman. SW, 681, suggests that he has just replaced Maximus (27 and 85) as Virdius' senior assistant.

the arguments which are maintained on the opposite side. T. is aware that Nicaea's memorandum presents only one side of the case and is unwilling either to reach a decision without giving the city's opponents a chance to make their case or to put the latter to the expense of coming to Rome. Hence his commission to P. and the procurators. If it were the procurators who were contesting Nicaea's privileges, they would hardly be instructed to assess the merits of their own arguments.

Epistles 85–6 B

Three testimonials to the merits of imperial officials who have been serving in BP.

These three documents need to be distinguished from 26 and 87: the latter were written on behalf of men who were not serving in the province, but with whom P. had personal ties. Two of these three appear to be written on behalf of men whose period of service in BP had ended, to judge by the words "I send him on his way with my recommendation to you"(*prosequor*): **85 and 86A.** All three seem to be composed in a standard form, beginning with the name of the man concerned and ending with "in that good faith which I owe to you". These testimonials are one of the main pieces of evidence adduced to support the hypothesis that the emperor's secretary for correspondence (*ab epistulis*) kept files on all imperial appointees, that governors were required to submit reports on their subordinates every year for inclusion in these files, and that promotions were made on grounds of merit and based on the evidence in such files (see E. Birley, *Roman Britain and the Roman Army*, 142f; A.R. Birley,*Marcus Aurelius*, 162–3; H.G. Pflaum, *Les procurateurs équestres*, 198f.) However, very powerful criticisms of the view that appointments were made by emperors on what would be regarded in the modern world as grounds of objective merit have been advanced by R.P. Saller in *Personal Patronage under the Early Empire*, 94–111. The only evidence adduced for the existence of files on individuals, Statius, *Silvae* V, 1, 94–8, merely refers to the *ab epistulis'* job of informing junior officers of their appointments (see Saller, 105–6; and H.M. Cotton, *Chiron* 11,230). As for P.'s three testimonials, the standard formula at the end of 85, 86A and 86B does indeed suggest that governors regularly supplied their subordinates with letters of recommendation, but the adjectives used of the three men are banal and no attempt at critical evaluation is made. Saller points to a fatal flaw in SW's suggestion that "P. uses stock epithets, but qualifies or varies them so that T. can read between the lines" (681–2): this would involve T. having to compare new testimonials from P. with all the earlier ones from him filed in the archives. Saller is right to stress that it is in 87 (as in 26) that P. is really pressing T. to promote a man to whom he has a personal obligation; by contrast these three texts (even 86B) seem routine in tone, with P. just doing what was expected of him for men who just happened to have served in the same province as himself.

Epistle 85

Written not long before 18 Sept., 111
Maximus. See 27–28.
to send him on his way with my recommendation. *Prosequor* means literally "to accompany" or "attend upon"; hence SW deduces that Maximus had left his post and had been replaced by Epimachus (see 84n.).

Epistle 86A

Written not long before 18 Sept., 111.
Gavius Bassus. See 21–22 nn.
to send him on his way. If SW's interpretation is correct, he too was leaving BP.

Epistle 86B

Written not long before 18 Sept., 111. This text is printed as a continuation of 86A by Avantius and Aldus but the linked passage is meaningless. The formula "in that good faith etc." evidently marked the end of the testimonial for Gavius Bassus, and the beginning of another epistle, with the name of another official at its head, has been lost in the transmission of the text.
both as individuals and as communities. For the terms *privatim* and *publice* see 58,9 n. Of course only the civilians could testify collectively, "as communities".

Epistle 87

P. requests an appointment for the son of one of the advisers who accompanied him to BP. Written not long before 18 Sept., 111.
87,1
the former chief centurion. A *primipilaris* was a man who had formerly been *primus pilus* in a legion (just as a *consularis* was a man who had once been consul). Every legion had one centurion in command of each of its 60 centuries: the centurion of the first century of the first cohort was known as the "first javelin" (*primus pilus*), and was the senior centurion of the whole legion. Centurions promoted to this rank received a large enough

bonus on discharge to qualify as *equites*, and some of these *primipilares* were eventually appointed by the emperors to equestrian military and civil posts in their service (see B. Dobson in ANRW II (1), 392 ff., and in C. Nicolet (ed), *Recherches sur les structures sociales dans l'Antiquité classique*, 99f).

When I was a tribune and he a prefect. For P.'s service as a military tribune in Syria c.81/2 see Introd., IVB. Since Nymphidius had already finished his career as a centurion by 80, he must have been into his seventies by 110 (which explains P.'s phrase about making his claim on his retirement, sect.2). The post with the title *praefectus* which Nymphidius was most likely to have held after his retirement as a *primus pilus* was that of *praefectus castrorum legionis*. There was normally one such prefect to each legion, and he ranked third in seniority after the legion's *legatus* and the one *tribunus militum* out of six who was an aspiring senator (*laticlavius*). See B. Dobson, in ANRW II (1), 413–4, and G. Webster, *The Roman Imperial Army*, 117–8. It seems very probable that Nymphidius had been *praefectus castrorum* in the legion in which P. had served as *tribunus laticlavius*.

87,2

to help me with his advice in Bithynia. There is an interesting parallel to P.'s action: when the orator Fronto was preparing to take up the proconsulship of Asia, he informed Antoninus Pius that "I have called to my side also from Mauretania a man with the greatest affection for me and dear to me in his turn, Julius Senex, in order to avail myself not only of his loyalty and diligence but also of his military capacity for hunting down and suppressing bandits" (Fronto, Loeb edition, Vol.1, p. 236).

87,3

he has earned as prefect of a cohort the fullest commendation of those distinguished men Iulius Ferox and Fuscus Salinator. The younger Nymphidius was evidently qualified to start his career with equestrian status: the prefecture of a cohort of auxiliary infantry was the first of three military posts (*tres militiae*) normally held by equites, who often subsequently served the emperor as civilian procurators (see E. Birley, *Roman Britain and the Roman Army*, chap. 13). The "fullest commendation" was presumably expressed in testimonials similar to 85–86B. The two senators ("most distinguished men": see 56, 2 n.) are likely to have served in turn as consular legates of the province in which Lupus' cohort had been stationed. Tiberius Iulius Ferox had been consul c. A.D. 99 (mentioned as consul elect in II, 11, 5, and perhaps the recipient of VII, 13; see *PIR*, Vol.4, I no.306). Pedanius Fuscus was a much older man, consul before 86, and father of a pupil of P.'s who married a niece of Hadrian (see VII, 26, 1, with SW's n.).

Epistles 88–9

P. sends, and T. acknowledges, congratulations on T.'s birthday.

Epistle 88

Written on 18 Sept., 111.
On the celebration of the emperor's birthday, see 17A, n.

Epistle 89

*T. modestly changes P.'s reference to T.'s own merit (*virtus*) to an allusion to the prosperity of the Roman state.*

Epistles 90–1

P. asks for, and receives from T., permission to construct an aqueduct at Sinope.

Epistle 90
Written not long after 18 Sept., 111, probably from Sinope (the description of the ground implies autopsy): it appears that it is only now, at the beginning of his second year in the province, that P. is paying his first visit to Pontus.

90,1

Sinope: see Introd. III(C)ii

are short of water. See 38, 1 n. on the contrast between Italy and eastern cities in this matter; it even applies to a colony of Roman citizens.

whether it can take and support a structure. I.e. arches supporting a water channel: see 37,2–3 nn.; and, on problems of subsidence, 39, 2.

90,2

Money, collected under our supervision: see 17B,2; 23,2; and 39,5, for P.'s activity in calling in debts to the cities.

if you permit. For T.'s instruction that all new building projects in the province should be referred to him for approval, see 23,1 n.

Epistle 91
provided only that it can in fact carry the work through out of its own resources. P. had already given his assurance on this point but here as elsewhere T. still wants to emphasise his anxiety about civic improvidence (see 24 nn.; 40,2; 98).

Epistles 92–3
P. sends on to T. a memorandum from the free city of Amisus about its right to keep its dining-clubs, and T. makes a grudging acknowledgement of that right.

Epistle 92
Written between 18 Sept., 111 and 3 Jan., 112, from Amisus (see "in this city", below)

The free and allied city of the Amiseni. On Amisus and its status, see Introd. III(C)ii.

employs its own laws through the benefit of your generosity. Once the city had been described as "free", it appears tautologous to say that it used its own laws (see J. Reynolds, *Aphrodisias and Rome* no.8, ll.46–7, with n. on p. 82: the "freedom" of Aphrodisias is defined by the Senate as "using its own law and judgements"). SW, 687, argues that, since the Latin words *beneficium* and *indulgentia* were technical terms for specific grants by the emperor, P. must refer to some specific improvement in Amisus' status granted by T. himself. However, T. should not need to be reminded of a grant he himself had made and T.'s own response gives no indication that he had done any such thing. The sentence was probably intended to do no more than point out to T. the fact that Amisus was a free city, in flattering, courtly language: all existing privileges are enjoyed by cities through T.'s generosity since he has refrained from cancelling them (so, by implication, Hardy, 207).

I have appended. In fact, since this was an original document, it was "attached" (i.e., glued) to P.'s letter. T. has the correct term in his reply. See 22,1 n.

a memorandum. See 47,2 n.; 83 n.

concerning eranoi. The Greek word appears in the original in P.'s epistle, but is transliterated and given a Latin ending in T.'s. In classical Athens *eranoi* were clubs whose members paid subscriptions to provide communal meals, but *eranos* in the singular was also used to refer to a subscription collected by the friends of an individual in financial difficulties (Liddell-Scott-Jones, *Greek-English Lexicon, eranos* II). T. seems to believe that the ostensible aim of the *eranoi* of Amisus was to help the less well-off.

handed to me in this city. This phrase shows that P. was visiting Amisus (SW, 688, deduces that P. was empowered by T. to inspect the accounts even of a free city). P.'s presence is a little surprising in the light of evidence from the free city of Aphrodisias, in Asia: the emperor Commodus expressed some reservations about agreeing to a request from the Aphrodisians to allow the proconsul of Asia to visit the city, and under Alexander Severus a proconsul accepted an invitation to visit the city only "if no law of your city or resolution of the Senate or imperial edict or epistle prevents the proconsul from visiting your city" (see J. Reynolds, *Aphrodisias and Rome*, 120–2, 175–6).

what you think should be forbidden etc. The existence of any kind of club violated the ban included in P.'s edict at T.'s instruction (see 33–34 nn.; 96,7). It appears that Amisus had taken advantage of P.'s visit to claim exemption from the ban on the grounds that it was a free city, and, since P. did not have the authority to disregard either a free city's privileges or T.'s explicit instructions, he had to refer the issue to T. For the word order in the Latin, see 96, 1n.

Epistle 93

If the Amiseni, etc. As in 66 and 80, the precise issue is spelt out carefully, in anticipation of a copy being supplied by P. to the Amiseni and of their using it as a binding precedent.

we cannot stand in the way of their having one. Jones, *GC*, 132, cited T.'s words as evidence hat "the constitutional status of free cities ... was ... observed in so meticulously legal a spirit that it gradually came in practice to be restricted". He claimed that T. was insisting that any activity of which Rome disapproved had to be expressly allowed in a free city's constitution, if such activity was to continue. SW, 689, is right to say that Jones "presses the wording too hard", and the new evidence from Aphrodisias shows that the rights of free cities were carefully safeguarded by T.'s successors, despite what Jones claims (see above).

not on crowds and unlawful assemblies. As in 91 T. reverts to one of his fixed ideas about the cities of this province, this time to his belief that clubs of any sort would become a cover for political intrigue and planning mob violence (see 34 nn.). This leads him in his final sentence to emphasise for P.'s own benefit that his decision in this case should not lead P. to "soften"their policy elsewhere.

Epistles 94–95

P. applies to T. for a grant of the privileges of a parent of three children for Suetonius, and T. agrees to make such a grant.

Epistle 94

Written between 18 Sept., 111, and 3 Jan., 112, possibly from Amisus (see 92).
94,1
I have long since, sir, included .... among my friends. The Latin phrase means literally"brought into tent-sharing". The word *contubernium* originally referred to sharing a tent while on campaign, but here it is used metaphorically to refer to friendship: see the use of *contubernalis* to mean "friend" in I,2,5; 19,1 and 24,1 (where it is applied to Suetonius; see *OLD contubernalis* 2a). P. cannot be using the phrase in a more technical sense to refer to a recent recruitment of Suetonius to serve on his staff in BP because of the adverb "long since"(the word order in Latin makes it very unlikely that this adverb was in-

tended to be taken with "having admired"). See Syme *RP* III, 1339; A. Wallace-Hadrill, *Suetonius*, p. 5, n.6.

Suetonius Tranquillus. The author of biographies of twelve Caesars and of eminent teachers of grammar and rhetoric which are extant, as well as of a large number of lost works of antiquarian scholarship (for a most illuminating analysis, see A. Wallace-Hadrill, *Suetonius*, chaps.2–3). For his earlier relations with P. see I,18; I,24; III,8; V,10; IX,34. He subsequently held senior posts on the emperor's staff as an equestrian, the last of which was that of secretary for correspondence (*ab epistulis*); he was dismissed from this post by Hadrian, while the court was in Britain, after the empress Sabina complained of his impertinence (*Augustan History, Hadrian* 11,3; see Syme, *RP* III, 1340 f.).

now that I have had a closer insight. "Now", Latin *nunc*, is an emendation of the first printed texts, which have *hunc* ("him" or "this man"). This is syntactically superfluous, and an adverb of time provides an appropriate contrast to "long since" earlier in the sentence. If P. did write "now", he clearly meant that Suetonius was a member of his entourage in BP. It is very likely that this was the case: (i) it makes good sense of "a closer insight" (i.e. roughing it together in the provinces is a good test of character and friendship); (ii) it would have given Suetonius a strong claim to get P. to use his influence with T. (see 87 for a recent request on behalf of the son of a member of the entourage); (iii) that a cultured governor might well recruit companions of scholarly tastes (perhaps as much for company during their hours of leisure as for practical assistance), as well as men with military experience, is shown by Fronto's reference to the "most learned men" he has sent for from Alexandria to join him in Asia (Fronto, Loeb ed., Vol. 1, p. 237).

94,2

The rights of a parent of three children. The emperor Augustus had proposed one law (the *lex Iulia de maritandis ordinibus* of c.18 B.C.) and sponsored another (the *lex Papia Poppaea* of A.D. 9), which were intended to encourage Roman citizens, especially of the propertied classes, to produce more children. The legislation imposed disabilities upon the unmarried (*caelibes*) and the married but childless (*orbi*), especially in the matter of qualifying for inheritances or legacies from testators who were not agnatic kindred. It also offered privileges to parents: if they were senators, they could stand for election to magistracies below the minimum ages required by other laws. To qualify for the full range of benefits one needed to be the parent of three children. Emperors from Augustus onwards had granted these privileges en bloc to favoured individuals who did not technically qualify for them: the empress Livia and the two consuls who proposed the law of A.D. 9 were said to have received this privilege. P. himself had written to thank T. for the grant of the *ius* some years earlier (X, 2). See *Cambridge Ancient History* Vol. X, 448–55.

he earns the good opinion of his friends. In this context *iudicia* is a euphemism for *suprema iudicia*, "the final judgment", i.e. legacies left to one's friends in one's will as a testimony to their good qualities (see VII, 20, 7; *OLD iudicium* 10b). This was the more valued since it could be thought to be wholly disinterested: see A. Wallace-Hadrill, *Proceedings of the Cambridge Philolological Society* 1981, 67–78, who (p. 79, n.50) stresses P.'s remark in a letter to Tacitus (VII,20,6),"unless someone happens to be a very close friend of one or other of us, we receive the same legacies ... ", as evidence of the widespread practice of making numerous legacies as tokens of friendship. Suetonius was, perhaps, like Tacitus and P., because of his literary renown, being named in numerous wills but, as an *orbus*, was only permitted by the law to take half of the sums specified by the testators.

(he) has had rather an unfortunate experience of marriage. Either one long-lasting marriage or a succession of marriages had produced no children who survived; the latter was P.'s experience.

94,3

I should not be asking for it when not face to face with you. This indicates that etiquette required a senator to make such requests of the emperor in person rather than in writing. Such a rule would be necessary to keep the floodgates closed against an endless stream of written applications. This hypothesis is confirmed by the very small number of written requests made by P. to T. between 98 and his departure for BP: six in all (4; 6; 9; 12; 13; 14).

Epistle 95

how sparing I am in granting these favours. It would be wise for an emperor to stress this when agreeing to such a request, to deter the petitioner from taking the emperor's agreement as an encouragement to make further requests.

since I am in the practice of stating in the Senate itself that I have not exceeded the number etc. T. implies that as a senator P. should have especial reason to know of his attitude. The device of informing the Senate that he would limit himself to a fixed number of grants (presumably during a limited period such as a year) and in due course reporting that he had done so would serve two purposes: (i) to flatter the dignity of the Senate as a corporate body (T. was anxious to distinguish his régime from the hated Domitian's); (ii) to help the emperor to withstand requests for the privilege from senators as individuals, who could hardly be offended if turned down on the grounds that T. had to keep his promise to the Senate.

(I) have given orders for an entry to be made in my registers that I have given etc. On "registers" (*commentarii*) see 66,1 n. If Suetonius wanted written proof of his grant he would have had to obtain an authenticated copy of the entry in the particular register which listed all grants of this specific privilege. The text of such a copy of a grant of Roman citizenship was itself copied on a bronze tablet found at Banasa (see *JRS* 1973, p. 86) and this reveals the form of such an entry: the date and place of the grant, the names of the recipients, the names of those who had recommended them (perhaps P.'s name was recorded in this case), and "to these we have given Roman citizenship"; in this case it would have been some such statement as "to him I have given the rights of a father of three".

subject to that proviso which I have been in the habit of making. The grant on the Banasa ablet ended with what were evidently two standard limitations, "without prejudice to the rights of their tribe and without reduction in their taxes". One can only conjecture what the limitation was in this case. It could have been a simple time limit such as Galba had imposed (Suetonius, *Galba* 14,3), but another possible proviso would be that the grant would lapse on the death or divorce of Suetonius' present wife.

Epistles 96–7

P. reports to T. that he has executed Christians who were persistent confessors and suggests that apostates from Christianity should be pardoned; T. approves the procedures followed by P. and agrees that apostates should be pardoned.

This exchange of letters is the earliest surviving "gentile" (i.e. neither Christian nor Jewish) evidence about the Christian church, and has inspired a very large body of scholarship, only a small portion of which can be cited here. Behind the exchange there lies a historical problem which remains unsolved, and is probably insoluble for lack of evidence: how did Roman courts come to treat being a Christian as a crime to be punished by death? The evidence of the *Acts of the Apostles* shows that Christians were not being punished for this in the 40s and 50s A.D. At Rome in A.D. 64 (Tacitus, *Annals* 15, 44; Suetonius, *Nero* 16, 2) Nero had many Christians put to death, but the crime with which they were (falsely) charged was arson, because Nero needed scapegoats for the great fire of Rome in that year. The next reliable evidence comes from T.'s reign, when the punishment of Christians is established practice. One school of historians has maintained that, in Crook's words, "'the equation Christian = man to be punished' can only have been established by government directive" (Crook, 279). Hence it has been maintained that a resolution of the Senate or an emperor's edict must have explicitly outlawed Christianity (the favoured date being 64, in the aftermath of Nero's persecution). However, P. does not seem to have been aware of the existence of any such "general law", and, more important, T. does not refer him to such a regulation (contrast, for example, Ep.66). Hence the majority of recent historians, at least in the English-speaking world, have taken the view that Crook's "equation" was established by Roman judges and that the definition of the crime was built up in a body of "case-law". Provincial governors had very wide discretion to punish anyone whom they might choose to regard as "troublemakers" disturbing the peace of their provinces: when Christians were brought before governors less scrupulous than P. by their hostile pagan neighbours, and the Christians proved "uncooperative", such governors would have had no hesitation in having them executed. See SW, Appendix 5; G.E.M. de Ste. Croix and SW in M.I. Finley (editor), *Studies in Ancient Society*, 210 f.; de Ste. Croix, in A.J. Toynbee (editor), *The Crucible of Christianity*, 345 f.; T.D. Barnes in *JRS* 1968, 32f.; Barnes, *Tertullian*, chap. 11; D.L. Stockton in B. Levick (editor), *The Ancient Historian and his materials*, 199f.

Epistle 96

Written between 18 Sept., 111 and 3 Jan., 112, from Pontus, either from Amisus (92) or Amastris (98)

96,1

It is my custom, sir, etc. The first two sentences contain an elaborate apology for troubling T. P. may have thought this necessary for two reasons: (1) the exceptional length of his letter; see also 81, which ends with a similar apology; (2) a belief that he could be expected to know what the standard procedure in trials of Christians was, as his explanation in the third sentence indicates.

I have never been present at trials of Christians. This implies that such trials had taken place during P.'s public career at which P. could have been present, i.e. at Rome, given P.'s lack of provincial experience since his military tribunate. There is no clear-cut evidence of particular trials at Rome since the Neronian persecution of A.D. 64 (see Barnes, *JRS* 1968, 35–6).

What the charge usually is and to what extent it is usually punished. A literal rendering of the Latin would be "what and how far it is customary for it either to be punished or to be investigated". As in 92 (*ad fin.*) P. is using an inverted word order in which the two outer elements ("what ... to be investigated") and the two inner ones ("how far ... to be punished") are intended to be taken together. P. elaborates, in the next section, first on the second question, and then on the first.

96,2

Whether any distinction should be made between different ages. Roman jurists did allow for an "excuse of age" (D 29,5,1,32; 29,5,14; 48,19,16,3), but at Lyons in 177 a boy of 15 from a Christian family was executed (Eusebius, *Ecclesiastical History* 5,1,53–4). De Ste. Croix (*Crucible of Christianity*, 345) comments that T. rightly ignored this question because it was "the kind of thing about which a provincial governor was given a complete responsibility".

whether pardon should be granted for repentance. This was probably the main question on which P. wanted a ruling from T., and he returns to his reason for raising it at the end of his letter (see sect.10 n.); it was when he was faced with "apostates" (sect.6) that P. decided to look more deeply into the whole matter.

Whether it is the name itself ... or the crimes associated with the name. P. turns to the first of his two questions, about the nature of the charge. The "crimes" or "abominations" (*flagitia*) which popular rumour attributed to Christians were incest, infanticide and cannibalism. These allegations are fully reported by Christian apologists who were concerned to refute them: e.g. Minucius Felix, *Octavius* 9–10; Tertullian, *Apology* 8. Similar fantasies had been invented about the Jews by Greeks of Alexandria (see J. Sevenster, *The Roots of Pagan Anti-Semitism in the Ancient World*, 140–2), and the same accusations which Tertullian had mocked while he was still a "mainstream" Christian he himself flung at Catholics after he had become a Montanist (see Barnes, *Tertullian*, 135–6). The medieval church levelled similar charges at heretical or dissident sects: on the whole topic, see N. Cohn, *Europe's Inner Demons*, chaps.1–3.

those who were prosecuted before me. This shows that, when P. was conducting assizes in Pontus, private prosecutors brought alleged Christians before him, under the normal procedure for criminal trials; P. did not "seek out" Christians or have any instructions from T. about them.

I followed this procedure. In sections 3–6 P. distinguishes between three categories of persons charged: those who admitted being Christians ("confessors", in Christian terms), those who denied it (conveniently labelled "deniers" by de Ste. Croix, in *Crucible*, 346) and those who said they had given it up ("apostates", in Christian terms). Each category was supposedly accused in a different way: the first by formal prosecution (*delatio*), the second in an anonymous broadsheet, the third named by an "informer" (*index*). De Ste. Croix, *loc. cit.*, is right to suspect that "P. has oversimplified and that in practice the situation was not quite so tidy".

96,3

Those who admitted that they were. Christians inherited from Judaism the duty to acknowledge only one true God, and to deny that one was a Christian, when challenged, was to violate the First Commandment: see Barnes, *Tertullian*, chap. 12; W.H.C. Frend, *Martyrdom and Persecution in the Early Church*, chaps 2–3.

a second and a third time, warning them of the punishment. P.'s motive, as a judge, was presumably to ensure that persons pleading guilty were fully aware of the consequences. After T. had approved the principle of pardoning apostates, later Roman judges used such repeated questions as a means of pressing Christian confessors to apostatise (see H. Musurillo, *The Acts of the Christian Martyrs*, nos.1, 9–11; 2B, 2 and 6; 6, 1–13; 7, 1–13).

to be executed. Literally, "to be led away", but this is a standard idiom for being taken away to be beheaded with a sword (see *OLD*, *duco* 4b).

their stubborness and unyielding obstinacy certainly ought to be punished. It is very odd for a judge to say that criminals who persist in pleading guilty deserve punishment for their persistence. But, if the offence was the mere profession (the "name itself"), by changing his plea to "not guilty" a former confessor would be renouncing his Christianity. P.'s comment would make better sense if his aim from the start had been to obtain apostacies, but, according to his own chronology, that was an idea which only came to him later (sections 9–10). This is surely a retrospective account of his attitude, written, of course, after he had become convinced of the desirability of making

Christians apostatise rather than confess: hence his (retrospective) comment about obstinacy.

96,4

to be sent on to the city, because they were Roman citizens. The standard deduction from this passage, from the governor of Judaea's response to St Paul's "I appeal unto Caesar" (Acts 25,11), and from passages in the Roman jurists, is that Roman citizens could appeal from a capital sentence imposed by a governor to the emperor's court, and that governors such as P., aware that citizens were very likely to exercise their right, either sent them off to Rome or asked the emperor's permission to execute (as was done in the case of Christians at Lyons in 177: Eusebius, *Ecclesiastical History* 5,1,47). Hence SW's comment (699) that "the circumstances in which a provincial governor could execute a Roman citizen without appeal to the Princeps were extremely limited." See SW, 164–5, and his *Roman Society and Roman Law in the New Testament*, 57f.; A.H.M. Jones, *Studies in Roman Government*, chap.4, and *The Criminal Courts of the Roman Republic and Principate*, 101–5. For a dissenting view see P. Garnsey, *JRS* 1966, 167f. and 1968, 51f. See also Millar, 507–16.

96,5

made offerings of incense and wine to your statue ... along with the cult-images of the gods. This "sacrifice test" is only used to verify the sincerity of those who denied that they were, or ever had been, Christians, and is one among three such tests, whereas later governors tried to induce confessors (sometimes by use of torture) to apostatise by offering such sacrifices (see de Ste Croix, in *Studies in Ancient Society*, 232). The use of T.'s statue is thus not evidence to support the theory that Christians were persecuted specifically for their refusal to worship the living emperor as a god: P. does not require confessing Christians to do this. For more general criticism of this theory, see F. Millar, in W. den Boer (editor), *Le culte des souverains* (*Entretiens Fondation Hardt*, Vol.19, 1972), 143f, and, on this passage, 152–3. In this instance T.'s statue was included alongside images of gods from local shrines, presumably as a sign of respect and allegiance.

it is said. P. disclaims personal knowledge and was presumably taking the word of one of his advisers, who claimed some expertise in the matter.

96,6

Named by an informer. This person's name was presumably known to P., but P. did not require him to act as prosecutor (as had happened with the first group: sect.2). P. must have had the persons named brought to him and questioned them himself. For T.'s reaction to this procedure, see 97,2 n.

96,7

They maintained that this had been the sum of their guilt or error .... Barnes (*JRS* 1968, 37) suggests that Roman judges before P. had simply discharged apostate Christians without more ado. It is typical of P.'s conscientiousness to question persons about exactly what they had got up to while they had been Christians, and then to consult T. about whether it was proper to release them.

the habit of gathering together. Neither of the ceremonies described by P. (hymn-singing and oath-taking) appears in the earliest full description of the Sunday service at dawn given in Justin Martyr's *First Apology* some 50 years later (chap.67: readings, sermon, prayers, communion and collection). The widely differing hypotheses advanced by liturgical scholars who attempt to reconcile P.'s account with evidence from Christian sources (summarised in SW, 702–8) disregard the possibility that Christian practices may have varied from region to region and period to period, as well as the certainty that P.'s reporting of what he was told is highly selective.

on a fixed day. This would be on the day following the Jewish Sabbath (= the English Sunday), because this was the weekly anniversary of the Resurrection: "we all gather together on the day of the sun ... Jesus Christ our saviour rose from the dead on this same day" (Justin, *1st Apology* 67). The seven-day week was a feature of the Babylonian and Jewish calendars, but not of traditional Greek or Roman ones. In late antiquity the week did come into use in the Roman Empire. P. does not, however, refer to this system, although in the late first century the Jew Josephus could claim that "there is no city, Greek or barbarian, to which our custom of abstaining from work on the 7th day has not spread" (*Against Apion*, 2, 39, 282). See E. Bickerman, *Chronology of the Ancient World*, 58–61; F.H. Colson, *The Week*, esp. chap. 8.

binding themselves by oath etc. This assertion was presumably stressed by P.'s informants in order to establish their moral respectability. There appear to be no parallels in Christian sources for such a ceremony as part of any Sunday services, so it has been argued that this is a garbled account of an oath taken by Christians at baptism (Justin, *1st Apology* 65). P., however, clearly supposed that what the apostates described was a ceremony in which all Christians took part every Sunday. It has been argued that the apostates, if they spoke to P. in Latin, used *sacramentum* in the sense in which it was used by Christian Latin writers, beginning with Tertullian, to refer to sacred ceremonies such as communion (Tertullian, *Corona Militis* 3; *Adversus Marcionem* 4, 34), or baptism (*De Baptismo* 5; *Adversus Marcionem, loc.cit*). There can be no certainty that Christians had already come to use the word in this specialised sense by 111. If they did use it in such a way, P. completely misunderstood them, and it would be impossible to reconstruct the actual ceremony they were describing to him.

not to some wickedness: i.e., any of the "crimes" (see sect.2n.).

not to commit acts of theft or robbery or adultery. These correspond to the seventh and eighth of the Jewish "Ten Commandments", and it has been suggested that the recitation of all 10 was taken over into Christian services from the practice of the Jewish synagogues (on which see E. Schürer, *History of the Jewish People* Vol.2 (rev. ed. 1979), 447). However, the next two items have no exact parallels in the Ten Commandments (see SW, 706).

not to refuse to return money placed in their keeping. On "deposits" as a widespread practice in the Roman world, see Crook, 209: "given the slow rates of travel in the ancient world, the shortage of police ... men had a frequent need to call on the goodwill of a neighbour to look after their property. One of the nastiest and most dishonourable things a man could do was to deny a deposit ...". Nevertheless, it must have been a very great temptation, and Juvenal jeered at a man of sixty who was angry and surprised when a friend succumbed to it (*Satire* 13, ll.5–18).

to meet again to take food. This appears to be a reference to the communal meal described by Christian sources as a "love-feast" (*agape*): on this meal, which was wholly distinct from the communion service, see H. Lietzmann and R.D. Richardson, *Mass and Lord's Supper* (1979), 161–71 and 271.

but food that was ordinary and harmless: i.e. not the flesh of murdered infants (see sect.2, n.).

they had given up doing even this. The natural way of interpreting the Latin would be that this referred only to the meal just described, and that it applied to all Christians. SW holds that, since it is incredible that faithful Christians should have abandoned communion, communion must at this point have become part of the dawn service (as it was in Justin's day: see above), and that Christians had continued to meet for this service. If so, P. did not regard such a meeting as a serious breach of his ban on "clubs", whereas a communal meal was a characteristic activity of such clubs.

my edict, in which, in accordance with your instructions, I had banned secret societies. On edicts and *mandata*, see Introd.II(G)iii; on clubs, 33–4 nn.

96,8

to ascertain what the truth was from two slave women who were called deaconesses, and under torture. P. implies that he would not really be confident of the
truth of the reports unless they were confirmed by evidence obtained under torture. The
traditional prohibition on the torture of witnesses who were free persons was still being
upheld by T.'s successors, Hadrian and Pius (P. Garnsey, *Social Status and Legal Privilege
in the Roman Empire*, 213–6). The evidence of slaves, on the other hand, was not admis-
sible except under torture. The Latin word *ministrae* is probably used to translate the
Greek word *diakonoi*, for Paul refers to Phoebe as the *diakonos* (servant) of the church at
Cenchreae (Romans 16, 1).

superstition. Also applied to the Christians by P.'s friends Tacitus (*Annals* 15, 44) and
Suetonius (*Nero* 16,2). The word is used to allude disparagingly to forms of religious ac-
tivity not approved of by the Roman establishment, but *not* to *all* forms of religion (see
R. MacMullen, *Paganism in the Roman Empire*, 70–3).

96,9

the number of people who are endangered. P., the prudent administrator, may be
worried at the upheavals which might result from mass executions, but he was also a no-
tably humane man for his age and class: the reference to "every age" echoes his first question to T. in sect.2.

96,10

It is well established that temples which just now were almost abandoned
have begun to be thronged. P. is only reporting what he has been told by his informants (presumably interested parties such as those responsible for the temples, as SW,
709, suggests), and he had no reason to tone down their exaggerated contrast between
"before" and "after", since it supported the case he is arguing to T. for pardoning the apostates. However, epigraphic evidence from regions of Phrygia, just to the south of Pontus,
indicates the presence of numerous Christians in rural villages in the second century: see
Vol 10 of *Monumenta Asiae Minoris Antiqua* (forthcoming in *Journal of Roman Studies
Monographs*).

the flesh of sacrificial victims. The word "flesh" is an insertion into the early texts,
proposed by Körte, and it is a conjecture which makes excellent sense of the passage. The
portions of sacrificial animals burnt as an offering to the gods were in general those which
humans found least appetising (see R.M. Ogilvie, *The Romans and their Gods*, 42) and the
remainder must have been the main source of "butchers' meat" for a population whose diet
was mainly confined to vegetable foods, fish and poultry (see Ogilvie, 50; R. Lane Fox,
Pagans and Christians, 70), as well as an important source of income for the temples and
the middlemen who traded the meat. Christians were forbidden to eat such meat because of
its association with idolatry (I Corinthians 10, 14–22).

what a host of people could be reformed, if room were given for repentance. P. is arguing in support of his proposal to discharge apostate Christians, which
he assumes would be an innovation requiring the emperor's consent (see section 2). He
has established that the alleged "crimes" are not committed by Christians, and encouragement of apostasy would revive the traditional cults in Pontus. He assumes that T. would
regard this as an important objective, and this sheds light on the motives of Roman emperors and governors in putting Christians to death, even after the "crimes" were shown to
be a fiction: as Gibbon said, the Christians were "a sect which deserted the religion of
their fathers". This "godlessness" or "atheism" of Christians in some cases provoked the
anger of pagan neighbours who feared that the wrath of the gods would be visited on them

(but there is no hint in P.'s letter of mass demonstrations against the Christians of Pontus), and Roman governors had an overriding obligation to maintain public order. Some later records show that some governors shared the religious fears of their subjects (see Musurillo, *op.cit.* no.6, 3–5; and de Ste Croix, *Studies in Ancient Society*, 243). P., however, gives no sign of sharing such fears, and for both P. and T. the traditional cults, both of Rome and of non-Roman communities, are part of the established order which it is their duty to maintain (for this attitude on the part of the Roman governing class, see J.H.W.G. Liebeschutz, *Continuity and Change in Roman religion*, chaps.1–2; and de Ste Croix, *Studies in Ancient Society*, 245–8).

Epistle 97

97,1

You followed the procedure which you ought to have followed. T. does not give a direct answer to P.'s question about punishment for the name alone, but the implication of this blanket statement of approval is that Christians are to be punished just for being Christians (since P. was convinced that the Christians he had had executed were innocent of any "crimes").

For no rule with a universal application ... can be laid down. For T.'s reluctance to limit governors' initiative by over-specific definitions, see 109, 113 nn. This sentence could also be taken as a response to P.'s question about the young Christians (96,2): it is left to P. to exercise his discretion in specific cases.

97,2

They should not be sought out; if they are prosecuted etc. T. is, by implication, criticising P.'s procedure in dealing with those named in the anonymous pamphlet and by an informer. P. had presumably given orders for those named to be brought before him and questioned them in person (96,6 n.). In T.'s view the appropriate procedure was for P. to act as an impartial judge when private prosecutors brought alleged Christians before him (*delatio*: see 96,2 n.). T. may have had two reasons for taking this line:

(a) Christians were not important enough for a governor to devote special efforts to hunting them out;

(b) such a procedure, by relying on anonymous informers, would stimulate malicious and vindictive accusations, whereas the private prosecutor (*delator*) had to provide evidence and argument in person, and was liable to a counter-charge of making an unfounded and malicious accusation (*calumnia*) from a defendant who had been acquitted (see Crook, 276–7).

the man who denies that he is a Christian ... shall obtain pardon for his repentance. T. does not give his reasons for accepting P.'s proposal about the apostates: presumably he accepted P.'s arguments and shared his concern for the prosperity of traditional cults (see 96,10 n.). The publication of P.'s correspondence with T. must have made T.'s ruling widely known, and it served as the legal basis for the execution of confessing Christians and for the release of apostates until the first "General Persecution", launched by Decius in A.D.250 (see Barnes, *JRS* 1968, 48).

For they both set a disgraceful precedent, and are not in keeping with the spirit of our age. For another case where T. seizes on a minor detail of P.'s original report and ticks P. off, see 38. For the objection to anonymous informers, see above. For the emphasis on the spirit of T.'s régime, especially in contrast to Domitian's, see 55 and 82.

Epistles 98–9

P. asks, and T. grants, permission to have an open sewer at Amastris covered over.

Epistle 98

Written not long before 3 Jan., 112 (see no.100) from Amastris (sect.1).

98,1
The city of the Amastrians. See Introd. III(C)ii.

98,2
if you permit it. See 23, 1 n. and 90,2.
we will ensure that money also is not lacking. See 23,2 and 90,2 for the same assurance accompanying similar applications for "building permits".

Epistle 99

99,2
I feel certain that with your usual diligence you will ensure. In this third case
  T. is more complimentary to P. than in 24 and 91, where, despite P.'s assurances, his
  replies included clauses which began "provided only that ...".

Epistles 100–1

*P. reports, and T. acknowledges, the fulfilment of the New Year vows for
T.'s well-being, and the undertaking of fresh vows.*

Epistle 100

*Written on or soon after 3 Jan., 112, probably from Amastris (see 98–99; Amastris, as the
seat of the council of Pontus (Introd. IIICii), is a more likely place for representatives of the
cities of Pontus to have assembled to take the vows than Amisus (92 and 110); see the gather-
ings at Nicomedia the year before (35 and 52)).*

  For the New Year vows, see 35–36 nn.
my fellow-soldiers and the provincials: in the previous year only the latter are
  mentioned in T.'s reply about the New Year ceremony (36), but both groups were present
  on 18 Jan. (52). For the provincials, see 35 n.

Epistles 102–3

*P. reports, and T. acknowledges, the ceremonies on the anniversary of T.'s
accession.*

Epistle 102

Written on, or soon after, 28 Jan., 112, probably from Amastris (see 100 n.).
  For the accession day ceremonies, see 52–53 nn.

Epistle 103

my fellow-soldiers and the provincials. T. takes it for granted that P.'s "we" in 102
  included both groups (see 100): the year before P. had specifically mentioned their presence (52).

Epistles 104–5

P. asks T. to grant full Roman citizenship to three freed slaves of Latin status, and T. agrees.

Epistle 104

Written after 28 Jan., 112.

Valerius Paulinus. Gaius Valerius Paulinus was a senator from Forum Iulii (Fréjus in modern Provence), who held the consulship in 107 (Smallwood, no.20, line 10, and no.356); he had been the recipient of five of P.'s published letters (II,2; IV,16; V,19; IX, 3 and 37). In V,19, P. had described his anxiety about the health of his own freedman Zosimus and asked that Zosimus might convalesce at Paulinus' estate near Fréjus. The letter begins, "I see how gently you treat your people" (i.e. freedmen: see 15 n.). Paulinus' motive in making P. one of his heirs must have been to ensure that his freedmen continued to be "treated gently", and he knew that P. shared his own humane attitude.

having excluded Paulinus. This was the text printed by Avantius, and also what Aldus read in the MS., but he indicated that he thought Paulino should be corrected to *uno* (i.e. "having excluded one (of the freedmen)"): SW rightly points out that this bit of information would be of no concern to T. Paulinus was probably Valerius Paulinus' son : T. would know the family connections of a consular and P. had no need to mention the exact relationship (so Hardy's objection, that mere "Paulinus", without "his son", is too vague, is invalid). SW, 714, points out that Hardy, 220, is also wrong in saying that the phrase "must mean 'excluded from the will'". In fact Paulinus the younger was probably joint heir with P., but the rights over the freedmen were reserved for P. alone by a legal procedure known as *praeceptio* (see 75, 2 n.).

his rights. A freed slave (*libertus*) remained under a number of obligations to his former owner (now his *patronus*), which were legally enforceable: an impoverished "patron" could demand financial support from a freedman; he could require the freedman, in the event of the patron's death before his children came of age, to act as *tutor*, i.e. to manage the property on the children's behalf; above all, the patron could claim a share in the freedman's property at his death, regardless of the freedman's own wishes (see Crook, 51–3).

over his Latin freedmen. Slaves set free by Roman owners at a formal ceremony before a magistrate who had *imperium*, or by will, themselves became Roman citizens. Owners also often freed slaves in their lifetimes by an informal ceremony "before friends" (access to qualified magistrates was no doubt hard to get). A law passed in the reigns of Augustus or Tiberius (a *lex Iunia*) regulated the status of such freed slaves: they did not become Roman citizens, but free men with the same rights as freeborn Romans who had joined Latin colonies. Hence they came to be called "Junian Latins" (see Gaius 3,55; Crook, 43–5). The relationship between Latins and their patrons differed from that between citizen freedmen and theirs in two significant ways: patrons could claim the entire property of a Latin freedman at his death (see Crook, 53); and a patron could institute an heir who was not a member of his family (*extraneus heres*) as his successor to the rights of a patron over Junian Latins (or even sell those rights), whereas a patron's sons or sons' sons could claim the rights of a patron over citizen freedmen even if they had been disinherited in the father's will (see Gaius 3, 58; Crook, 53). So it was only because these freedmen were Latins that P. was able to succeed Paulinus as their patron, and P. stood to benefit financially if these freedmen owned any substantial property.

the rights of Roman citizens. For the word *Quirites* as a term for Roman citizens, see 58, 7n. The legal phrase "by the right of a Roman citizen" (*ex iure Quiritium*) is used especially to refer to a form of full ownership which only Roman citizens possessed (see

Crook, 139–40), but *ius Quiritium* had since the *lex Iunia* come to be used to describe the package of rights enjoyed by citizen freedmen and denied to Junian Latins. Just as emperors exercised the privilege of granting the rights of parents to the childless (see 94, 2 n.), so they made individual grants of this 'package' of rights to Junian Latins, thus promoting them to full citizen status and enabling them to make wills (by making this request P. may have been sacrificing a potential gain). P. had earlier made similar requests to T. on behalf of other patrons (5,2; 11). See Gaius 3, 72; *Tituli Ulpiani* 3, 2.

For I fear etc. P. will have recalled T.'s own remark, "how sparingly I bestow these benefits", in the reply about Suetonius (95).

C. Valerius Astraeus etc. All three freedmen had the same personal name (*praenomen*) and "clan-name" (*gentilicium*), viz. Gaius Valerius, because, as was the usual practice, they had adopted those of their former owner, Paulinus, when they were manumitted; as slaves they will each have had only one name, which they converted to a Roman "family-name" (*cognomen*) at the same time (Astraeus, Dionysius, Aper). See A.M. Duff, *Freedmen in the early Roman empire*, 52.

Epistle 105

an entry to be made in my registers. On the imperial *commentarii* see 66,1n. There must have been a separate *commentarius iure Quiritium donatorum*, (register of those endowed with Quiritary right), similar to that for foreigners granted Roman citizenship (see 107 n.). It probably recorded, in addition to the names of the beneficiaries, those of the person making the application and of the patron (the same in this case, but different in the cases mentioned in 5,2 and 11).

Epistles 106–7

P. transmits to T. a petition from a centurion of an auxiliary cohort, and T. sends his response for delivery to the centurion.

Epistle 106

Written after 28 Jan., 112.

P. Accius Aquila, centurion of the sixth mounted cohort. A "mounted cohort" was a unit of probably 600 auxiliary soldiers, with 480 infantrymen and 120 cavalrymen (see P.A. Holder, *The Auxilia from Augustus to Trajan* (British Archaeological Reports, International Series 70, 1980), 7–8). The presence of a cohort with this title in BP is also attested by inscriptions: R. Cagnat, *Inscriptiones Graecae ad res Romanas*, Vol.3, nos.2 and 1396. Aquila's full set of three Latin names (*tria nomina*) show that he is a Roman citizen, despite the fact that auxiliary units were originally recruited exclusively from non-Romans (and auxiliaries received grants of citizenship only upon discharge from the army). From A.D. 70 onwards an increasing number of auxiliary centurions were Roman citizens (see P.A. Holder, *The Auxilia*, 87, and the table of known centurions of the period A.D. 70–117 on p. 102, with 16 citizens to 3 non-citizens). Such centurions could be (a) Romans commissioned from civilian life, (b) Romans transferred from a legion, (c) Romans recruited into the auxiliaries as ordinary soldiers (these increased in numbers in A.D. 70–117), and promoted from the ranks (Holder, 86–8).

to send on to you a petition. Since this was a separate document, it was probably attached/glued to P.'s letter (22,1n.). On the word *libellus*, see 47,2 and 59 nn. In this case the text clearly contained a request to the emperor (T. was "moved by his appeal"), and *libellus* is used in the technical sense of a "petition".

the status of his daughter. It is clear from T.'s reply that she was a non-Roman, and this was because her mother was not a Roman. Serving soldiers were not permitted to be married in this period, but the child of an illegal union with a Roman woman would still have had Roman status (see B. Campbell, *JRS* 1978, 153–4). No Roman man could contract a legal marriage with a foreign woman (unless there had been a special grant of *conubium*), and the children of any such union would have the nationality of their mother (see Gaius 1, 75; Crook, 40).

I thought it harsh to refuse, since I knew etc. P. feels it necessary to justify his use of an official pass to assist a private petitioner (see 45–46 nn.). The Code of Justinian preserves a very large number of imperial responses to such petitions, and there has been a widely-accepted theory that most of these petitions were forwarded to the emperors from the provinces by their governors, and indeed that governors were obliged to do this (the basic article is that by U. Wilcken, *Hermes* 1920, 1f.; the theory has been restated by A. d'Ors and F. Martin, *American Journal of Philology* 1979, 111f.). This letter of P.'s has been one of the main pieces of evidence used to support this theory. However, P.'s language here proves that (a) he was free to refuse to allow Aquila access to the official courier system, and (b) in doing so P. was granting an exceptional favour, because Aquila was a soldier, and T. was an emperor especially concerned with the interests of soldiers; hence P. was not following a standard procedure. Most petitioners, especially civilian petitioners, had to deliver their petitions to the emperor in person, or through an agent (see Williams, *JRS* 1974, 93–8; *ZPE* 40, 284–7; Millar, 469, 475–6).

Epistle 107

I have granted Roman citizenship to his daughter. See 106 n. There is no reference to a copy of the entry in the imperial register of such grants being sent with this epistle; such a copy was sent by Marcus Aurelius to a Mauretanian chieftain who had secured a grant of citizenship for his wife and children (*JRS* 1973, pp.86–7, ll.22–33).

I have sent you the petition with its rescript for you to hand over to him. Whereas emperors (and governors) responded to epistles by composing separate epistles of their own, the response to a petition was added at the bottom of the original text: the Latin and Greek terms used for such a response (*subscriptio* and *hypographe*) mean "thing written below". It is certain that by A.D.139 the standard procedure was for all petitions to the emperor, when the subscripts had been added, to be displayed in a public place near the emperor's residence for a short period and then to be stored in the imperial archives. It was left to the petitioner's own initiative to have an attested copy made of the petition with its subscript while it was on display (see U. Wilcken, *Hermes* 1920, 1f.; Williams, *JRS* 1974, 98–101 and *ZPE* 40, 287–94; *id.66*, 181–7). U. Wilcken argued that, from the time of Augustus until that of Hadrian, petitioners received back the original texts of their petitions with the imperial subscripts added, but this sentence of T.'s was the only direct evidence he had for this hypothesis (see *Hermes* 1920, 19–20; *JRS* 1974, 98). However, since the present text is such an isolated piece of evidence, it is not adequate proof of Wilcken's theory that until Hadrian's reign all petitioners to the emperor were treated like Aquila. T.'s action was not standard procedure, but an exceptional favour to a serving soldier, just as P.'s original despatch of his petition to T. had been a favour. This exchange of letters should not be used to argue that before A.D.139 most petitioners to the emperor did not have to deliver their petitions in person and obtain their own copies, as they certainly had to do thereafter (see Williams, *ZPE* 40, 283–94, and 66, 198–207).

Epistles 108–9

P. asks T. to consider granting all the cities of the province a prior claim on the assets of debtors, but T. replies that the existing laws in each city should be maintained.

Epistle   108

Written after 28 Jan., 112.

108,1

in recovering sums of money. For the cities' difficulties in doing this see 17A,3; 17B,2; 23,2; 39,5. Dio of Prusa claimed that "in all the cities there are public moneys, and a few persons have them in their possession, some through ignorance, some for other reasons" (*Or.*48,9).

from leases or from sales. *Locatio* (offering for rent or leasing out) and *venditio* (offering for sale) were used by Roman lawyers in conjunction with the corresponding terms *conductio* (leasing or hiring) and *emptio* (buying) to describe two types of contract (see Crook, 214–22; and Gaius 3, 139–147). In the Flavian charters of Spanish municipalities these terms are used to describe contracts between municipal governments and private individuals or partnerships for the farming of municipal taxes and the provision of services to the municipality: *JRS* 1986, 161, chap. J (trans. p. 187) and 167, chap. 63 (trans. p. 190). J. Gonzalez comments that the language of hire (*locatio/conductio*) is applied to *publica* (collection of taxes) and the language of sale to *ultro tributa* (contracts to supply services), "because collection of taxes was auctioned out for a limited period whereas a contract for public works was a once for all act" (*JRS* 1986, 212). P.'s "leases" must also cover leases of land and buildings owned by the cities: chapter 76 of the charter of Irni deals with "visiting and inspecting the territories (*fines*), fields (*agri*) and sources of revenue (*vectigalia*)" of the municipality (*JRS* 1986, 173, chap.76, trans. p. 193); rents from municipal property and payments by tax-farmers of the indirect taxes were two of the chief sources of revenue of the cities (see Jones, *GC,* 244–6). "Sales" thus refers to contracts to provide the cities with services, e.g. putting up public buildings; see 17A,3 and 17B,2, for the way such contracts could lead to sums of public money being misappropriated by private persons.

the right of prior claim. P. has transliterated the Greek accusative form of a technical term which meant "first exaction", *protopraxian* (the Greek form is found in an edict of a Prefect of Egypt of 68: Smallwood, *Documents of Gaius, Claudius and Nero,* no. 391, ll.19 and 25). T. uses a Latin periphrasis, "a privilege whereby they take priority over all the other creditors". In Egypt this privilege was reserved for the imperial fiscus (see the document just cited); in the third century the jurist Paulus asserted that "the privilege of the fiscus is to keep first place among all the creditors" (*Sententiae Pauli,* 5, 12, 10), and the jurist Marcianus wrote that "no city has a privilege similar to that of the fiscus over the property of a debtor, unless it has been specifically given (to a city) by the emperor" (D 50,1,10).

108,2

some rule ... through which their interests may be safeguarded for ever. P.'s recommendation is wholly in character. (a) For the sake of tidy administration he wants a rule which will be uniform throughout the province and permanent in effect (see 65, 72, 112). (b) He is quite ruthless in sacrificing the interests of private creditors to protect the funds of the cities (see 54,2; 112,3).

Epistle   109

What rights ... must be determined in accordance with the law of each city. T. is equally in character in refusing to impose a uniform rule, but instead directing P. to maintain the law of each city: see 69; 97,1; 113. It was presumably up to P. to discover what the law had been in each case before the proconsuls started granting *protopraxia*.

it will not be appropriate for this ... to be granted by me to the detriment of private persons. See especially the tone of 55, with the phrase about "not being in accordance with the justice of our age", and also 111, ad fin. However, T.'s concern for fairness towards private citizens does not override his respect for long-established local rules, so *protopraxia* will not be taken away from those cities which had exercised the privilege in the past.

Epistles 110–1

P. asks T. whether a city can sue to recover a grant made from civic funds twenty years earlier; T. replies that grants made so long ago should not be reconsidered.

Epistle 110

Written after 28 Jan., 112.

110,1

The public advocate. *Ecdicus* is a Latinised form of a Greek title, the original meaning of which was "avenger". The Latin form was used by Cicero to describe barristers acting for Greek cities in Asia (*Ad fam.* 13, 56, 1), and the Greek form appears in inscriptions. In some cases an appointment was made ad hoc for a particular lawsuit, and was an unpaid compulsory service (i.e. a "liturgy" imposed on a wealthy citizen: see D. 50, 4, 18, 13); but in some cities, such as Amisus, the post seems to have been a regular annual office (see Jones, *GC*, 244–5; SW, 719).

the city of the Amiseni. See Introd. III(C)ii. Presumably the kind of payment Iulius Piso had received was not recoverable under the local law of Amisus, and the only way the city could get its money back was to get P. to enforce on Piso the rule laid down in T.'s *mandata* (and presumably made public in P.'s own edict; see 96, 7). On the relationship between the governor and this free city see 92nn.

before me. I.e., before P.'s tribunal at the assizes (possibly being held at Amastris, the city most recently mentioned (98–9) and one which was an assize centre: Introd. IIICii).

with the agreement of the Council and the Assembly. I.e., a formal resolution proposed by the former and ratified by the latter, what is referred to by P. in 43 by its Greek name *psephisma*. This is P.'s only reference to a city assembly: see Introd. IIE.

your instructions in which grants of this kind are forbidden. This was presumably a special clause inserted in P.'s own *mandata* as part of T.'s plan to clean up corruption in local government in BP: T. regarded such payments as another means by which local leaders could "do each other favours" (38). By the early third century the principle had come to be universally applied: "self-seeking resolutions of decurions ought to be vetoed, whether they have released some debtor or bestowed a gift" (Ulpian, *On the duty of a city auditor*, D 50, 9, 4 praef.).

110,2

he had made very many gifts to the community. Piso must have been a member of the ruling aristocracy (as his status as a Roman citizen would suggest), and must have been involved in the competitive expenditure on public amenities called for by the "desire for honour", Greek *philotimia* (see Jones, *Dio*, chap.12). The late 3rd century jurist Hermogenian allowed an exception from the principle enunciated in the passage from Ulpian quoted above: "a subsistence grant is allowed to be voted to decurions whose funds are exhausted, especially if they have used up their property in munificence to their native city" (D 50, 2, 8).

to the ruin of what was left of his standing. The reference to Piso's *dignitas*, his "standing" or "rank", probably alludes to his continued membership of the council at Amisus. As SW, 720, pointed out, it suggests that there was a minimum property qualification for council membership in BP, just as there was for the Senate at Rome (see Talbert,

10), and for municipal councils in Italy (P.'s letter to a decurion of his native Como shows that there the minimum sum was 100,000 sesterces: I, 19, 2). 40,000 denarii was equivalent to 160,000 sesterces, well above the minimum at Como.

what course you think should be followed. P. gives no explicit expression of his own opinion, but his full and eloquent statement of the case presented by Piso makes it clear he hoped to elicit from T. the ruling which T. did in the event make.

Epistle 111

Although the instructions do forbid ... yet .... As in other letters in which T. allows exceptions to a general rule (e.g. 93) he restates that rule, so as to make it clear that he wants it enforced in all other cases (i.e. to grants made within a shorter period than twenty years!).

twenty years ago. As SW, 721, points out, this period was chosen because that was the one mentioned by P. (110,1), so that this ruling would protect Piso. Jones, *GC*, 135, argued that the ban on such payments had been in force in BP when Piso got his grant: "for Trajan, in allowing grants made over twenty years ago, implies that even then they were illegal". However, it seems more probable that it was a new rule introduced to the province by P. on T.'s instructions, and that this prompted Piso's enemies at Amisus to take action. There is no evidence that T. would object in principle to retrospective action against people whom he had described in 38 as "doing each other favours": in 115 he only rejects such action on practical grounds (so SW, 721).

the interests of individuals in each place. Cf. similar expressions of concern for private persons in 55 and 109.

Epistles 112–3

P. asks T. to consider imposing a compulsory entrance fee on new councillors in all the cities of the province, but T. refuses to lay down a uniform rule.

Epistle 112

Written after 28 Jan., 112.

112,1

The Pompeian law. See Introd. IIGi

enrolled in a Council by censors. See 79,1 nn.

to pay money. The technical term for an entrance fee paid by new councillors is used by T. in his reply: *honorarium decurionatus*, "the fee for a decurionate" (also called *summa honoraria* or *summa legitima*). The patchy evidence for the history of this payment was analysed by P. Garnsey, in *Historia* 20, 1971, 309 f. The reason for the silence of the Pompeian law is probably that such payments were unknown in the municipalities of Italy in the first century B.C. There is some evidence that during the first century A.D. men co-opted on to municipal councils in Italy, with the honorary rank of ex-magistrates but without having held office, had to make payments at entry, because their fellows who had held office would have had to pay out large sums, on public amenities. Such payments had been unknown in BP until the enlargement of some councils under T. (see below). In the course of the second century "the entry-fee (paid by all decurions) was .. at least widespread, and it is a reasonable assumption that it was, or became, universal".

those whom your generosity has allowed some of the cities to add over and above the lawful number. The "lawful number" must have been a maximum size for each city council in BP laid down in the Pompeian law. Whether there was a single figure for the whole province, and, if so, what it was, is not known: in the municipalities of

Italy and the western provinces, 100 was the standard size for councils, but in the eastern provinces councils were often much larger (see Jones, *GC*, 171; but in the Macedonian city addressed by Antoninus Pius (below) the council was only 80 in number. Prusa's council probably numbered several hundreds before T. allowed another 100 councillors to be added: see Jones, *Dio* 107).

Two cities which were allowed by T. to enlarge their councils are attested: Claudiopolis (39,5) and Prusa (see Jones, *Dio*, 96 and 107). Dio's own orations show that he represented Prusa on an embassy to T. which must have asked for an enlargement of the council (40, 14) and that Dio got what he asked for from T. (40,15; 45,3; see 44,11). 100 members were added to the Council (45,7), and these were apparently chosen by election by the whole citizen-body (45,9).

have paid one or two thousand denarii each.   As P.'s account of Anicius' measures (sect.2) shows, different amounts were collected in different cities. The immediate acquisition of substantial lump sums for city funds was one of the motives for Prusa's request to T. Dio wrote of "having made my native land more esteemed by providing an accession of funds, as from the councillors' money ..." (48,11). The emperor Antoninus Pius, in an epistle to a city in Macedonia, wrote: "let your council number 80, and let each of them pay 500 Attic drachmas, in order that prestige may accrue to you from the size of your council, and revenue from the money which they will pay" (*I.G. Bulgaria* 4, 2263, 8–12; trans. in *American Journal of Philology* 1958, 52–3; despite Garnsey's doubts (*Historia* 1971, 312, n.8), it is clear that Pius was responding to a request from an existing city to enlarge its council, since a formal embassy from an organised community had been sent to the emperor).

112,2

Later the proconsul Anicius Maximus ordered those who were enrolled by censors to pay as well, but only in a very few cities.   Anicius must have served during T.'s reign, after T.'s concession to "some cities". Anicius presumably agreed to requests from the "very few" cities, which were probably the same ones as those which T. had allowed to enlarge their councils.

112,3

whether in all the cities all those who will henceforward be enrolled as councillors ought to pay some fixed sum.   This idea had presumably occurred to P. because the censors elected the year before (see 79, 4 n.) were now enrolling new councillors to fill gaps left in the ranks since the previous census. It is typical of P. (a) to pursue his mission of improving civic finances by imposing financial burdens on the councillors (see 54,2; also 108, 2 n.); (b) to wish to apply a uniform rule to the whole province (see 65; 72; 108,2).

Epistle 113

No general rule can be laid down by me.   It is equally typical of T. to refuse to impose uniformity on the cities (see 69; 97,1; 109).

the law of each city should be followed.   See the very similar formulation in 109. The "law" presumably means a civic resolution ratified by a proconsul (viz. Anicius), and the effect of T.'s decision is that, in the "very few cities" to which Anicius' ruling applied, the councillors enrolled by the censors will have to pay up, but in the other cities they will not.

but indeed I am sure etc.   The rest of this sentence presents the most difficult and contentious textual problems to be found in Book X; see the full discussion in the Appendix.

Epistles   114–5

P. asks whether city councillors who are by origin citizens of another city in the province should be expelled from the councils by censors;   T. replies that men of this kind who are already councillors should not be expelled, but that the Pompeian law's provisions must be observed in future.

Epistle   114

Written after 28 Jan., 112.

114,1

the Pompeian law. See Introd., IIGi.

to enrol ... as honorary citizens. In the Greek-speaking world of the Hellenistic period it was quite common for individuals to hold multiple citizenships: cities granted (or even sold) citizenship to resident aliens or to eminent natives of other cities, and by grants of *isopoliteia* whole cities exchanged citizenship (see Jones,*GC*, 160,172). Pompeius simply allowed the cities of the new province to continue with their traditional practices.

provided that none of them came from those cities which are in Bithynia. A convincing motive for this measure has been proposed by A.J. Marshall (see *JRS* 1968, 108). In parts of the new province he had organised, Pompeius had had to found new self-governing cities to take over the work of local government hitherto carried out by officials of the kings of Pontus, and such cities needed wealthy councillors to function effectively: "it would be especially important for him to forbid the cities to attract fresh citizens at each other's expense and to discourage the richer members, who provided magistrates and capital, from migrating to more established cities ... " (*loc.cit.*). See Introd. III(A)iii.

for what reasons men may be expelled from a senate .... Like other provisions of the law these must have been based on a Roman model (see 79, 1 nn.), presumably the practice of the censors at Rome: for a parallel, see the section of Julius Caesar's regulations for the municipalities of Italy which lists the reasons for disqualifying men from serving as decurions (*ILS* 6085, ll.104–25, trans. in Lewis and Reinhold, Vol.1, 418–9).

114,2

some of the censors. For their functions and the motives of the present censors in consulting P. about what were long-standing breaches of the Pompeian law, see 79,3–4 nn.

114,3

yet did not order a man to be expelled from a senate for that reason. Since the reason for the law's silence was obviously that, if its ban on enrolling as citizens natives of other cities was enforced, there would be no such senators, P. appears to be rather pedantic in advancing this silence as a reason for doubt and for his need to consult T. The next clause supplies the main reason for referring the question to T. (and, by implication, inviting him to condone the breaches of the law).

I was assured that in every city there were very many councillors from other cities. Dio of Prusa's references to himself and his relatives confirm that grants of citizenship to wealthy natives of other cities of the province had been an accepted custom (see *Or.* 38,1: 41,2; 41,6). In a speech addressed to the people of Apamea on the need for harmony with Prusa Dio claims that "you have made very many of those from that place (i.e. Prusa) citizens (i.e. of Apamea), and you give them a place on your council" (*Or.* 41,10).

I have appended the chapters of the law. See 79, 5 and for "appended", 22, 1 n.

Epistle 115

You had good reason. A rare expression of approval by T. (see 16; but T. now becomes more effusive: see 117 and 121).

whether ... ought to remain in a senate. "Ought to remain" translates a supplement proposed by Hardy 230, to fill what was evidently a gap in the MS (Avantius printed no verb at all in the "whether" clause). The precise issue is again spelt out, probably in case copies of the imperial epistle alone were transmitted to the censors and used as precedents (see 66, 1 n.; 80 n.).

for the future, however, the Pompeian law should be observed. Marshall (*loc.cit.*) sees in T.'s insistence on this a sign that "the movement of the rich from their native cities caused even more severe problems as municipal office came to be regarded as an unwelcome burden". There is virtually no reliable evidence that it was so regarded in T.'s time (see Appendix), and T. may equally have been moved by respect for "the authority of the law": in regulations for the councils of Athens Marcus Aurelius speaks of an earlier attempt to bring the Areopagus back to its "ancient custom" of insisting on its members having three generations of freeborn ancestors (*ZPE* 8, p. 177, ll.58–60, trans. pp.178–9).

Epistles 116–7

P. asks T. whether and how far individual provincials should be allowed to invite large numbers of people to celebrations and is told by T. to make up his own mind.

Epistle 116

Written after 28 Jan., 112.

116,1

Those who put on the toga of manhood. The toga was the distinctive gown which all Roman men ought to wear, in the view of traditionalists such as Augustus (Suetonius, *Divus Augustus* 40, 5). Adult males wore a plain white one (*toga pura*); boys, as well as magistrates in office, wore a *toga praetexta* with a purple stripe (see *Oxford Classical Dictionary: toga*). Youths celebrated their "coming of age" by wearing the former instead of the latter, normally at some time between the ages of 14 and 16 (SW, 106, on I,9,2). The persons concerned must come from the wealthiest and most aristocratic families in the province, many of whom would by this date be Roman citizens.

to give them two denarii or a single denarius apiece. The practice of distributing "pocket-money" on such occasions was so common, at least in Italy and the West, that there was a special Latin word for these "tips": *sportulae* (used by T. in his reply). Apuleius refers to his wife spending 50,000 sesterces on distributions to the people of her native city, Oea in Africa, when one of her sons was married and the other put on his toga of manhood (*Apologia* 87,2). Inscriptions from cities in the West record endowments set up by wealthy benefactors to provide in perpetuity for such cash distributions at local festivals: in these cases it is stipulated that decurions should receive larger sums than ordinary citizens (see R.P. Duncan-Jones: *Economy of the Roman Empire*, 139–41; Jones,*GC*, 180). It is therefore likely that what P. means is that in Pontus the usual practice was to give decurions 2 denarii on such occasions, but non-decurions (i.e. "members of the plebs") only one denarius: see 79,3, for the view of the local curial families on the difference of caste between themselves and outsiders.

116,2

may be thought ... to fall into a type of bribery. P. explains why he cannot make up his own mind whether to ban this practice or let it continue, and so has to ask T.

for a ruling: on the one hand (*sicut*), it is an established custom on such traditional occasions; on the other hand (*ita*), he has certain fears. P.'s use of the Greek term *dianome* (with the basic meaning "distribution") must mean that it was the fact of cash being handed out to large numbers which was the objectionable feature. The word *dianome* is used in Greek texts of the 2nd century A.D. to refer to gifts distributed to the masses to win support (e.g. Appian, *Civil Wars* 1, 27; Marcus Aurelius 1, 16). P. himself would have been alert to the dangers of the votes of councillors being bought: in VI,19,1 he reported demands voiced in the Senate during an election that "candidates should not provide entertainments, send gifts, put money on deposit".

Epistle 117
gathers people together ... in organised bodies, as it were, not as separate individuals on the basis of personal acquaintance. The only corporate bodies to which P. had referred were the city councils, and it must be the councils to which T. is referring: only some members of the plebs were invited, not the whole citizen body, and there is no sign that those "commoners" who were invited received their invitations as members of corporate bodies. T.'s indirect reference to the councils shows that he took P.'s *dianome* to refer to gifts made in exchange for votes.
But it was for this purpose that I chose a man of your wisdom. T. rebukes P., although he is in agreement with him about the undesirability of the practice (see the emphatic "you had good reason" at the very beginning: also 115), because he thinks P. should have acted on his own responsibility. For a very similar response to P.'s hesitations, see 32,1; and 82,1.

Epistles 118-9
P. asks T. about the date from which athletes victorious in 'triumphal' games are entitled to claim their rewards, and about retrospective claims to such rewards by athletes whose victories preceded T.'s own promotion of the status of some games. T. rejects the retrospective claims, and fixes the day of an athlete's triumphal entry into his native city as the date when he is first entitled to his rewards.

Epistle 118
Written after 28 Jan., 112.
118,1
The athletes. These included boxers and wrestlers as well as competitors in track events. P. Weiss, *ZPE* 48, 126, plausibly suggests that P. must have been approached by the local provincial officers of one of the associations of professional athletes, which are attested in inscriptions and papyri (see Millar, 456–62; H.W. Pleket, *ZPE* 10, 197 f.; C.A. Forbes, *Classical Philology* 50, 238 f.), acting on behalf of members of their association whose native cities lay in BP.
the rewards which you established for triumphal games. I.e. the rewards due to athletes who won first prizes at such games. (a) **Games** is the conventional English translation of Latin *certamina*, which, like its Greek counterpart *agones*, means "contests", or "competitions". In many cities in the eastern provinces such "games" were held at intervals of 1, 2 or 4 years, in association with local religious festivals, and included competitions for musicians, poets and actors as well as athletes (see Jones, *GC*, 230–4; H W. Pleket, *Arena* 1 (1976), 53f.): e.g., in T.'s reign a new festival with "games", to be held every four years, was set up at Pergamum, to be paid for by one of T.'s generals, Iulius Quadratus (consul II in 105), and dedicated jointly to Jupiter, god of

friendship, and T. himself (Smallwood, no. 450). (b) **Triumphal** is used to translate *"iselasticis"* in the Latin: Latin case-endings are attached by P. and T. to an adjective transliterated from the Greek (*eiselastikos*), which derives from a Greek verb meaning "drive into" (*eiselaunein*), a verb which P. uses in Greek in the next sentence. The emperor Marcus Aurelius, more of a linguistic purist than P. or T., used a periphrasis in Latin to describe what was meant by *"eiselastic"*: "games from which men returning to their native land as victors [make a triumphal entry]" (*Istanbul.Mitteilungen* 25, p. 150, ll.31–2; *JRS* 1976, 80–1). The terms of this privilege were already established by the time of the Augustan writer Vitruvius: "the ancestors of the Greeks established such great honours for the noble athletes who have won at the Olympian, Pythian, Isthmian and Nemean games that ... when they return in victory to their own cities, they are borne in triumph on four-horse chariots into the walls and their native places, and enjoy lifelong subsistence at public expense" (*De Architectura* 9, pref.). After winning prizes at all the main games in Greece, Nero entered Rome through a special breach made in the walls, alleging that this was the practice for *"iselastic"* victors (Dio Cassius 63,20,1; Suetononius, *Nero* 25,1; see Plutarch, *Quaestiones Conviviales* 2,5,2, "and the permission given to victors making their entry to demolish part of the walls"). (c) **Rewards** is used to render Latin words whose literal meaning is "those things which you have laid down in return for". P. is referring to what he calls *obsonia* in section 2: Vitruvius (*loc.cit.*) refers to "lifelong subsistence at public expense" and Dio Cassius to the provision of an "eternal food supply" to victors, and to their "being fed" (52,30,4). Papyrus texts from Hermopolis in Egypt of A.D. 267 include applications from athletes for payment of their "opsonia" because of past victories in *"eiselastic"* games (e.g. *Select Papyri* (Loeb), Vol.2, no.306). The "reward" was therefore an allowance, sufficient at least to provide subsistence, due for the rest of an athlete's life, and provided by his native city (see Jones,*GC*, 232). (d) **which you established.** At an earlier date T. must have fixed the amount of the *obsonia* due to *"eiselastic"* victors. Since this was apparently a regulation of universal application (see his revision of the list of such games: section 2), SW, 729, must be right to say that T. "probably standardised them so far as possible"; and, given T.'s concern for the finances of Greek cities, it is highly improbable that he increased them (as Hardy, 233, asserted).

are due to them from the very day on which they were crowned. Wreaths of olive or bay were the sole and symbolic rewards given to victors in the most prestigious games in classical Greece. This day would be the actual day on which the athlete won his victory. J. and L. Robert pointed out that professional athletes travelling around the "circuit" of games might pass months or years before their return home; so that an allowance due during the interval between the victory and the return might amount to a considerable sum (see *Revue des Études Grecques* 1961, 150).

on which they made a triumphal entry into their native city. It was presumably the authorities of the cities of the province who were insisting on paying the victors' allowances only from the later date, perhaps as part of an "economy drive" prompted by P.'s mission.

I myself, on the other hand ... . The Latin text printed here excises five words printed after *contra* in the Avantian and Aldine texts (viz., *scribo iselastici nomine itaque eorum*). It has proved impossible to extract any coherent sense from them as they stand, and P. Weiss has made a convincing case for excising them all as marginal glosses composed by scribes, which had crept into the main text of the MS; as he points out, 3 of the 5 words were usually excised in 17th and 18th century editions (see *ZPE* 48, 125–31).

118,2

allowances. These are the "rewards" mentioned above. The Latin plural *obsonia* derives from the Greek plural *opsonia*: this word was originally used to refer to rations provided for soldiers, but by the Hellenistic age could also simply refer to soldiers' pay in general (see Pleket, *ZPE* 10, 204, n.27). Pleket also points out that Fabius Persicus, proconsul of Asia in Claudius' reign, refers in a Greek edict to *opsonion* being paid to "holy victors" (Smallwood, *Documents of Gaius, Claudius* etc. no. 380, col. 6, 1.22–col.7, 1.2).

that contest which was made triumphal by you ... those games which ceased to be triumphal. Taken together, these two clauses show that T. had laid down a list of games entitled to "*iselastic*" status, promoting some games and demoting others. In view of T.'s concern for civic finances, one would expect the second category to have been larger than the first. This was presumably done in the same regulation as that which laid down the rewards (see above). It is not known whether any emperor before T. had drawn up such a list. In the Hellenistic world, with its numerous sovereign states, cities had to undertake extensive diplomacy to obtain such recognition (see Jones,*GC*, 232).

118,3

To explain your own benefactions. In his comments on both of the applications made by the athletes P. has made it clear that he thinks they should be rejected: this sentence explains why he did not venture to do so on his own responsibility. Since T. in his reply makes no criticism of P. (unlike in 117), he must have agreed with P. that a governor should not "interpret" an emperor's ruling unilaterally.

Epistle 119

the fact that they have ceased to receive etc. The first three sentences largely repeat P.'s own words and this fact fully justifies the emendations to this sentence printed in the *OCT* (see SW, 730, for details).

The allowances which they had collected before that are nevertheless not being reclaimed. This last sentence is T.'s only addition to the arguments in P.'s original letter. The implication may be that the athletes should be grateful for not being made to repay these sums. Hardy, 235, must be right: T. is being "a little ironical", and, as SW, 731, suggests, "provoked by the sophistical insolence of the requests", which came from a group aptly characterised by Weiss (*art.cit.*) as the spoilt children of imperial society. Neither T. (41,2n.) nor P. (IV,22,7) had any sympathy with the Greek taste for athletics.

Epistles 120–1

P. reports that he has provided his wife with a pass to use official transport to return to Italy, and T. assures him that he approves.

Epistle 120

Written after 28 Jan.,112.

120,1

passes. See 45–46 nn.

120,2

my wife. Calpurnia, P.'s third wife (IV, 1 and 19). Had she not had to leave the province, we should not have known that she had accompanied P. to BP. Under the Republic Roman officials had been forbidden to take their wives with them to posts in the provinces; it was probably Tiberius, who kept governors in the same province for long periods, that first relaxed this ban (see A.J. Marshall, *Greece & Rome* 22, 1975, 11f.and Tacitus, *Annals* 3, 33–4, for an unsuccessful motion in the Senate to have the ban reimposed in A.D.21).

her grandfather. L Calpurnius Fabatus of Comum. His son, Calpurnia's father, had died before her marriage to P. (IV,19,1; V,11,2).

her aunt. Calpurnia Hispulla, daughter of Fabatus, who seems to have been virtually a mother to Calpurnia: P. addressed to her letters about his wife's education (IV,19) and a miscarriage (VIII,11).

Epistle 121

You were right ... . P.'s notification to T. was clearly just an act of courtesy, and evoked the kind of polite acknowledgement which P. clearly expected (but may not have lived long enough to read). Millar,328, builds too much on this exchange when he cites it as evidence for a greatly increased dependence of provincial governors upon the emperor.

APPENDIX: Epistle 113.

The Latin text of the second half of the second sentence as printed by Avantius makes no sense, and drastic emendations have been proposed. In the text and translation above SW's emendations, which were incorporated in Mynor's *OCT*, have been reproduced, but these have been severely criticised by C.P. Jones (see *Phoenix* 1968, 137). Garnsey expressed very clearly what the overall purport of the passage must have been: "an expression of opinion, framed as a prediction, about the way in which a sub-group among local councillors, most probably the "supernumeraries", would react to the imposition of the entry-fee" (*Historia* 1971, 322, n.73). Garnsey's word "supernumeraries" is taken from SW, 723, who uses it to refer to the group of decurions described in P.'s first sentence, those added to the councils of some cities by T.'s special permission earlier in his reign: SW proposed to emend *qui inviti fiunt decuriones* (who become decurions against their will) to *qui invitati fiunt decuriones* (who become decurions by invitation), and to take this phrase as referring to the additional decurions mentioned in P.'s first sentence. Jones,*GC*, 343, n.62, had already argued that, since the first part of T.'s reply had dealt with the decurions enrolled by censors, "the second part should mention additional, not unwilling, decurions". However, P. had only mentioned the "additional" decurions for historical reasons, to explain why "ordinary" decurions paid fees in some, but only some, of BP's cities: there was no reason for T. to allude to the former at all in his reply. His immediate concern (like P.'s) was with the "ordinary" decurions who were being enrolled by the censors. The result of T.'s ruling would be that they would fall into two categories, one composed of those who had to pay (in some of the cities) and the other of those who did not (in the rest of the cities). T.'s prediction should apply to one or other of these groups, and to its relationship to the other (alluded to by the penultimate word *ceteris*, "the rest of them"). However, the errors in the text transmitted in the MS and copied by Avantius are so deep-seated that there seems no way of deciding for certain which group T. was referring to and what prediction he was making about it.

SW argued that there was no good evidence of any serious reluctance to serve as decurions among the wealthy at this period (it is a phenomenon very well-attested in the 3rd and 4th centuries). He held that the only text cited in support of the belief that there was widespread reluctance had been misinterpreted. One section of the Flavian charter for the municipality of Malaga in Spain laid down elaborate rules for the compulsory nomination of candidates for municipal magistracies in case there were not enough volunteers (*JRS* 1986, p. 162, para.51, trans. p. 188). To quote SW (*The Roman Citizenship*, ed. 2, 1973, p. 256), "the lawgiver ... had to provide against any possibility of accident due to whatever cause, whereby for some years there might come a gap in the governmental system." He is clearly right that legislation often provides remedies for what are in practice very remote contingencies. Furthermore, when P. had earlier consulted T. about the enrolment of new decurions by the censors, he gave no indication that either the aristocrats who were under the minimum age or the commoners who were over it would be reluctant to serve. So far from regarding the decurionate as a burden to be evaded, the local aristocracies did not want it to be "polluted" by volunteer commoners. Garnsey is right to conclude that SW "appears to have the best of the historical argument" (see his discussion of the decline of the urban aristocracy in ANRW II (1), 229 f.; quotation from 232, n.11).

There are, however, objections to SW's proposed emendation and interpretation of the clause (*qui invitati fiunt decuriones,* "those who become decurions by invitation", taken as referring to the "supernumeraries" alluded to by P. in section 1 of his letter). (a) Why should T. describe such decurions as *invitati*? Were they "invited" in any significant sense that decurions enrolled by censors were not? At Prusa the "supernumeraries" were apparently chosen by popular election (see 112,1 n.), which implies some competition among candidates who put themselves forward. It could be argued that it would be more appropriate to describe decurions nominated by the censors as "becoming decurions by invitation." (b) There was no good reason for T. to refer to the "supernumeraries" at all, since they were not the subject of P.'s enquiry (see above). It was argued above that T. should have been referring to the decurions newly nominated by the censors, and distinguishing between some, who would, under his ruling, have to pay fees, and others, who would not. It can also be conjectured that he predicted that the latter would voluntarily spend money on their own cities, even if not compelled to pay fees. It must be admitted, however, that there is no obvious way to emend Avantius' text to yield this meaning, or, indeed, any other meaning. For the present the passage remains impenetrable, and it should not be used as historical evidence, to demonstrate, for example, a widespread reluctance to serve in the decurionate.